Theology and the
Boundary Discourse of Human Rights

Theology
and the
Boundary Discourse
of
Human Rights

∼

ETHNA REGAN

Georgetown University Press ⋄ Washington, D.C.

Georgetown University Press, Washington, D.C. www.press.georgetown.edu

Library of Congress Cataloging-in-Publication Data
Regan, Ethna.
   Theology and the boundary discourse of human rights / Ethna Regan.
       p. cm.
   Includes bibliographical references and index.
   ISBN 978-1-58901-642-2 (pbk. : alk. paper)
   1. Human rights—Religious aspects—Catholic Church. 2. Human rights—Religious aspects—Christianity. I. Title.
   BX1795.H85R44 2010
   261.7—dc22   2009024820

∞ This book is printed on acid-free paper meeting the requirements of the American National Standard for Permanence in Paper for Printed Library Materials.

15   14   13   12   11   10   9   8   7   6   5   4   3   2

First printing

Printed in the United States of America

For my mother, Áine

Contents

∿

Acknowledgments   *xi*

Introduction   1

CHAPTER ONE

A Dialectical Boundary Discourse: Secular and Religious   7

     Are Human Rights Ahistorical?   8

     Are Human Rights Universal?   9

     A Dialectical Boundary Discourse of Human Flourishing   13

     The Charter of the United Nations   16

     The *Universal Declaration of Human Rights*: A Fragile and Negotiated Consensus   17

     Human Rights and the Catholic Church since the Second Vatican Council   23

     Pope John Paul II and Human Rights   38

     The Direction of Pope Benedict XVI?   44

     A Crisis of Trust   45

     Conclusion   46

CHAPTER TWO

Theological Anthropology and Human Rights:
Karl Rahner's Concentration on the Human   63

     Theological Engagement with the Discourse of Human Rights   64

     Imago Dei: Indicative and Imperative   69

     Karl Rahner: A Concentration on the Human   71

     Human Capacity for God: Supernatural Existential   76

Human Goodness: The "Anonymous Christian"   78

Human Freedom   81

Human Experience and the Experience of God   84

Human Dignity   85

Human Suffering   87

Conclusion   89

CHAPTER THREE

Human Rights in Time: Realism between Memory and Hope   100

Memory   100

The Ethics of Memory   101

Trials and Truth Commissions: Just Memory?   102

Toward Just Memory: A Guatemalan Case Study   107

Theology toward Just Memory: The Haunted Tardiness of Johann Baptist Metz   114

The Influence of Karl Rahner   115

Political Theology   117

Memory: Dangerous Memory   118

Narrative: Dangerous Stories   122

Solidarity: Dangerous Responsibility   123

Auschwitz: An Interruption That Orients   125

Challenge: A Future Based on the Memory of Suffering   129

Silence and Interruptive Realism   130

Conclusion   132

CHAPTER FOUR

Liberation Theology and Human Rights: From Interruptive Realism to the Centrality of La Realidad   143

Liberation Theology and Human Rights   146

The Preferential Option for the Poor   151

Who Are the Poor?   153

The Rights of the Poor   157

A Mysticism of Human Rights   161

From Interruptive Realism to the Centrality of *La Realidad*   163

The Weight of Reality: Ignacio Ellacuría   164

Conclusion   166

CHAPTER FIVE

Rights-Holders or Beggars? Responding to
the Postliberal Critique   178

"Disdain" for the Secular: The Refusal of a Rival   179

A Preference for a Theological Politics over Political Theology   189

Impatience with the Provisional   199

Conclusion   204

Conclusion   215

Select Bibliography   223

About the Author   233

Index   235

Acknowledgments

~

THE ROOTS OF THIS BOOK are in the Caribbean; the research was carried out in the University of Cambridge; and it was prepared for publication in Dublin. In each of these places there are people who helped shape the book, and I would like to acknowledge their various contributions.

My reflection on human rights emerged particularly from the experience of working with the Credo Foundation for Justice in Port of Spain, Trinidad, in its response to the needs of children on the streets and advocacy for the abolition of the death penalty in the Caribbean. From the Holy Faith Sisters, staff, and young people of Credo Centre, I learned much about both compassion and resilience. It was reflection on the praxis of Credo's work that taught me about the important link between a concern for human rights and a commitment to the larger questions of human flourishing. My years in both Samoa and the Caribbean shaped my theological reflection and my priorities as a theologian, and I acknowledge the enrichment of these experiences. I would like specifically to thank my former colleagues and students at the Regional Seminary, the University of the West Indies, for what they taught me about theological reflection and the priorities of theology.

I would like to express my appreciation of the wise and challenging guidance of the late Professor Dan Hardy, my doctoral supervisor in Cambridge. Thanks are also due to Janet Soskice, who supervised me in the Lent term 2003. I am grateful for a doctoral bursary from the Cambridge European Trust. To the Faculty of Divinity, University of Cambridge, I express thanks for the award of the Burney Studentship in 2003 and for awards from the Bethune Baker and the Theological Studies funds. Within the Faculty of Divinity and from other faculties, there were many graduate students whose friendship and collegial conversation enriched my own research and reflection. Among these I give special mention to the late May Ling Tan-Chow, whose friendship and insight are missed by many in her native Singapore and in the wider theological community. I enjoyed the international life of Wolfson College, Cambridge and the warm friendships there across the boundaries of cultures and academic disciplines.

Colleagues at the Mater Dei Institute of Education in Dublin offered helpful comments on different parts of the final text, and I would like to acknowledge here Eoin Cassidy, Gabriel Flynn, Dermot Lane, Elaine McDonald, Fainche Ryan, and PJ Sexton. I would also like to acknowledge the helpful comments from the expert readers commissioned by Georgetown University Press to read the manuscript. I would like to thank Don Jacobs, my acquisitions editor at the press, for his helpful and courteous guidance along the way to publication.

To my parents, Jim and the late Áine Regan, and my brothers Brian and Colm and their families, I offer my gratitude for their love and support.

I am grateful above all to my religious community, the Sisters of the Holy Faith, for their generosity in granting me leave to do the initial doctoral research and for their ongoing support. My home for many years was with the Holy Faith Sisters in Trinidad, and their commitment to a faith that does justice has always been a source of inspiration.

Introduction

~

THE DISCOURSE OF HUMAN RIGHTS HAS EMERGED as the dominant moral discourse of our time. Reflecting on this often contentious discourse, with both its enthusiasts and detractors, led me to consider the following questions: What constitutes an intelligible definition of human rights? What place should this discourse occupy within ethics? Can theology acknowledge human rights discourse? How is theological engagement with human rights justified? What are the implications of the convergence of what are two potentially universalizable discourses?

I came to this research with a worldview that has been profoundly enriched by living and working in the Caribbean and in Samoa, learning something of cultural differences and what I will refer to as "situated universalism." Involvement in the campaign against the death penalty in Trinidad and Tobago raised important questions about justice, punishment, the rights of victims and of perpetrators, and the brutalizing effect of capital punishment on society as a whole. The campaign also pointed to complex religious-secular allegiances leading to intellectual and practical solidarity in the *saeculum* where Augustine's two cities, the *Civitas Dei* and the *Civitas terrene*, overlap.[1] But if there is one experience that has been the touchstone of this book, it is involvement in the work of Credo Centre with children who live and work on the streets of Port of Spain. The "street children" of our world are one of our most vulnerable human groups. Working with them taught me that the denial of basic rights to food, shelter, safety, and education, and the various kinds of exploitation that this denial exposes children to, both undermines their human dignity and damages their capacity to develop their potential. The resulting impoverishment both diminishes their flourishing as human beings and denies the human community the gifts of those who never reach their potential.

This book defines human rights as a "dialectical boundary discourse" of human flourishing, attributing to rights the position of protective marginality in ethics; rights are necessarily "marginal" in that they are not ends in themselves, but in this marginal position they play a crucial protective role. Rights do not simply guard the limits below which we should not fall in terms of ethical conduct but are protective of the conditions in which the "more" of ethics—love, virtue, community—can flourish.

I do not hold with the view that rights "trump" all other considerations in ethics or with what could be described as "inverse trumping," which invokes a more "authentic" tradition of virtue and community to triumph over the fiction of human rights. Human rights discourse has an intrinsic communitarian dimension, and there must also be concern for the conditions in which the capacity to be virtuous flourishes. Although the concept of *eudaimonia*, human flourishing, is implicit in this work, a positive exposition of such flourishing is not outlined in detail. Instead it is approached by way of absence, negation, and darkness: a *via negativa* exposition of that which prevents, distorts, and damages the capacity to flourish as individuals and as communities. However, this *via negativa* also makes implicit claims about what is necessary for human flourishing and challenges a simple juxtaposition of *eudaimonia* and human rights.

This book does not attempt to construct a theology of human rights, nor a theological foundation for human rights but to justify and explore theological engagement with the discourse of human rights. A broad understanding of theological engagement with human rights discourse is proposed that includes (a) explicit engagement with rights discourse in terms of both foundational questions and historical implementation; and (b) implicit engagement in areas of shared concern for both discourses, concerns about the human person and community, about human dignity and freedom, about justice and politics. It highlights where the themes and concerns of key modern theologians converge with the themes and concerns of those committed to the advancement of human rights. It also aims to counter some of the "disdain" for rights discourse that is found in postliberal theological and philosophical currents.

In the light of some common objections to human rights discourse, chapter 1 briefly explores two examples of its use in public discourse: in the foundational documents of the United Nations and, in more detail, in modern Roman Catholic social teaching, just one example of religious use of human rights discourse. It is argued that, despite their apparent "groundlessness," the foundational documents of the United Nations—seminal for subsequent human rights documents worldwide—are forged out of the particular historical crucible of twentieth-century totalitarianism and are examples of the fragile and negotiated consensus that marks the human rights project. Roman Catholic engagement with human rights discourse is marked by significant movement from hostility to nuanced acceptance and active promotion of human rights. Both of these examples of public discourse about human rights are bruised by failures of implementation, notably the failure of the United Nations to prevent genocidal acts in Srebrenica and Rwanda and the failure of the Catholic Church in the face of extensive child abuse. Although religious and secular human rights discourse differ in their foundational suppositions, their commonality is more than simply pragmatic; both can be enriched by reciprocity of critique.

Theological engagement with human rights is ecumenical, complex, and diverse; four examples of this engagement are explored at the beginning of chapter 2. The most common theological justification for human rights is the doctrine of *Imago Dei*. This doctrine underpins discussion about the dignity of the human person and the role of human rights in the protection of that dignity. Karl Rahner, a theologian who did not use the language of human rights, is not someone whose work is normally appealed to in the engagement between theology and human rights, but Rahner's concentration on the human develops a transcendental Thomist version of the doctrine of *Imago Dei*. Some aspects of his theological anthropology are discussed, including the supernatural existential, the oft-misunderstood concept of the "anonymous Christian," and his reflections on human dignity, freedom, and suffering. Rahner's theological anthropology points to the necessity of taking human rights discourse seriously and of understanding rights not as the foundation of a minimalist anthropology but as protective of the ultimate luminosity of the human person. However, I also argue that Rahner's theology is characterized by a kind of idealism: it does not sufficiently acknowledge what might damage the human capacity for God, does not elucidate threats to human dignity and freedom, and does not adequately recognize the paradox of grace and dis-grace that constitutes human reality.

In a more "realistic" vein, chapter 3 engages with issues of human rights violations and their individual and communal impact. The memory of suffering was the catalyst for the formulation of the Universal Declaration of Human Rights in 1948. Societies and cultures are defined in terms of memory and the handling of memory, particularly the memory of suffering. Recent truth-seeking initiatives in postconflict situations, which point to the difficulties inherent both in the "excess" of remembering and in the obliteration of memory, are briefly explored. These pragmatic attempts to engage with the memory of suffering and the impact of damage mark a kind of travail toward developing what Paul Ricoeur calls a "culture of just memory."[2] The Recovery of Historical Memory Project of the Human Rights Office of the Archdiocese of Guatemala exemplifies, in its bleak narration of human rights violations, the praxis of an ethic toward just memory.

The question of a theology toward just memory is one that Johann Baptist Metz grappled with, a grappling that took him on a journey from silence to speech about the Holocaust. His theological response to the Holocaust is marked by a "haunted tardiness," and as he moves gradually from transcendental to political theology, a fissure emerges in his work born of this late explicit "interruption" by Auschwitz. I describe this movement in terms of "interruptive realism," not considering it a sufficient category but one that raises questions about the cultivation of a *habitus operativus bonus* of vigilance toward suffering, injustice, and violations of human dignity.

Chapter 4 turns to liberation theology, a theology born of ethical indignation in the face of poverty and oppression in Latin America. Whether or not one considers liberation theology to be the most significant theological movement of the twentieth century—some would say since the Reformation—I contend that it has irretrievably changed the theological landscape. Its key theological principles—the preferential option for the poor and the primacy of praxis—remain as a persistent challenge to theology in the church and in the academy. This chapter outlines the initial rejection of and gradual engagement with the discourse of human rights within liberation theology, drawing from Catholic, Marxist, and liberal approaches to human rights. Human rights discourse becomes increasingly associated with the preferential option for the poor, and the focus of liberation theology is on the rights of the poor. It is argued here that the emphasis on the rights of the poor unveils the paradoxical question of partiality in human rights, a partiality that does not negate the universality but rather points toward authentic universality in the form of historical and concrete realization. A focus on the rights of the poor as the key issue in human rights discourse is not only the preoccupation of liberation theologians. The philosopher Thomas Pogge holds that "the great human rights deficits persisting today are heavily concentrated" among the global poor.[3]

Chapter 5 explores theologians who think differently about theological engagement with secular discourse. It responds to the postliberal critique of

John Milbank and Stanley Hauerwas, challenging Milbank's attempts to build a comprehensive system on the ruins of secular reason and Hauerwas's views on political theology and human rights. Hauerwas and Milbank represent a particular kind of postliberal theology united in their engagement with an Augustinian view of theological politics and their opposition to human rights, liberal democracy, and politics as "statecraft." This chapter also offers a critical reading of Daniel M. Bell's critique of liberation theology, specifically addressing Bell's contention that liberation theology reduces justice to the position of guarantor of rights and his dismissal of the classical conception of justice as *suum cuique* in favor of the gift of forgiveness.

I argue that although the streams in this postliberal theology are not homogeneous, three common characteristics can be identified: (a) a disdain for the secular, including human rights; (b) a preference for a theological politics over political theology; and (c) an impatience with the provisional. I suggest that these characteristics lead this postliberal current to an overextended ecclesiology. Their engagement with an Augustinian view of theological politics neglects Augustine's own ambiguity about the relationship between the *Civitas Dei* and the *Civitas terrena* and also his conclusion that the question of distinction between the cities is ultimately an eschatological one. The result is that they neglect the ethical possibilities within the overlapping space shared by the "sacred" of the *Civitas Dei* and the "profane" of the *Civitas terrena*.

I conclude that it is precisely within this overlap of cities that theological engagement with human rights—with its positive discourse and with the reality of violations—takes place. Human rights is a discourse for the provisional time, in the overlapping space of the intermediate realm, an effort to make the best city possible, knowing it is not a lasting city. Human rights, in this context, could be interpreted as a boundary discourse of *vera iustitia*.

Notes

1. Augustine, *The City of God against the Pagans*, edited and translated by R. W. Dyson (Cambridge: Cambridge University Press, 2003).
2. Paul Ricoeur, "Memory and Forgetting," in *Questioning Ethics: Contemporary Debates in Philosophy*, edited by Richard Kearney and Mark Dooley (London: Routledge, 1999), 5–11.
3. Thomas Pogge, "Recognized and Violated by International Law: The Human Rights of the Global Poor," *Leiden Journal of International Law*, 18 (2005): 717–45.

∿

Chapter One

A Dialectical Boundary Discourse

SECULAR AND RELIGIOUS

A child found wandering in the woods, the remnant of a slaughtered nation whose temples have been razed and whose books have been burned, has no share in human dignity.

—Richard Rorty

HAS THIS CHILD NO SHARE IN HUMAN DIGNITY? Has he or she no appeal to human rights, the dominant moral discourse of our time? Richard Rorty describes the contemporary moral landscape as one primarily inhabited by "Kantians" or "Hegelians." Those who hold that there are such things as intrinsic human dignity and universal human rights are Kantians. They also uphold an ahistorical distinction between the demands of morality and those of prudence. Rorty identifies a particular type of contemporary Hegelian as one who seeks to uphold the institutions and practices of liberal democracies without an appeal to their foundations in the Western philosophical tradition. He describes this as "postmodernist bourgeois liberalism." These Hegelians have no justification for an appeal to the dignity of the wandering orphan, so Rorty, self-described as a "free-loading atheist," is content to invoke the Jewish and Christian ethic of the treatment of the stranger that still resides in the Western tradition.[1] Rorty's analysis points to some of the difficulties of doing ethics in our time.

This chapter begins by examining what kind of discourse human rights is and what place, if any, it should occupy in contemporary ethics. Before offering a definition of human rights, I will briefly respond to two questions that are commonly raised in this context: Are human rights ahistorical? Are human rights universal? A definition of human rights discourse will then be proposed, and two examples—one secular and one religious—of its use in public discourse will be explored.

Are Human Rights Ahistorical?

Human rights discourse is often perceived as operating within a false universality that is ahistorical at best and marked by Western colonial pretensions at worst. However, rights discourse has always arisen from conflict within a particular historical and geographical context and has found expression at different times in terms of liberties, natural rights, and human rights. The Magna Carta limited the power of the monarch, thus establishing basic legal rights for the freemen of thirteenth-century England; in the face of the sixteenth-century violence of the *conquistadores*, Francisco de Vitoria and Bartolomé de las Casas appealed to a doctrine of natural rights for the defense of the Amerindians; John Locke's *Two Treatises of Government* were published in the context of the English Glorious Revolution and the subsequent practical transition of power from monarch to parliament; and the seminal modern document on human rights, the *Universal Declaration of Human Rights*, was drafted in the shadows of the Holocaust and the destruction of so many lives in the Second World War. Rights, then, present themselves as an historical product, but rights are not without significant universal validity.

This book assumes a broad and complex history for the modern notion of human rights, one that looks behind the major contribution of Enlightenment liberties to what John Witte describes as "the deeper genesis and genius of many modern rights norms in religious texts and traditions that antedate the Enlightenment by centuries, even by millennia."[2] Brian Tierney locates the origins of Western rights theories in the natural rights thinking of medieval law and religion.[3] Both Witte and Tierney are part of a considerable body of scholarship that points to "liberty before liberalism,"[4] and the contribution of this scholarship to a richer and deeper history of human rights is important in the light of the persistence, in some quarters, of a one-dimensional approach to the history of human rights.[5]

Aversion to the concept of human rights is sometimes expressed by dismissing them as "inventions," as if this automatically rendered them philosophically irrelevant. The Latin *invenio* (to discover) points to creativity in discussion and argument. There are many ways in which philosophy and theology "discover" or "come upon" words, structures, and systems that articulate, in particular times and places, truths considered natural and supernatural. Human rights are such a construct, an "invention," a construction born of an intuitive conviction, a creative attempt to articulate the protection of the human person, an articulation that is not necessarily at odds with natural law theories in philosophy or theology.

Are Human Rights Universal?

Richard Rorty, a nonfoundationalist, argues that a human rights culture, independent of transcendental universalism, can be developed on the basis of sentimentality rather than moral knowledge.[6] Rorty is representative of postmodernist rejection of any "ahistorical" concept of human nature and of the possibility of transcultural norms regarding human dignity; however, the questioning of such universals is not the prerogative of postmodernism. As Isaiah Berlin outlines in his essay "The Counter-Enlightenment," opposition to the universals of the Enlightenment is as old as the movement itself. He identifies not just the opposition of the churches and religious thinkers but a "more formidable" ancient relativist and skeptical tradition that surfaced in various "romantic and irrational" creeds and movements, "political and aesthetic, violent and peaceful, anarchic and totalitarian, the most violent and pathological forms being the fascist and totalitarian doctrines of the twentieth century."[7] Although the antiuniversalist Nazi rejection of a common human nature and the ensuing horror born of that rejection was the impetus for the drafting of the *Universal Declaration of Human Rights* (1948), from the very beginning the project was questioned regarding the validity of such universals.[8]

It is important to acknowledge the issue of genuine and perceived conflicts between the universality of human rights and the reality of cultural diversity, but I also contend that a "cultural preference" approach to human rights exists often among those who are not obviously under threat and among those who, wanting to control power and liberty, perceive human rights as an obstacle. A nonfoundationalist philosophical approach to human rights, such as that advocated by Rorty, contains a potentially essentialist view of the role of culture in morality, a role that tends to reduce the person to a passive receptor of inherited values rather than a subject who is part of the dynamic process of "traditioning." This view of the role of culture in morality, a view influenced by both postcolonial thought and postmodern perspectivalism, can also mask differences *within* cultures and can legitimate oppressive practices on the basis that they are embedded in a particular culture. This cultural essentialism also risks becoming an unwilling ally of those who invoke cultural values to justify authoritarian regimes and violent or exclusionary practices. Indeed, this invocation of cultural values by such regimes is criticized by scholars and nongovernmental organizations (NGOs) across the world from within a variety of traditions and cultures.[9]

Appeals to nationalism and specific cultural identity can be a genuine call to unmask a universalizing of human rights theory that does not pay sufficient heed to the diversity of religious and cultural contexts in which human persons seek justice. Working with the campaign against the death penalty in the Caribbean, I have seen this cultural dismissal of aspects of human rights discourse used specifically for the purpose of expediting hanging. Rights groups and organizations of international law were perceived by some local leaders as threats to the political sovereignty of Caribbean nations. "The issue of capital punishment has . . . provided the opportunity for the more generalized and dangerous erosion of human rights, and it has done so under the banner of a false nationalism."[10]

Dissent in the face of oppression, be that the protest of workers, philosophers, theologians, artists, poets, or that of long-suffering mothers of disappeared children, is born of the conviction that the difference between good and evil, between humane and inhumane treatment, is not reducible to cultural preference. A hermeneutic of suspicion is needed in defining cultural difference regarding human rights and justice, a hermeneutic that gives priority to the voices of the violated and the excluded. Human rights discourse finds a point of convergence in the "solidarity of the shaken"—to borrow a phrase from Jan Patocka[11]—those shaken by violation, by deprivation, but also those shaken by witness of and participation in violation, and the responsive solidarity *with* the shaken that is the mark of much contemporary action on behalf of human rights.

The aim here is to avoid the poles of extreme relativism and extreme universalism. Jack Donnelly argues for a form of "weak cultural relativism" that does not undermine the fundamental universality of human rights norms and suggests that "deviations should be rare and their cumulative impact relatively minor."[12] Divergence in terms of philosophical conceptions and cultural traditions can coexist with a convergence that is not identical with Western hegemony.

Caution about conceding too much to the claims of cultural relativism is echoed by the Muslim scholar Abdullahi A. An-Na'im, whose work examines the cross-cultural legitimacy of universal human rights. An-Na'im suggests that this universal legitimacy can be enhanced by exploring the possibilities of "cultural reinterpretation and reconstruction through *internal cultural discourse* and *cross cultural dialogue*."[13] Rather than a "weak relativism," he suggests a reasonable degree of cultural relativism provided it does not prevent action against injustice and oppression. Bassam Tibi also holds that the idea of human rights lies at the hub of an international morality based on an irreducible cross-cultural consensus, but he contends that Muslims—and this argument could be extended to others—must seek to speak the language of human rights "*in our own tongues*."[14] Instead of Donnelly's "weak relativism," and wanting to avoid the problematic of "relativism," I suggest the term "situated universalism," which places the emphasis on universalism without denying that the formulation and explication of that universalism are always situated somewhere.

Exploring the feminist contribution to moral philosophy, Seyla Benhabib distinguishes between "substitutionalist" universalistic moral theories and "interactive" universalism. The former, found in most moral theories in the Western tradition from Hobbes to Rawls, "dismisses the concrete other, while interactive universalism acknowledges that every generalized other is also a concrete other."[15] In proposing the term "situated universalism," I am trying to respect this idea of concrete subjectivity, that is, being a subject whose human nature is concretized in terms of race, gender, class, and culture, without allowing any dimension of that concreteness to undermine the inalienable dignity of the human person or limit that person's human rights.

Brooke A. Ackerly offers a feminist engagement with universal human rights theory in *Universal Human Rights in a World of Difference*.[16] She draws on women's human rights activism as a resource for a normative theory of social justice that relies on the universality of human rights but a universality that is "politically constituted, derived by engagement with the politics of epistemology, diversity, and dissent."[17] Arguing for an imminent moral universal and cross-cultural inquiry as a form of nontranscendental theorizing, Ackerly holds that transcendental arguments—religious or philosophical—"are a mask for political arguments for human rights."[18] Although a thorough response to this argument is not possible here, concern must be raised that, notwithstanding the challenges of interpreting the various proposed metrics of human rights—dignity, autonomy, agency, *Imago Dei*, human functioning—and the power dynamics involved in such interpretation, the dismissal of all transcendental arguments risks essentializing context even in the desire to expand universality.

The concept of "situated universalism" also attempts to acknowledge that the implementation and promotion of universal human rights are situated in a variety of contexts, some of which have other moral "discourses of protection" and "discourses of provision" that can complement rights discourse or speed their practical and political implementation across a variety of cultural and political contexts.

Human rights discourse is not the only way to express violation and deprivation. Talal Asad holds that "cruelty can be experienced and addressed *in ways other than violation of rights*—for example, as a failure of specific virtues or as an expression of particular vices."[19] Asad does not attack the legitimacy of universalistic discourses regarding torture and inhuman treatment on ethical grounds, but he suggests that ethnographies of suffering may help the promotion of human rights in ways that respect discourses of protection and provision other than rights discourse. Such a complementarity of moral discourses means that human rights discourse need not seek to silence other ethical languages of protection and provision that may, in certain situations, do more to advance human rights than a sole appeal to rights discourse.

Holding fast to the term "universalism" keeps open the possibility of criticism of cultures on matters of human rights, for all cultures must be open to internal and external criticism, and to deny this in a "cultural-preference" approach to human rights is to render people vulnerable to oppression and exclusion. To focus on the "universalism" of human rights is not to advocate a kind of ethical imperialism; and to qualify this universalism with the term "situated" is not to succumb to ethical relativism. Thus, the intention in proposing the term "situated universalism" is not to advocate a cultural contraction of the universalizability of human rights but to expand the capacity of human rights discourse to protect and provide for the conditions in which concrete human beings can flourish in a multiplicity of contexts. As Kofi Annan has said, "Human rights are African rights. They are also Asian rights; they are European rights; they are American rights. They belong to no government, they are limited to no continent, for they are fundamental to humankind itself."[20]

A Dialectical Boundary Discourse of Human Flourishing

The argument here is that human rights language is a dialectical language that holds in tension the universal and the particular, the religious and the secular, the individual and community, theory and practice, emotion and reason, the abstract and the concrete. The dialectical tension between these various elements is necessary in order that human rights not become merely the discourse for the protection of the rights of individuals insofar as those rights not infringe upon the rights of other individuals. Human rights function as a dialectical boundary discourse for exploration of the notion of human flourishing. It is a discourse of possibility and reliability, of aspiration and alarm. It is a language that draws attention to suffering and sets the conditions and guidelines for the exercise of responsibility in response to the awareness of suffering.

The discourse of human rights provides guidelines for the exercise of responsibility with or on behalf of those who suffer as a result of violations. There is a tendency to interpret rights and responsibilities in an oppositional way. Jonathan Sacks describes rights as "passive" and responsibilities as "active" and suggests that a "responsibility-based culture . . . emphasizes giving over receiving, doing not complaining."[21] Although Sacks writes beautifully on the ethics of responsibility, he tends to present selfish and trivial appeals to rights as normative, overlooking both the fact that much human rights advocacy and activism is done on behalf of others and the important fact that human rights persist even where there is a failure of responsibility by others.

Envisaging human rights as a boundary discourse resonates with other philosophical views of rights. John Finnis, for example, holds that human rights are a contemporary expression of natural rights and that rights facilitate the basic goods of human flourishing. Despite the abuse of rights language by "fanatics, adventurers, and self-interested persons from the eighteenth century to today," human rights emphasize equality, that is, "the truth that everyone is a locus of human flourishing which is to be considered with favor in him as much as in anybody else."[22] The importance of human rights discourse consists in the fact that it includes "everyone" within the potentiality of human flourishing.

Apart from placing before us a reminder of this equality, Finnis suggests that human rights discourse also tends to undercut the calculations of consequentialists and clarifies undifferentiated reference to the common good. Offering an altogether different perspective, Ronald Dworkin suggests that the term "rights" marks off that special consideration that operates as a check on maximizing the general good and that rights play the role of "trump" in the game of moral reasoning.[23] Defining rights discourse as a boundary discourse, located at the margins of ethics, pointing toward the larger questions of human flourishing and ecological sustainability challenges this view of rights as a trump in the game of moral reasoning.

As a dialectical boundary discourse for discussion of human flourishing, human rights discourse upholds the indivisibility and interdependence of civil and political, and social and economic rights, for it challenges all the economic, cultural, social, and political conditions that limit the opportunities for human flourishing.

The question of qualification or the limitation of rights tends to be addressed mainly in terms of the legality of state restriction of human rights, but in a world where six million children die each year as a result of hunger, it is a question for global economics as well as a matter of distributive justice. R. J. Vincent holds that subsistence rights have a strong claim over other rights: "When, as in contemporary world society, we plainly cannot take the provision of subsistence for granted, the liberal theory of human rights should play its part in repairing the neglect."[24] The issue of the priority of subsistence is raised not as an extension of the Cold War tension between the Eastern approach to human rights and the Western emphasis on civil and political rights but as a reminder that perhaps the worst violation of human rights in our contemporary world is the suffering of those who are starving and malnourished. There cannot be significant discussion of human flourishing without our taking adequate account of the priority of sustainable subsistence and the implications of this for our understanding of human rights, a theme to which we shall return in chapter 4.

Human rights discourse can be understood as a boundary discourse that has arisen historically and that, at this time, articulates and encapsulates the possibility of the protection of human dignity. It is to be used with caution, however, and with an awareness of the dangers of extremism, self-righteousness, and lack of concern for relationality and sociality. The tradition born of Locke reassigns absolute right from the sovereign to the parliament to the individual. Absoluteness in any of these assignments has been shown to be dangerous, and a competition between or among sovereignties does not nourish human flourishing. However, the balance remains in limited favor of the individual, who can appeal to human rights without the need for begging or special pleading.

In the ancient world, virtue constituted a common discourse for Greeks, Romans, and Christians; the discourse of human rights has become a common discourse for many contemporary philosophers and religious ethicists. The recovery of the language of virtue is seen by some philosophers and theologians to be a recovery that will trump the language of rights and expose its emptiness and lack of roots. This view is exemplified, in different ways, in the writings of the philosopher Alasdair MacIntyre and the theologians Stanley Hauerwas and John Milbank, whose perspectives on human rights will be discussed in chapter 5.

However, the ethical dilemma cannot be reduced to a simple choice between human rights discourse and virtue ethics. I propose that this boundary discourse of human rights does more than merely protect the boundaries of human flourishing, enable the pursuit of the common good, and flesh out what that common good might mean for those who inhabit the "common." It also protects the conditions within which virtue can be nourished and provides opportunities for the exercise of virtue: the virtues of courage, hope, justice, prudence, and temperance.

Human flourishing consists in a generosity of existence, a dynamic of giving and receiving. This generosity of existence, the capacity to live ethically, can also be expressed in terms of situated universalism, for the explication of flourishing, of *eudaimonia*, is always situated somewhere. Human flourishing defined as a "generosity of existence" gives both credibility and limitation to the notion of human rights. Human rights, in this context, are not simply about what the individual can "claim," but, rather, they are about what we have a duty to give to, or protect in, others.

Rights thus become an obligation of justice and generosity, a "means" in pursuit of the common good, a matter not just of strict justice, but also of friendship. It is a discourse that opens the possibility for greater generosity beyond the "mere" implementation of declarations and conventions; however, those who are dismissive of these instruments need to recognize that they are the means to publicly recognize and legally protect the human dignity—of the social and relational human person—that philosophers and theologians so prize. Human rights discourse is concerned with the protection of the dignity of the human person, not simply with regard to the minimal conditions necessary for that dignity, but with all that potentially distorts or thwarts the capacity for giving and receiving that marks the generosity of existence to which the human person is called.

At the same time that we conclude that rights provide the best available contemporary moral discourse for the protection of human dignity, it is nonetheless important to maintain a healthy skepticism: not the skepticism of the cultural relativist, nor that of the antifoundationalist postmodernist, but skepticism reminiscent of the classical definition of Sextus Empiricus who saw the skeptic as one who continues the investigation.[25] It is imperative that we critically engage with contemporary rights discourse and that we continue to investigate the most effective means of protecting human dignity, challenging poverty and injustice, and ensuring that everyone is included within the potentiality of human flourishing.

We will now explore two examples of the use of human rights in public discourse, the secular foundational documents of the United Nations and the religious appeal to human rights in Roman Catholic social teaching since the Second Vatican Council.

The Charter of the United Nations

The Charter of the United Nations and the *Universal Declaration of Human Rights*, together with the 1966 International Covenants on Civil and Political Rights, and on Economic, Social and Cultural Rights, remain the most significant contemporary secular instruments for the international protection of human rights.[26] They emerged from the tragedy of war that had been etched on the consciousness of the delegates from fifty nations who gathered for the San Francisco Conference that marked the founding of the United Nations in 1945.[27]

Germany was on the brink of surrendering, but war with Japan would continue for another four months, and the photographs emerging from the liberated concentration camps constituted a "negative epiphany" that haunted the deliberations.[28] Many of the delegates from less-powerful nations felt the dominance of the Great Powers—the Soviet Union, United States, Great Britain, France, and China—but the contribution of these other nations was not insignificant. The "extraordinary and unprecedented influence" of religious and secular NGOs and private individuals (both those present in San Francisco and those sending submissions from a distance), those normally considered outside the pale of diplomatic affairs, was a major feature of the Conference.[29] This international and diverse assemblage challenged the plans of the Great Powers and resulted in the relatively strong provisions on human rights being incorporated into the Charter, which was signed on June 26, 1945.

The tone of the opening words of the Charter, the pledge to "save suc-ceeding generations from the scourge of war," is reminiscent of Adorno's post-Kantian appeal, that Hitler's barbarism imposes a new categorical imperative on human beings, so to arrange their thought and action that "Auschwitz would not repeat itself, that nothing similar would happen."[30] The poignancy of this imperative is striking in the shadow of the violence that has marked the period since the inauguration of the United Nations.

The Charter introduces motifs that occur throughout subsequent human rights documents: faith in the *dignity* and *worth* of the human person, in *inalienable fundamental human rights,* in the *equality* of man and woman, and the equality of all nations, large and small.[31] The Charter contains seven references to human rights,[32] but Latin American proposals to include a bill of rights in the Charter were opposed by the United States, although the latter eventually agreed to the establishment of a Human Rights Commission.[33] The Great Powers, although acknowledging the validity of universal human rights, insisted on the protection of the domestic jurisdiction of every state[34]; however, the limits of that protection in the light of other parts of the Charter are the subject of controversy among scholars of international law.[35] In terms of politics, the Charter, in establishing a relationship between the legitimacy of a state and its treatment of its own citizens, marks a shift from the Westphalian system,[36] with its emphasis on the principle of national sovereignty, to the elevation of human rights to the level of international law. Although the references to human rights in the Charter were general in nature, providing no specific definition of rights, they became the basis for the 1948 *Universal Declaration of Human Rights* and the guiding principles for international protection of human rights.

The Universal Declaration of Human Rights: *A Fragile and Negotiated Consensus*

> In the United Nations Declaration on Human Rights of 1949 [*sic*] what has since become the normal UN practice of not giving good reasons for *any* assertions whatsoever is followed with great vigour.
>
> —Alisdair MacIntyre, *After Virtue*[37]

Alasdair MacIntyre's dismissal of human rights is born of his conviction that modern ethical discourse is in ruins and that the solution rests in a retrieval of the premodern tradition of the virtues, a tradition displaced by liberal modernity with its emphasis on rights. Belief in rights, for MacIntyre, is akin to believing in witches and unicorns. The paucity of common philosophical justification in the *Universal Declaration* (hereafter, the Declaration) does not, however, mean that such justifications were not explored in the complex discussion that led to its formulation, nor that the decision not to endorse one particular philosophical justification of human rights was based on a practice of "not giving good reasons." The reason for the absence of a common philosophical justification in the Declaration lay in the desire for a negotiated and wide-ranging consensus, behind which were very definitive historical reasons. The Declaration is ultimately, as Jacques Maritain—one of the drafters—observes, a political rather than metaphysical document.[38] The Declaration also needs to be read not as a series of disconnected rights but as a whole piece, a tapestry in which each thread plays a significant role in the overall picture. This chapter addresses just some aspects of that tapestry.

The drafters were anxious that a declaration of universal human rights be based on a firm international basis; thus, there was an attempt to make the drafting process, which consisted of seven stages, as geographically inclusive as possible.[39] Despite this attempt, large areas of the world, including Africa and Asia, were underrepresented. The first draft, written by the Canadian John Humphrey, drew from existing documents such as that of the Inter-American Juridical Committee, and this draft was the basis for all other developments.[40] Humphrey is described as *primus inter pares* of the drafters. Later, more credit was given to René Cassin than to Humphrey, a situation that also overlooked the significant intellectual contribution of the philosophers Charles Malik from Lebanon and Peng-chun Chang of China.[41]

As with the Charter, the Declaration was drafted in the shadow of the Holocaust. The impact of the horrors was not articulated in a general way but found expression in very specific articles that address the incremental assaults on human dignity, liberty, and human life under Nazism and fascism. The continuum of horror that was euthanasia, the concentration camps, the dramatic increase in capital punishment inside the Third Reich, the treatment of prisoners of war, medical experimentation, and torture were all responded to with the extensive range of human rights expressed in the Declaration.[42] Almost a quarter of the rights deal with legal human rights in response to the Nazification of the German legal system, and many of the social, cultural, and economic rights were influenced by Nazi distortion of labor rights, marriage law, education, and cultural activities.[43] The Declaration is not simply historical in a general sense but is born of the specifics of that historicity. Thus, a close examination of the drafting of the Declaration gives the lie to MacIntyre's suggestion that it consists in assertions "without good reasons."

If the Charter laid out the general principles for a morality of human rights, the Universal Declaration outlined the normative content. It begins not with an enunciation of rights but with a statement about the human person and of what is common to humanity:

> *Whereas* recognition of the inherent dignity and of the equal and inalienable rights of all members of the human family is the foundation of freedom, justice and peace, in the world,
>
> *Whereas* disregard and contempt for human rights have resulted in barbarous acts which have outraged the conscience of mankind, and the advent of a world in which human beings shall enjoy freedom of speech and belief and freedom from fear and want has been proclaimed as the highest aspiration of the common people. . . .[44]
>
> All human beings are born free and equal in dignity and rights. They are endowed with reason and conscience and should act towards each other in a spirit of brotherhood.[45]

The appeal to "dignity" seems to presuppose a latent common grasp of its meaning, and no specific definition is offered.[46] Dignity, of course, is not a univocal term, and it is well to heed Gabriel Marcel's observation that "dignity" often suffers from a "verbal inflation" that aims to compensate verbally for actual widespread deterioration.[47] In the Declaration, there is an implicit defining of dignity, a definition that comes via the way of darkness and barbarism. It may offer a thin normative basis, but such a basis is nonetheless important and, together with the sociohistorical rationale of the Preamble, constitutes potentiality for agreement about human rights across the boundaries of difference of faith and culture. The importance of the word "recognition" lies in its challenge to the perspective of legal positivism, which held that the only rights were those conferred by the laws of states, a view that rendered the individual vulnerable to legally sanctioned violations of his or her rights.

The subject of the Declaration is "everyone"; but this "everyone" is a located person whose rights find expression in the context of family, marriage, country, community, and in the dynamics of association, public service, trade unions, and educational and cultural life. The exercise of the rights of this situated "everyone" is subject to limitations, and "everyone" "has duties to community *in which alone* the free and full development of his/her personality is possible."[48] Without denying that the individual precedes the state, Article 29 thus states that community is necessary for the flourishing of the human personality.

This article was originally a part of three articles covering the communitarian dimensions of human rights located at the beginning of the document. It was the Latin American delegates, supported only by Chang and a few others, who pushed for the inclusion of a list of duties in the Declaration. Only very late in the drafting process was it relocated to the end of the document. Ironically, it was Chang's proposal that an article that dealt with the limitations on the exercise of rights and freedoms proclaimed in the Declaration should not appear at the beginning before those rights and freedoms had been enunciated, which led to the moving of the reference to duties to the penultimate article.[49] If these three original articles had remained at the beginning and not been reduced to one penultimate article in the Declaration, the deontological and "communitarian" aspects of human rights might then have appeared as a more constitutive dimension of the Declaration.[50]

The Declaration does not specify human duties in the way that it does human rights; rather, it leaves duties to domestic law and governance.[51] The concept of duty is considered more ancient than rights, but reciprocity of duties and rights (even if not so named) is also constitutive of ancient ethical codes. Johan Galtung suggests that "rights" is a misnomer and that the preferred term is the more complete, albeit awkward, "human rights/duties."[52] Although it has been suggested that our time is marked by a "twilight of duty,"[53] the language of human rights can also be the way in which contemporary people express their sense of duty to others, or explain their participation in the struggle for justice, or are galvanized into the exercise of responsibility with and on behalf of others, perspectives evident in the work of many religious and secular groups that toil in the area of human rights and social justice.

The rights and freedoms of others, together with "the just requirements of morality, public order and the general welfare in a democratic society," are stated as the conditions for legal limitation of the exercise of one's rights.[54] This is the difficult issue of permissible limitations, sometimes termed "restrictions" or "exceptions." The Declaration does not discuss the difficult issue of derogation, that is, the partial revocation of a law, or the withdrawal from a human rights article in a convention, in times of national or international emergencies.

The Declaration is not a guide for the rights-bearing and radically autonomous individual who sees the court as the arena for the securing of claims and the acquisition of compensation without due regard for the common good and the flourishing of others in community and society. Notwithstanding the difficulties with the document, or, more explicitly, with its implementation, the Declaration echoes human aspirations and hopes. It upholds, however falteringly, the rights of a human person based on his or her entitlement to freedom and equal dignity, contextualized in community, limited by the need for justice and social harmony, and bound by duties to others, although the scope of these duties is not enunciated. Human rights are not envisaged simply as the exemplification of the concerns of a radically autonomous individual in a postdeontic age.

The Preamble states that the protection of human rights is the business not just of the state but also of "every individual and organ of society." Although the concepts of duty and responsibility remain undeveloped, the Declaration is neither individualistic nor statist. It entails notions of responsibility and subsidiarity.[55] The goods outlined in the earlier part of the Declaration, Articles 3–10, are enforceable by law; but the later goods of livelihood, care, education, and participation could have been expressed in terms of duties of solidarity, so that rights could be understood as not only concerned with the avoidance of violation, but also with the doing of the good. There is some confusion in the appeal to both rights as endowments and rights as claims.

Despite the intense conflict, particularly between the Soviet bloc and the West, there was a remarkable degree of consensus attached to the Declaration. It is often suggested that this is attributable to the Declaration's aspirational nature, that is, not being a traditional treaty and not made available for signatures. However, having become part of international policy, the Declaration remains a solemn declaration of intent to respect and promote human rights. The language of cooperation and promotion speaks of a moral duty, while the language of legal obligation binds states to certain actions. Legally, the Declaration can be regarded as part of international customary law as result of the frequency with which it has been used as a reference in, or incorporated into, other legal instruments. This constitutes a shift in international law from the absolute sovereignty of nation states to the principle of humanity.[56] A narrow concern with the rights of states broadens to a concern for the rights of persons. Nations are accountable to the international community for the way they treat their own people, and failure to protect the rights of its citizens weakens the claims of a state to political legitimacy.

In establishing human rights as the "foundation of freedom, justice and peace," there is a meeting of legal and ethical theory. The resulting Declaration shows surprising moral and philosophical coherence, despite the obvious lack of a common foundation or justification for the rights. It is grounded in an appeal neither to God (the most controversial issue), to human nature, nor to nature. Although more political and less metaphysical than earlier Western approaches to human rights, it is not so much philosophically "groundless" as permissive of a mixed approach to justification of human rights.

The Declaration quickly began to make an impact, influencing the setting of standards and the establishment of norms through declarations and legally binding conventions covering a wide variety of specific aspects of international human rights. The United Nations Educational, Scientific and Cultural Organization (UNESCO) has played a key role in both the dissemination of information and promotion of human rights through education and production of materials in various media. However, legal instruments and consciousness raising did not easily translate into the reality of transformative action. Over two hundred local, regional, and international covenants, declarations, charters, treaties, protocols, and agreements have come into being to facilitate the implementation of the foundational UN documents and the realization of human rights throughout the world. There are nations that have ratified only one of the 1966 Covenants; however, no nation has withdrawn from its recognition of the Declaration.

The Declaration's greatest weaknesses are not a fragile philosophical or moral coherence but, rather, the failure to implement the Declaration and the lack of adequate enforcement mechanisms. The idealism of the Declaration is overshadowed by the failure of the United Nations, particularly its Commission on Human Rights, to protect victims of human rights violations. Human rights organizations have been critical of the failure of the United Nations Commission on Human Rights—replaced in 2006 by the intergovernmental Human Rights Council—to investigate reports of abuse, to adopt resolutions on pressing national situations, and to monitor and implement protocols and agreements.

A report issued in 2000 on United Nations Peace Operations stated, "No failure did more damage to the standing and credibility of the United Nations peacekeepers in the 1990s than its reluctance to distinguish victim from aggressor." The report holds that this failure may amount to "complicity in evil"—complicity of omission rather than commission, but complicity nonetheless.[57] The failure to prevent ethnic cleansing in Bosnia (1992–95), in particular the genocidal Srebrenica massacre, damages not only the credibility of the peacekeepers but the credibility of the organization as a whole. In 1994, when genocide was obviously imminent in Rwanda, the small group of UN peacekeepers were withdrawn from the country, and there was a deliberate decision by government representatives from a number of countries, including the United States, not to use the word "genocide," because they had an obligation under the 1948 Convention on the Prevention and Punishment of the Crime of Genocide, to act in a preventative way. The ongoing situation in Darfur, Sudan, is but one example showing that the lessons of Srebrenica and Rwanda have yet to be learned.

This public discourse of the United Nations needs a commitment to ongoing reflection and far greater implementation, a fact recognized in the November 2004 report *A More Secure World: Our Shared Responsibility*.[58] The report highlights, among other things, the need for an expanded and more proactive Security Council, a new doctrine of intervention where a government has failed in "responsibility to protect," and the restoration of credibility to the Commission on Human Rights. Richard Falk, reflecting on half a century of the modern human rights movement, identifies the "prime challenges" on the human rights agenda for the next fifty years: "improving the process of implementation, separating geopolitical practice from the domain of human rights, and enhancing the impression that leading states are as subject to comparable criteria of evaluation as are weak and vulnerable states."[59] Although much has been achieved since the founding of the United Nations, it is clear from the continued and large-scale violation of human rights that the promise of its foundational documents awaits fulfillment.

Human Rights and the Catholic Church since the Second Vatican Council

Belief in the inherent dignity of the human person is the foundation of Catholic social teaching and the starting point for its vision of society. Human rights are recognized as essential for the protection of human dignity and the building of community. Catholic discourse in the area of human rights draws together the basic themes of human dignity, respect for human freedom, the relationship of this freedom to the common good, fulfillment of basic needs, and participation in community. The development of this social teaching constitutes an attempt to discover and articulate—in terms of foundational justification, norms, and praxis—the concrete implications of human dignity in interpersonal, social, structural, and international terms. However, the acceptance of the notion of human rights by the Catholic Church and the incorporation of that discourse into its social teaching have been a slow and complicated process. The relationship between the Christian churches and human rights has been characterized as a movement from reluctance and hostility to acceptance: "reluctance" was the general response of Protestantism and "hostility" the general Catholic response.[60]

It is outside the scope of this work to trace the genealogy of this hostility of Catholicism to democracy and human rights since the French Revolution, but one example, in papal teaching, of the hostile response would be Gregory XVI's 1832 encyclical *Mirari vos*.[61] This encyclical issued condemnations of liberalism, individualism, democracy, the madness (*deliramentum*) of freedom of conscience, freedom of opinion, press freedom, and the separation of Church and state.

The defensive ultramontanist position of the Catholic Church in the nineteenth century perceived the Enlightenment as the enemy, for it proposed an idea of freedom that seemed to lack any normative framework that would maintain a proper relationship among freedom, justice, and order.[62] Bryan Hehir contends that the "neuralgic point" was the idea of religious freedom.[63] The Catholic transition from an ultramontanist position to acceptance of human rights was influenced by a number of factors, but within the limits of this chapter, the influence of just two figures, Pope Leo XIII and Pope Pius XII, will be very briefly mentioned.

Leo XIII, a man whose hierarchical view of civil society made him fearful of modern notions of freedom and equality, became the founder of modern Catholic social teaching, setting that teaching in a direction that would eventually lead to wholehearted acceptance of religious freedom, human rights, and democracy. In a series of texts from 1880 to 1902, Leo offered a modern exposition of the position of Gelasian I on the "theology of the two powers" wherein Leo "transcended the historically conditioned medieval conception of the two powers in the one society called Christendom," making it clear that there are two societies, two distinct orders of law, as well as two distinct powers, thereby establishing a position for the claim of the freedom of the Church in the context of the rightful secularity of society and state. [64]

Leo's 1891 encyclical *Rerum novarum* on the rights of the worker taught that "the human being is prior to the State and has natural rights that do not depend on the State."[65] It established the basic right to a living wage, that is, "a wage [that] will enable him, housed, clothed, and secure, to live a life without hardship."[66] Leo XIII also legitimated the role of trade unions.[67] Although his position may be described as paternalistic, defensive about socialism, and entailing a distorted view of private property, Leo moved the Church in the direction of social and economic rights, and brought the sufferings of the poor, especially the exploited industrial workers, into official Church teaching.

In the face of twentieth-century totalitarianism, the complex and controversial Pope Pius XII addressed the question of civil and political rights particularly in his Christmas Messages of 1941–45.[68] The Church was fearful of both left-wing and right-wing totalitarianism, and although the greater fear seemed to be of the former, experience with both kinds led to a more positive assessment of human rights in the political order (in both the national and the international community), and the freedom of the individual.

Pius XII stressed the distinction between society and the state as an essential bulwark against totalitarianism, accepting what would have been unthinkable to Leo XIII, a juridical or limited constitutional state. Although this more positive assessment of rights was not developed because of the continued influence of nineteenth-century antiliberalism, Pius nonetheless made a significant contribution that set the stage for the positive engagement of Catholicism with human rights.

However, it is his failure to clearly denounce the persecution and extermination of the Jews that is ultimately the legacy of Pius XII. Although a thorough analysis of this complex and contested question is not possible here, it could be suggested that Pius's failure had less to do with anti-Semitism and moral cowardice than with his concentration on diplomacy, the intense fear of communism, fear of reprisals, and an ecclesiology that saw the Church as essential for salvation and therefore in need of protection in order to facilitate access to the sacraments.[69]

Both Leo XIII and Pius XII, in different ways, contributed to the Catholic transition from hostility toward the discourse of human rights to acceptance of and positive engagement with this discourse.[70] In the time between the end of

World War II and the Second Vatican Council (1962–65), there was considerable Catholic intellectual engagement with the themes of democracy, human rights, and religious freedom, engagement that laid the groundwork for the first systematic treatment of human rights in official Catholic social teaching in the encyclical of Pope John XXIII, *Pacem in terris*.

PACEM IN TERRIS (1963)

When Pope John XXIII—then Angelo Roncalli—was papal nuncio in Paris in the 1940s, he participated, with René Cassin, in discussions about the drafting of the Universal Declaration. This was the time of the establishment of UNESCO in Paris, and Roncalli was influential in ensuring that the Catholic Church would make connections with the United Nations and its organizations. In calling the Second Vatican Council, the desire of Pope John XXIII was for *aggiornamento*, a renewal of the Church, particularly in terms of its relationship with the world.[71] It has been suggested that one of his major contributions to the Church was a "new spirituality of commitment to the world, a spirituality that contains the seeds of a new theology."[72] *Aggiornamento* was not mere accommodation to modernity but a commitment to engagement that does not exclude prophetic critique. Part of this *aggiornamento* involved new reflection on themes such as democracy, freedom of religion, and human rights.

Pacem in terris—On Establishing Universal Peace in Truth, Justice, Charity, and Liberty—issued by John XXIII between the first and second sessions of Vatican II, marks the first systematic treatment of human rights in official Catholic social teaching.[73] It is the first papal encyclical to be addressed not just to Catholics but also to "all men and women of goodwill."[74] John appeals to a basic anthropological principle upon which human society depends: each individual is truly a person, endowed with intelligence and free will, with rights and duties that are universal and inalienable. The consideration of this human dignity from the viewpoint of Revelation "incomparably increases" our estimation of it, but the first and basic appeal is to a philosophical anthropology, indicative of the methodology of *Pacem in terris*.[75] In addressing the question of the dignity of the human person, John moves from the neoscholastic approach of Leo XIII and Pius XII, who only obliquely refer to human dignity, to a greater reliance on the concept of the dignity of the human person, grounded in reason and natural law.

The only reference to the New Testament is Romans 2:15, the classical scriptural justification of the existence of the Natural Law.[76] A natural law approach is in continuity with the Catholic position that the authentic demands of morality are accessible to human reason reflecting on human experience, a position that opens possibilities for conversation about human rights and justice with interlocutors outside of the Christian tradition. As part of its appeal to natural law, *Pacem in terris* recognizes the role of the United Nations. It makes special reference to the Universal Declaration, seeing therein a profound recognition of the dignity of every person, and the assertion of "everyone's rights to be free to seek out the truth, to follow moral principles, discharge the duties imposed by justice, and lead a fully human life."[77]

The human person, member of the human family, has rights and duties flowing from a common human nature. The document is not an endorsement of a minimalist liberal rights perspective, which narrowly defines the right to life as the right to noninterference and protection from aggression. It offers a comprehensive list of natural rights, beginning with the "right to live": rights pertaining to bodily integrity, moral and cultural values, to worship God according to one's conscience, freedom regarding choice of state in life, economic rights, rights of association and movement, and political rights, including the right to participation and to express one's dignity by contributing to the common welfare of fellow citizens.[78] The right to life and the living conditions worthy of human dignity are woven together, avoiding thereby the dichotomy that was inherent in much debate about human rights. Although the document's broad canvas of rights does not clarify how these rights are to be prioritized, it marks an important contribution to Catholic discussion of human rights and links it with the debate within the United Nations, at that time, about the primacy of particular rights.

As a result of the reference to economic rights in Leo XIII, and other influences including the work of the American Catholic social reformer, John A. Ryan, the Catholic tradition did not have the same difficulty with socioeconomic rights as it did with the concept of civil and political rights.[79] *Pacem in terris* is a major development because of its endorsement of civil and political rights.[80] Its distance from the older Catholic view of preference for the union of Church and state led also to the endorsement, by the Vatican, of democracy and pluralism. Furthermore, there is a change in the perception of state authority, a shift from a paternalistic role of directing its subjects in the ways of truth, justice, and religion, to an understanding of its function in terms of the protection of human rights. All states are equal in dignity, and each state has the right to play the leading part in its own development.[81]

Pacem in terris also upholds a more positive and comprehensive view of the constitutional state than is normal in natural rights theories. Rights are discussed in the context of some contemporary issues: racism, the arms race (mentioned for the first time in official Catholic social teaching), industrial progress, social welfare, economic sharing, and political participation. The encyclical does not propose a single model of society, but, rather, it teaches that the mechanism for protection of human dignity in various social and political contexts is the promotion of human rights.

Pacem in terris stresses the relational character of rights and the reciprocity of rights and duties. The encyclical calls for "many-sided collaboration" out of a sense of responsibility.[82] Although it is not clear how rights and duties are to be adjudicated when they are in conflict, the focus on the relationship between rights and duties places the discussion about human rights in a framework of sociality and responsibility. Pope John holds in tension the dialectic of the social and the individual: the self-in-society. The rights of the human person are affirmed within the context of interdependence and solidarity, thus avoiding an atomistic or individualistic understanding of human rights.

John XXIII issues a subtle challenge to those who make ideological use of Catholic social teaching in order to prevent greater social justice, for example, where the appeal to the right to private property is being claimed without any sense of social responsibility. He particularly addresses those who "derive special advantage from the fact that their rights have received preferential protection."[83] He had in mind the neglected rights of the poor in situations of injustice and landlessness. In the encyclical *Mater et magistra* (1961), Pope John made a significant contribution to the development of Catholic social teaching by shifting from the traditional Catholic opposition to state intervention and the "Welfare State," and, in combination with his treatment of human rights in *Pacem in terris*, he contributed to what is described as a "decisive move away from the right" in Catholic social teaching.[84] This movement in Catholic social teaching would eventually bear fruit in the adoption, by liberation theology, of the theological concept of the "preferential option for the poor."

Only six months after the Cuban missile crisis, and against the background of the Vietnam War, John XXIII opened the door for dialogue between East and West, "by distinguishing between false ideological teachings and movements that address social and economic questions."[85] This distinction allows for the possibility of dialogue and the belief in the possible fruitfulness of such dialogue. The manner and the degree of collaboration in the attainment of economic, social, cultural, and political advantage are matters for the virtue of prudence to decide.

The question could be raised as to whether Pope John was realistic about the profound differences between West and East and about the fears engendered by the reliance on arms as the basis of peace. Even his great ally, John Courtney Murray, wondered if the confident hope of Pope John took "realistic account of the fundamental schism in the world today."[86] However, the principle of prudential conversation across the boundaries of ideological differences, for the sake of justice, is a crucial ethical principle, with profound ecclesiological implications.

The political philosopher Maurice Cranston read *Pacem in terris* not as an appeal to the Christian imagination, but "to the Christian conscience, and beyond that to the conscience of mankind."[87] Cranston admired the document for its fresh appeal to natural law, seeing the papal approach as grounded in the Stoic tradition—rather than what he perceived as the orthodox Catholic and dominantly clerical approach to natural law—with its reference to the order of the universe and its appeal to something discernible by the eye of reason alone and pertaining to humanity as a whole.[88] *Pacem in terris* is thus a bridging document between natural law and natural rights perspectives on human rights. Its natural law framework, incorporating elements of the natural rights tradition, shows a progression from the papal rejection of the concept of modern political liberties associated with democratic revolutions in the eighteenth and nineteenth centuries.

There were approving references to *Pacem in terris* in the Soviet Press, and it was lauded by both the president of the United States and the secretary-general of the United Nations. Reinhold Niebuhr offered a Protestant critique—though not the only Protestant response—charging the encyclical with failure to face the reality of sin and the effects of sin in terms of conflict and injustice, a result of what he describes as its more Pelagian than Augustinian spirit.[89] There were criticisms of its natural law methodology; the strength of natural law methodology is its perceived weakness from a theological perspective, specifically the neglect of the centrality of Christ. The references to Christ and the gospels are placed at the end of the document and do not substantially contribute to its ethical framework. This difference is not simply a matter of perspective but substantially affects "interpretations of what is practically possible in the human rights field and influences determination of strategic priorities in the effort to implement human rights."[90] The document also lacks a sustained analysis of the dynamics of power in the world, a general weakness in modern Christian social ethics, which is later challenged, to some extent, by the ethics of liberation theology.

Although the references to scripture and the explicitly theological references may not contribute substantively to the document's ethical framework, and seem almost like a postlude, there is inherent in the document what might be called an implicit or "presumptive" pneumatology. *Pacem in terris* presumes the working of the Holy Spirit in the hearts of men and women of goodwill and the capacity of that Spirit to work through ideological differences. This implicit and presumptive pneumatology has implications for ecclesiology and ethics, for the Church's understanding of its role in the world, and for how it engages in conversation and praxis regarding the protection of human rights.

Pacem in terris places human dignity at the heart of Catholic social teaching. The encyclical stresses the social and structural mediation of that dignity, so that dignity becomes increasingly associated with human rights. Subsequent Catholic social ethics—both in the official teachings and in the broader theological discourse—focuses on the ongoing discovery of the demands of this human dignity. *Pacem in terris* influenced the position of Vatican Council II on human rights and on the relationship between the Church and democracy. The contribution of two of the documents of Vatican II to the development of the engagement of Catholic social teaching with the discourse of human rights will now be examined: The Pastoral Constitution on the Church in the Modern World, *Gaudium et spes*, and the Declaration on Religious Liberty, *Dignitatis humanae*.

GAUDIUM ET SPES (1965)

The cornerstone of *Gaudium et spes* is the dignity of the human person. The preface to the document locates the mission of Christians not in a general philosophical reflection on humanity, but in "the joys and hopes, griefs and anxieties" of the people of the age, "especially those who are poor or in any way afflicted." A historically conscious and inductive methodology is introduced in an attempt to ground natural law specifically in the human person, not in an abstract conception of human nature, seeking to hold in tension the commonality of natural law and the specifics of historicity. Nature is not viewed as consisting of fixed and changeless essences; nor is ethics the deduction of decisions from unchanging principles. It points to a dynamic understanding of natural law engaged in an ongoing search to understand what it means to be a human person—in his or her totality—in the world. It is a watershed in the movement from an emphasis on human *nature* to the human *person* in official Catholic documents, marking what Bernard Lonergan describes as a shift from a classicist, deductive natural law approach to a historically conscious, inductive, personalist approach.[91]

The personalism that pervades the document is a transposition of natural law into philosophical anthropology, a transposition that marks a renewal within the tradition of natural law itself, enabling reasoning about the human person in a new key. Personalism as a perspective places anthropology at the center; the human person, considered in his or her entirety in what is unique to the individual human person and common to the human condition, becomes the key to social justice and peace.[92] Social and political systems exist to meet human needs and to contribute to the development of human persons. Personalism, and a new theological anthropology influenced by the work of Karl Rahner, meant that theological consideration of the human person led not only to greater engagement with human rights in general but also to engagement with the particularity of the subject as woman, man, child, black, indigenous, or poor.

Gaudium et spes recognizes that the human race "has passed from a rather static concept of reality to a more dynamic, evolutionary one" and affirms the historical and developing character of the human person.[93] It is the human person, therefore, who is the key to this discussion, each individual human person in her or his totality, "body and soul, heart and conscience, mind and will."[94] The anthropology of the document is unitary, avoiding the fragmentation of a human "nature" into distinct and separate faculties. The person is understood as historical, embodied, relational, unique within the context of equality with others, a fundamental equality that is the basis for holding that the fundamental moral demands are universalizable. Human rights protect these dimensions of the human person in their vulnerability and in their potentiality.

Historical consciousness is a delicate balance that seeks to take history seriously without reducing to historical or cultural relativism. This consciousness also brings less certainty that any one rationality can adequately speak to and of the nature of the human person in her or his complexity. The responsibility the Church carries is that of "reading the signs of the times and of interpreting them in the light of the Gospel."[95] John XXIII begins with the hopeful signs and then reflects on the alarming signs of the times. This phrase, "the signs of the times," an echo of Matthew 16:3–4, is given theological and methodological significance in this document. It is a simple phrase, one that can fall prey to superficial interpretation and facile application; however, the actual working out of the issues addressed in *Gaudium et spes* demonstrates the complexity of the term. Deductive reasoning from an immutable natural law shifts toward a prudential discernment of the present reality in the light of the Gospel and the teaching of the Church. Reading the signs of the times is, however, a risky enterprise: one risks being wrong, not so much in terms of ethical principles, but in concrete situational analysis and the development of normative responses.

The human person and the urgent problems of the day—cultural, economic, and political—are to be examined "in the light of the Gospel and of human experience."[96]

This identification of history and human experience as the *locus revelationis* presents a challenge to the chosen *locus* of the theologian. Not only is the duty to discern these signs essential for understanding the mission of the Church in the world, but it also challenges us to evaluate what, in fact, are the concerns of theology. If the passion for the dignity of the human person and the protection of that dignity in human rights are signs of our time, then the theologian must engage with this.

The liberal philosophical anthropology inherited from the Enlightenment has been described as that of the free, equal, and rational "man." Although *Gaudium et spes* does recognize, some would say uncritically, these pillars of the liberal anthropology, it is inadequate to say that this is the anthropology of the document, for its central motif is the human person as *Imago Dei*. While reaffirming natural law tradition that human dignity is evident in the human intelligence, freedom, and conscience common to all, its inherently personalist perspective links this tradition with the biblical and theological vision of the human person as the image of God. The Council's affirmation of modernity is a nuanced one. It is not a capitulation to an individualistically autonomous self—indeed, it challenges this interpretation of human dignity—but is rather an affirmation of the Aristotelian and Thomistic emphasis on the social nature of the human person and on the practical reality of interdependence, stressing that an individualistic ethic is not sufficient: "We are witnesses of the birth of a new humanism, one in which the human person is defined first of all by their responsibility toward their brothers and sisters and toward history."[97]

This new humanism of *Gaudium et spes* is Christological humanism, for Christ is "the focal point and goal of the human person, as well as of all human history."[98] The energy that motivates and sustains human beings in their efforts to make life more human, peaceful, and just is an en-Spirited energy, Christ at work in the hearts of men and women.[99] "He taught us by example that we too must shoulder that cross which the world and the flesh inflict upon those who search after peace and justice."[100] This pointer to a theology of the cross is not developed, perhaps because of the optimism in the document about the possibilities of reform and goodwill to bring about justice and peace. The shouldering of the cross in the search for justice and peace, a shouldering that leads to an extensive martyrology, later finds expression in Latin American liberation theology, whose engagement with the discourse of human rights will be examined in chapter 4.

Gaudium et spes reflects on the social and communal dimensions of the human vocation, the call to humanity to be "one family," whose basic equality must "receive greater recognition," necessitating a denunciation of racism, sexism, and any other exclusionary ideology.[101] The growing awareness of the "sublime dignity of human persons," whose *rights and duties are universal and inviolable*, is highlighted.[102]

Although many of the optimistic statements about humanity and the modern world are, in fact, qualified, the document is marked by an overly confident humanism. This confidence is later modified by the reading of the oppressive signs of the times offered by key sections of the documents produced at the 1968 meeting of Latin American bishops at Medellín. These documents influenced the Church worldwide, particularly through the inspiration they gave to Christians who were committed to social justice and peace.[103] Their sharp analysis of the situation of "institutionalized violence" offered a challenge to the whole Church to take seriously the option for the poor and social justice.[104]

The promotion of human rights is one of the ways in which the Church carries out her role as "champion" of the dignity of the human vocation.[105] The Church sees itself as having a vocation to contribute toward making the human family more human: through proclaiming and fostering human rights, building up the human community, and the initiation of action for service of all people, especially the poor.[106] There is an insistence on the right of the poor to their share of the Earth's resources and on the responsibility of the rich that goes beyond the giving of charity out of superfluous wealth. The desire to fulfill this vocation has led the postconciliar Church into greater active participation in the struggle for human rights around the world.

The Council places the protection of human rights at the heart of politics, a politics requiring limited government and respect for the principle of subsidiarity. This shift has been described as a "preferential option for constitutional democracy."[107] Without abandoning the traditional Catholic themes of the primacy of the common good and natural law, the Council endorses modern politics on the basis of the organization of people in pursuit of "a dynamically conceived common good" with respect for rights and the possibility of democratic participation. It offers a clear account of the nature and limits of human authority. People are entitled to defend their own rights and those of their fellow citizens against the abuses of a tyrannical regime. However, the document then goes on to qualify these entitlements in such a way that it dilutes the strength of the initial statement: "within limits laid down by natural law and the Gospel" and obedience to the common good.[108]

One of the most significant contributions of *Gaudium et spes* was to ground the protection and promotion of human rights theologically and thus to place Catholic involvement in the struggle for human rights at the heart of the mission and ministry of the Church.[109] "In virtue of the Gospel entrusted to it, the Church proclaims human rights; it acknowledges and holds in high esteem the dynamic approach of today which is fostering these rights all over the world."[110]

Whereas *Pacem in terris* is an outstanding text in terms of the promotion of human dignity and human rights, *Gaudium et spes* transforms the involvement of the Church in human rights so that it has an evangelical and eschatological dimension. The Church saw itself called to be a "sign and safeguard of the transcendence of the human person."[111] The transcendental worth of the human person must be concretely recognized and realized in historical reality. Human rights, previously considered the ideology of liberals, now became the mechanism for the protection of this transcendence, reminding us that transcendentality and historicity are intimately connected, both being matters of ultimate concern. The defense of the human person, in all aspects of personhood, becomes the essential task of the Church. The abstract concept of human dignity becomes historicized dignity, which, through reflection on the signs of the times, becomes the dignity of particular persons in specific contexts of violation and deprivation. The call to be readers of the signs of the times is a reminder that the specific demands of human dignity cannot be outlined a priori.[112]

Whereas the Church is in a relationship of mutuality with the world, its single intention is "that God's kingdom will come and that the salvation of the whole human race will come to pass."[113] Importantly for the relationship between the efforts of the Church to protect human rights and the work of other religious and secular human rights agencies, there is recognition of the presence of the Holy Spirit in all those working for justice and peace. Earthly progress in the cause of justice, peace, and freedom is not seen as identical with the growth of the kingdom of God but is nonetheless of vital concern to it. The ministry of human rights is placed in relation to theological anthropology, to the mission of Christ, and to the ongoing renewal that is the work of the Holy Spirit. Our efforts to promote human rights are seen as participation in the continuing creative work of God, and the response to violations of human rights is the concern of God through Christ's identification with the least: "You did it for me."[114]

DIGNITATIS HUMANAE (1965)

The expressed intention at the beginning of *Dignitatis humanae* is that of developing "the teaching of recent popes on the inviolable rights of the human person and on the constitutional order of society."[115] This Declaration marks the Church coming to accept what had already been recognized in civil law and to acknowledge a principle that had been proclaimed in all the declarations of human rights. It may not be a milestone in terms of philosophical debate about human rights, but it had a major impact on the self-understanding of the Church and on the understanding of the nature of doctrine in history.[116] Interest in religious freedom arose particularly in contexts where Catholics were in a minority, but as the Church began to reflect deeply on the dignity and freedom of the human person, to develop its own social teaching in a more historical direction, to see value in the documents of the United Nations, and to struggle for the rights of those living under communist regimes, it became obvious that it was self-contradictory to continue to oppose such freedom.

Dignitatis humanae was the document that brought out the struggle, at the Council, between traditional Catholic views of freedom and more "liberal" views, for the rejection of the confessional state was anathema to those who defined freedom in terms of possession of the truth. There were difficulties in the drafting of the document with the distinction between the objective right of persons with regard to religious liberty and the traditional argument regarding the right to the existence of the one true religion. The Council had to stress that a person may have duties to the truth, but the truth has no rights. The subject of rights is the human person, in truth or error, based on the dignity of that human person in his or her discernment and decision making. Its starting point is thus the modern consciousness of the dignity of the human person, the basis of whose dignity is known by reason and revelation and is manifested in the gifts of rationality and freedom.

The methodology of *Dignitatis humanae* reflects the shift from the concept of human nature to that of the human person, and this shift enables the right to religious freedom to be grounded in the dignity of the person.[117] It uses the language of "protection and promotion of human rights," language that echoes strongly that of the United Nations documents.

Within *Dignitatis humanae*, the dynamic of freedom is one of movement from personal freedom to the freedom of the Church. The primary emphasis is the issue of religious freedom on formally juridical—rather than ethical or social—grounds, that is, religious freedom as freedom from coercion, or as an immunity. This civil right rests on the dignity of the human person who bears the responsibility to search for the truth. This search for truth transcends the authority of the State, and the human person is bound to follow her or his conscience faithfully. Even if a particular religious community is given special recognition, the rights of all must be recognized. Personal freedom is constitutive of the common good, the latter defined as "the sum total of those conditions of social life which enable people to achieve a fuller measure of perfection with greater ease. It consists especially in safeguarding the rights and duties of the human person."[118]

The dialectic of human rights and duties—including the right to religious freedom—provides the outlines of the common good, within the context of constitutional government. The foundation of religious freedom is the dignity of the human person, and this freedom is owed to the person in justice. Religious freedom, that "neuralgic point" in the relationship between the Catholic Church and Enlightenment liberty, is now held to be the primary freedom, which secures other human and civil freedoms.[119]

This suggests an ordering of human rights within the context of their interdependence. Religious freedom is not simply about the toleration of a lesser evil, nor is it identical with religious indifferentism or simple religious relativism. Religious freedom concerns the safeguarding of that which is most precious in the human person, the capacity for transcendence, for living out the orientation to God, which is the human vocation. The right to religious freedom moves from personal freedom to the freedom of the Church, not vice versa.

John Courtney Murray, the theologian who had most influence on this document, held that "the issue of religious freedom was in itself minor," maintaining that the hidden agenda of the document was the issue of doctrinal development and that the right to religious freedom was "simply juridical."[120] It may, indeed, have been a *simply* juridical matter, but it was not a *merely* or *exclusively* juridical matter. Murray also holds that the right to religious freedom is a "self-denying ordinance" on the part of both government and the Church. The former denies itself the right to interfere with the free exercise of religion, except where a civil offense against public order arises, and the Church denies itself any secular arm. "In ratifying the principle of religious freedom, the Church accepts the full burden of freedom, which is the single claim she is entitled to make on the secular world."[121]

Dignitatis humanae, a primarily pastoral, rather than specifically ethical, document, marks the first official recognition of doctrinal development within the tradition of Catholic social teaching, a corpus that normally emphasizes continuity. The acknowledgment, at the highest level, that the doctrine of the Catholic Church can change is extremely significant, marking what Murray calls "progress in understanding of the truth."[122] It points to the tradition as living wisdom, grounded in community, and refined in the context of worship, praxis, and conversation with others outside the community.[123]

Engagement with the doctrine of human rights has contributed to an ecclesiological ethic marked by receptive engagement with others committed to the ongoing discovery of responsibility engendered by the recognition of human rights as part of the demands of justice in an increasingly complex world. Without the promulgation of this document, human rights could not have taken a core role in the social teaching of the Church, nor could the Church have become the advocate of human rights that it has become in many parts of the world. *Dignitatis humanae* cleared the way for the Catholic Church to become an active defender of human rights.

Pope John Paul II and Human Rights

John Paul II showed a consistent concern for human rights throughout his pontificate, using the language of human rights to ground the discussion of justice in his social teaching and in the passionate appeals for justice in his journeys to various parts of the world. Given the vast amount of material (encyclicals, speeches, and homilies), the fact that human rights is a constant theme in his social teaching, and the length of his pontificate, only five aspects of his engagement with human rights discourse will be briefly explored: (a) John Paul's general view of human rights and the human rights movement; (b) human rights and his appeal for justice; (c) his treatment of religious freedom; (d) his methodological concerns; and (e) the ecclesiological implications of his teaching.

GENERAL VIEW OF HUMAN RIGHTS AND THE HUMAN RIGHTS MOVEMENT

John Paul had a generally positive view of the secular human rights movement, seeing therein evidence both of a universal human nature and also of a humanism that speaks to all people of good will. He described the Universal Declaration as "one of the highest expressions of the human conscience of our time"[124] and called for a culture of human rights—which is accommodating of legitimate cultural and political differences—to become "an integral part of humanity's moral patrimony."[125]

John Paul viewed the hunger for justice and peace that is characteristic of our time as evidence of a hunger for the Spirit of God,[126] and he believed the growing awareness among human beings of their inherent dignity expressed in the concern for human rights to be "the first positive sign of the time."[127] However this pneumatological perspective on social ethics and John Paul's positive assessment of the potential of the United Nations and of the impact of the global human rights movement coexist with an increasingly oppositional view of modernity that is especially evident in John Paul's later writings.

HUMAN RIGHTS AND THE APPEAL FOR JUSTICE

The language of human rights was usually the basis of John Paul's appeal for justice; in fact, rights became the dominant way in which he addressed social issues. In *Redemptor hominis*, the Universal Declaration is taken seriously as a companion for moral discernment, for it is not only a response to past horror, but it constitutes the basis for a continual revision of programs, systems and regimes from the point of view of the welfare of the person in community.[128]

It is the job of the Church—together with all people of goodwill—to be vigilant regarding the actual implementation of the Universal Declaration. Human rights thus become the measure by which social justice is tested in the life of political bodies, and the protection of human rights the criterion of authentic development and peace, for every violation of human rights contains the seeds of possible conflict.[129] John Paul saw no contradiction between the promotion of human rights and the commitment to the common good. The interconnection of human rights is seen as the expression of different dimensions of the human person, and ethics, for John Paul, is essentially the safeguarding of all that is human.

During his pontificate, John Paul II endorsed the broad range of political, social, and economic rights found in the United Nations documents, "thickening" the notion of human rights in the Catholic tradition.[130] The language of human rights becomes more nuanced than in *Pacem in terris*, with greater emphasis on the relationship between rights, obligations/duties, and truth. Rights are understood not simply as immunities but as indicators of the obligations of human persons toward one another. John Paul II deepens the notion of obligation, grounding it in his personalistic interpretation of the commandment of love, a commandment that he presents as an affirmative deepening of the negative Kantian imperative, and in this context he offers a view of human freedom as oriented toward being a gift for others.[131] "If we cannot accept the prospect of giving ourselves as a gift, then the danger of a selfish freedom will always be present."[132] Thus John Paul not only "thickens" the notion of human rights within the Catholic tradition, but he also deepens the understanding of human freedom that human rights are protective of. This perspective on freedom as oriented toward being a gift for others is consistent with the view of human rights as a boundary discourse in ethics, a discourse that is concerned not only with minimal protection and provision but is also protective of the *more* to which the human person is called.

In *Sollicitudo rei socialis*, John Paul II grounds the human rights debate in the intrinsically social character of human life and links liberal concerns about individual human rights to a broader social picture embracing socioeconomic and political concerns, taking seriously the role of structures and their impact on human life. This emphasis on the social nature of human rights calls forth what John Paul describes as the "virtue" of solidarity.[133] It is perhaps more accurate to speak of an ethic of solidarity, a gathering up of the traditional virtues as powers (*virtus*) to accomplish moral good, into a moral stance in response to the interdependence of humanity. John Paul has a very specific understanding of solidarity as not merely "a feeling of vague compassion or shallow distress at the misfortunes of so many people. . . . It is a firm and persevering determination to commit oneself to the common good."[134] This commitment to the common good calls especially for solidarity with the poor and those who suffer as a consequence of sinful structures and violations of human rights. The theme of solidarity is also central in the ethical discourse emerging from liberation theology. The struggle against human rights violations is not simply a legal-juridical battle, but it is part of the battle against evil and sin, at the personal and social levels, thus placing the struggle at the heart of Catholic moral theology.

HUMAN RIGHTS AND RELIGIOUS FREEDOM

For John Paul II, religious freedom constitutes the very heart of human rights; it is the cornerstone and safeguard of all other rights. This is because the basic identity of the human person consists in orientation to God, and, as *Dignitatis humanae* upheld, the living out of this orientation—even by those in error or those culpable of negligence—is a search for truth that transcends the authority of the state.

However, over time there is a shift in John Paul's reception of *Dignitatis humanae*. For many years, he placed the question of religious freedom in the context of the struggle against atheistic communism; however, in later years, while not denying that religious persecution still exists in many parts of the world, he saw religious freedom as under assault from the forces of secularism and relativism.[135] John Paul appeals for the rights of human conscience because of the persistence of old forms of totalitarianism in parts of the world, the increasing influence of utilitarian values in the developed world, and the threat posed by new forms of religious fundamentalism in other countries.[136]

During his papacy John Paul's reading of the secular became increasingly negative and oppositional. In *Centesimus annus* (1991) John Paul posits that the root of social problems lies in the turn of modernity to secularism, a concern that is augmented in *Veritatis splendor* (1993) and *Evangelium vitae* (1995). The only solution to social problems, he holds, lies in a return to religious values, for secular humanism cannot provide the answers. This view is a significant contrast with his earlier positive view of the secular human rights movement, of the moral significance of the Universal Declaration, and the perception of pneumatological presence in the modern striving for justice, peace, and development. It places John Paul more in line with Niebuhrian Christian realism than with the more hopeful perspective of Vatican II.[137]

Within his vision of the conflict between a "Culture of Life" and a "Culture of Death," there is increasing emphasis on the right to life, particularly in a society where "everything is negotiable . . . even the right to life."[138] John Paul offers a valuable critique of the "surprising contradiction" in human rights discourse and action between a growing moral sensitivity to the dignity of all human persons without distinction, on the one hand, and the undermining of that dignity "especially at the more significant moments of existence: the moment of birth and of death," on the other.[139] He suggests that this contradiction is rooted first in an extreme and distorted form of subjectivity that considers only the radically autonomous person as having rights and second in a "mentality which tends to equate personal dignity with the capacity for verbal and explicit, or at least perceptible communication."[140] This contradiction forges an individualistic understanding of human freedom that risks becoming "the freedom of the 'strong' against the weak who have no choice but to submit."[141] Notwithstanding the complexity of the issues and the often polarized discussions surrounding the ethical questions at the beginning and end of human life, John Paul issues an important challenge to the human rights movement to recognize this contradiction and the implications of the contradiction for our understanding of human dignity, freedom, and vulnerability.

The difficulty with John Paul's vision of a conflict of cultures is that it tends to overlook the elements in secular culture that are compatible with the Christian vision of the welfare of the human person and the justice of human community. This vision also tends to inflate the previous contribution of the

Church to the development of human rights, an inflation that is not consistent with the historical record of the hostility of the Catholic Church to democracy and human rights.

METHODOLOGICAL CONCERNS

Whereas his earlier encyclicals, for example *Redemptor hominis*, with its understanding of the human person as "the primary and fundamental way for the Church," continue the historically conscious methodology of Vatican II, over the years there seems to have been a diminishment of sympathy for this approach and a return to a traditional natural law basis.[142] This methodological shift has been criticized for giving precedence to permanent principles over local discernment of social morality.[143]

However, John Paul also had an acute sense of history and context, as evidenced in the fact that many of his international pastoral visits were at critical moments for human rights and democracy, for example, his visits to Central America in 1983 and to Poland in 1979, 1983, and 1987. His approach to the historicization of human dignity is nonetheless somewhat paradoxical. John Paul's preference for a Thomistic personalism appears to have led to an insistence on universal and absolute norms, but it is also this personalism that led to his championing human rights in specific contexts at critical moments.[144] In many ways his personalism is a two-edged sword, both tending toward an ahistorical approach to ethics that may not serve people well in the concrete particularities of moral discernment, yet also providing a discourse for discussion of human dignity across the boundaries of difference, and the bearing fruit of that discussion in action for the protection of human rights.

ECCLESIOLOGICAL IMPLICATIONS

John Paul II made the defense of human rights the primary mode of engagement of the Church with politics. That defense of human rights is Christologically grounded, for Jesus Christ is the source and center for any exploration of humanism.[145] His reference to an "apostolate of human rights" gives a pastoral-theological dimension to the promotion of human rights and the protection of those whose rights have been violated.[146] This apostolate is a form of service that facilitates ecumenical collaboration as well as collaboration with people of other faiths and secular convictions who actively promote human dignity. Thus, John Paul II has consolidated the relationship between the Catholic Church and democracy in a way that has facilitated both the challenging of inhumane authoritarian rule and offered a critique to democracy itself, pointing to an authentic democracy grounded in explicit recognition of human rights and decision making focused on the common good.[147]

The emphasis by Vatican II and subsequently by John Paul II on the protection and promotion of human rights as a key to and measure of justice led to the refining and application of these themes in the various documents produced by local churches throughout the world. In a 1998 survey of the social teaching of Episcopal conferences worldwide since *Rerum novarum* (1891), human rights emerged as one of the six major themes dealt with in the social documents of the bishops in Africa, Asia, Europe, and North America. The Latin American documents gave priority to the themes of poverty, property, and salaries, whereas Oceania focused primarily on education, government, and property.[148] Across the differences of time and topography, the theme of human rights, either explicitly or implicitly, is a key motif in modern Catholic social thought.

There has been discussion since the Second Vatican Council—both within and without the Church—about the relationship between the public position of the Church on human rights and social justice, and the internal practice of the Church. This discussion has focused on issues such as the tension between public teaching about equality of men and women and domestic ecclesial practice regarding the role of women in the Church, the contradiction between the emphasis on participation as necessary for human dignity and the decision-making structures within the Church, or the economic question of just wages for Church employees. The Church as an institution has a duty to uphold human rights within its own structures, and although the notion of protective rights is found within Canon Law, the Church should be answerable to civil law when it violates human rights. The discourse of human rights may not be the appropriate language to challenge exclusionary practices within the Church, but it could be suggested that John Paul's contribution to democracy, freedom, and human rights in the civil realm "will be enhanced or diminished in the public eye partly by his governance of his institution."[149]

The Direction of Pope Benedict XVI?

In 2008, which marked the sixtieth anniversary of the Universal Declaration of Human Rights, Pope Benedict XVI spoke to the United Nations General Assembly about the global significance of human rights and the accompanying responsibilities.[150] He specifically addressed the emerging doctrine in international human rights discourse, the "responsibility to protect," a responsibility specifically highlighted in Kofi Annan's 2004 report, *A More Secure World: Our Shared Responsibility*, which was referred to earlier.

Benedict upheld the importance of the UN's role in the defense of human rights, the promotion of which is "the most effective strategy for eliminating inequalities between countries and social groups, and for increasing security." In the context of the responsibility to protect, Benedict stated that it is not intervention that is a limitation on sovereignty—provided it is consistent with international law—but rather "it is indifference or failure to intervene that does the real damage."[151] Benedict was speaking not only to the General Assembly but to the international community at a time when international interventions to combat egregious human rights violations in places like the Democratic Republic of Congo and Sudan were (and still are) fraught with difficulties.

Pope Benedict's UN speech, while continuing the Catholic Church's support of the modern human rights project, also issued a caution against human rights becoming a "relativistic conception" that denies their universalism. He expressed concerns about a legal positivism that risks allowing rights to become "weak propositions divorced from the ethical and rational dimension which is their foundation and their goal." Questions about the foundations of human rights, their selective application, unlimited expansion, and the privileging of an individualistic approach are also interwoven in a speech of complex ideas. The right to religious freedom, he reminded us, is not limited to freedom of worship but includes the public dimension of religion and hence "the possibility of believers playing their part in building the social order."

Benedict concluded his speech to the United Nations with reference to his encyclical *Spes salvi*: "every generation has the task of engaging anew in the arduous search for the right way to order human affairs."[152] Christian engagement in the contemporary search for the right way to order human affairs is motivated by hope born of the message of Christ, and the Church is happy to be associated with the organization "charged with the responsibility of promoting peace and goodwill throughout the earth." The post–Vatican II emphasis on the protection and promotion of human rights as keys to and measure of justice may find a theological challenge in the direction that Benedict took Catholic social thought in his encyclical *Deus caritas est*, but this speech to the United Nations deepens Catholic engagement with the discourse of human rights, an engagement characterized by both commitment and critique.[153]

A Crisis of Trust

However, it is with a profound pathos that one approaches the major shift in Catholic engagement with human rights since Vatican II, for the recent child abuse scandals in the Church have led to a crisis of trust in the integrity of the ethic of the institution itself. The painful narratives of horrific and systemic abuse of vulnerable children expose the dissonance between theory and praxis, between the proclaimed ethic and the operative ethic of the Catholic Church. Stephen Rosetti describes a "slow awakening" within the Church, both to the prevalence of child sexual abuse and to awareness of the depth of the damage it caused victims, especially the wounding of the capacity to trust that results from sexual contact with a trusted adult.[154] Church responses, which tended to focus on legal issues, led to the further violation, or "the second injury," of those already violated by abusers. Distorted loyalty to the institution too often took precedence over the protection of the dignity of the human person, in particular that of vulnerable children, and the negative effects of being ignored or blamed constituted an exacerbation of the original trauma.[155] A desire to avoid scandal has overshadowed the Church with a scandal even worse than acknowledging the truth when these violations first came to light, evidence of a deafness to the words of Christ who warned that the harming of one of these little ones is the most profound scandal.[156]

No simple communitarian solution can be proffered to the crisis, for these children were usually members of the Christian community and experienced abuse at the hands of community leaders. A shameful collusion of Church and state in twentieth-century Ireland resulted in some of the poorest children of the nation experiencing abuse in institutions run by a number of religious congregations.[157] The Church failed to live out the personalism that Vatican II had committed it to, both in its moral analysis of the abuse and in its pastoral response to the children involved. Catholic moral theology did not take seriously the child as an ethical subject. And its own theology of human rights failed to prevent violations of human dignity, violations that damaged children in both their vulnerability and their potentiality. Disturbing images and narratives of abuse overshadow graceful praxis and important theological perspectives on human rights.

In the face of this crisis of trust, the temptation is to be silent on matters of human rights; but the challenge is to reflect on the failure of the Church and allow the lessons of that failure to forge our theology and our praxis. This involves persevering with the attempt to discover and articulate—in terms of foundational justification, norms, and praxis—the place of human rights in Christian ethics and continuing to strive for the concrete realization of those rights locally and globally.

Conclusion

Charles Taylor holds that the affirmation of radically unconditional universal human rights in modern liberal political culture could never have emerged from Christendom, a civilization where the institutions and culture are meant to reflect the Christian nature of society. He suggests that the reason for this lies not within Christianity itself but within the particular project of Christendom.[158] Taylor's thesis merits further discussion elsewhere, but the complex history of the relationship between religion and human rights, be that the "hostility" of Catholicism or the "reluctance" of Protestantism, does point to the vulnerability of otherness in a framework of Christendom.

This chapter has outlined two examples of how the dominant moral discourse of our time is expressed in public discourse, one secular, the other religious. Although there are significant foundational differences between both of these public discourses, their commonality is more than simply pragmatic. Faith communities and the narratives on which they are founded can offer critical grounding for human rights discourse protecting it from an infinite expansion of "conflicting subjective wants that have no real authority and, in reality can never be implemented."[159] The Catholic tradition has had to adopt a stance of humility toward the challenge that has come from secular discourse about human rights and the ongoing challenge born of its own internal failure to protect human rights. Secular discourse, particularly with its tendency toward the denial of transcendence and the subsequent reductionist anthropology, also needs challenging. What is called for is reciprocity of critique, a reciprocity that challenges contradictions in both religious and secular use of human rights discourse.

Both the religious and the secular public discourses of human rights are fragile, and both are bruised by failure of implementation. The strength of the religious discourse is that it has the capacity to hold in tension the Kantian–Hegelian dialectic. Catholic engagement with human rights has pointed to the capacity both to uphold the intrinsic value of human dignity and to be attentive to the historicization of that dignity. The secular discourse of human rights continually pushes what Taylor calls "the impulse of solidarity" beyond the frontiers of Christendom, or, indeed, beyond the frontiers of any communal entity that strives to define dignity, equality, and justice in self-referential terms.[160]

The discourse of human rights, this dialectical boundary discourse of human flourishing, positioned in ethics as protective marginality, remains both a catalyst and a meeting point for ethical conversation across traditions but is never dependent entirely on one tradition. Defining and locating rights discourse as a boundary discourse prevents it from eclipsing other forms of ethical and political discourse. Human rights thus can never be the center and goal of ethics, but rights discourse is positioned on the margins of ethics as a discourse of protection of the *more* of ethics to which we are called as persons and communities, nationally and internationally. We can respond to Rorty's remark, quoted at the beginning of this chapter, by saying that the remnant child of the slaughtered nation is not devoid of human dignity.

Notes

The epigraph for this chapter is drawn from Richard Rorty, "Postmodernist Bourgeois Liberalism," in *Objectivity, Relativism, and Truth: Philosophical Papers,* Vol. I (Cambridge: Cambridge University Press, 1991), 201.

1. Rorty, "Postmodernist Bourgeois Liberalism," 202.
2. Witte, *The Reformation of Rights,* 344. Witte outlines the human rights side of the Calvinist story without denying its bleaker side, showing how the distinct Calvinist theology and jurisprudence of human rights were gradually cast into enduring institutional and constitutional forms in early modern Europe and America.
3. Tierney, *The Idea of Natural Rights.*
4. Skinner, *Liberty before Liberalism.* Skinner explores the rise of what he calls the neo-Roman understanding of civil liberty in English political thought of the mid-seventeenth century, its subsequent fall, and the consequent hegemony of liberalism in Anglophone political philosophy.

5. An example of this one-dimensional approach to the history of human rights is to be found in A. C. Grayling's *Towards the Light: The Story of the Struggles for Liberty and Rights That Made the Modern West* (London: Bloomsbury, 2007).

6. Richard Rorty, "Human Rights, Rationality and Sentimentality," in *On Human Rights: The Oxford Amnesty Lectures 1993*, Stephen Shute and Susan Hurley, eds. (New York: Basic Books), 111–34.

7. Henry Hardy and Roger Hausheer, eds., *The Proper Study of Mankind: An Anthology of Essays* (London: Chatto & Windus, 1997), 243–68.

8. Consider the 1947 American Anthropological Association's "Statement on Human Rights," *American Anthropologist* 49, no. 4 (1947): 539–43. On hearing that the Commission on Human Rights was considering proposals for a declaration of basic human rights, the executive board of the Association wrote to the Commission asking: "How can the proposed Declaration be applicable to all human beings and not be a statement of rights conceived only in terms of the values prevalent in the countries of Western Europe and North America?" Expressing concern that the values of other peoples had been consistently misunderstood, the board stated that standards and values are relative to the culture from which they derive.

9. See Kam Weng Ng's "Human Rights and Asian Values" in *Christianity and Human Rights: Influences and Issues*, Frances S. Adeney and Arvind Sharma, eds. (Albany: State University of New York Press, 2007), 151–66. She deconstructs four aspects of the "Asian values" argument: the cultural specificity of human rights; the precedence of the community over the individual; the priority of social-economic rights over civil-political rights; and the reserve of the implementation of human rights as a matter of national sovereignty.

10. *On Capital Punishment* (Port of Spain: Antilles Episcopal Conference, 2000) n. 13.

11. See Jan Patocka, *Heretical Essays in the Philosophy of History*, trans. Erazim Kohák (Chicago: Open Court, 1996).

12. Donnelly, *International Human Rights*, 35–36.

13. Abdullahi A. An-Na'im, ed. *Human Rights in Cross-Cultural Perspectives*, "Introduction," 3. See also chapter I: "Toward a Cross-Cultural Approach to Defining International Standards of Human Rights: The Meaning of Cruel, Inhuman, or Degrading Treatment or Punishment," 19–43. An-Na'im suggests that both the international standards and the norms and values of culture must be open to revision. He does not advocate discarding the universal standards but simply questioning the upholding of these standards in absolute terms, without due concern for promoting the cultural legitimacy of human rights; see "Conclusion," 427–35. Amartya Sen, in an examination of the relationship between culture and human rights in Asia, highlights the key issue as "not whether these non-freedom perspectives are *present* in Asian traditions, but whether the freedom-oriented perspectives are *absent* there." Sen, *Development as Freedom* (Oxford: Oxford

University Press, 1999), 234. Addressing the question of the legitimacy of universal human rights from a legal perspective, with special reference to the African Charter, one of the regional instruments that adds complexity to human rights law, Lone Lindholt, in *Questioning the Universality of Human Rights*, concludes that a universal approach remains legitimate if one distinguishes between the essence and detailed formulations.

14. Tibi, *The Challenge of Fundamentalism*. See chapter 10: "Human Rights in Islam and the West: Cross-Cultural Foundations of Shared Values," 198–214, at 205. The importance of engaging with Islamic religious scholarship is highlighted in Irene Oh's *The Rights of God: Islam, Human Rights, and Comparative Ethics* (Washington, DC: Georgetown University Press, 2007). Through an analysis of the work of three Islamic scholars, Abul A'la Maududi, Sayyid Qutb, and Abdolkarim Soroush, Oh examines human rights issues of the contemporary Islamic world, particularly political participation, religious toleration, and freedom of conscience. All three scholars contend that Islam is capable of accommodating and advocating human rights.

15. Seyla Benhabib, "The Generalized and the Concrete Other: The Kohlberg-Gilligan Controversy and Feminist Theory," *Praxis International* 4 (1985): 402–24, at 416.

16. Ackerly, *Universal Human Rights*.

17. Ibid., 89.

18. Ibid., 76. Ackerly offers an important challenge to all those concerned about human rights to be vigilant about those whose voices are excluded or silenced in human rights discourse, but her dismissal of the transcendental appeal as a mere mask for power seems to overlook the important role that religion plays in feminist moral discourse.

19. See T. Asad, "On Torture, or Cruel, Inhuman and Degrading Treatment," in Arthur Kleinman, Veena Das, and Margaret Lock, eds., *Social Suffering* (Berkeley/London: University of California Press, 1997), 285–308, at 285. I concur with Asad but with the caveat that the use of experiences of torture and cruelty to explore questions of cultural relativism needs extremely sensitive handling.

20. Kofi Annan addressed the question of the universality of human rights from the perspective of his own continent, Africa. He challenged the suggestion that human rights were a luxury of the rich for which Africa was not ready, describing this as "demeaning of the yearning for human dignity that resides in every African heart." *UN Press Release*, SG/SM/6359, October 15, 1997. Quoted in William Korey, *NGOs and the Universal Declaration of Human Rights: A Curious Grapevine* (New York: St. Martin's Press, 1998), 490.

21. Jonathan Sacks, *To Heal a Fractured World: The Ethics of Responsibility* (London/New York: Continuum, 2005).

22. Finnis, *Natural Law and Natural Rights*, 221.

23. Dworkin, *Taking Rights Seriously*, 139, 269.

24. R. J. Vincent, *Human Rights and International Relations* (Cambridge: Cambridge University Press, 1986), vi. In chapters 6–8, Vincent deals with this question of the priority of subsistence rights.

25. Sextus Empiricus describes the most fundamental difference among philosophies: "When people are investigating any subject, the likely result is either a discovery, or a denial of discovery and a confession of inapprehensibility, or else a continuation of the investigation. This, no doubt, is why in the case of philosophical investigations, too, some have said that they have discovered the truth, some have asserted that it cannot be apprehended, and others are still investigating." *Outlines of Scepticism*, Book I, Cambridge Texts in the History of Philosophy, Julia Annas and Jonathan Barnes, eds. (Cambridge: Cambridge University Press, 2000), 3.

26. All references to United Nations documents on human rights are from *Blackstone's International Human Rights Documents*, 3rd ed., P. R. Gandhi, ed. (Oxford: Oxford University Press, 2002).

27. At the Yalta Conference in February 1945, Churchill, Roosevelt, and Stalin decided on the San Francisco meeting, to be called the United Nations Conference on International Organization, the purpose of which would be to develop the plan worked out at Dumbarton Oaks the previous year.

28. Susan Sontag used this phrase to describe the impact on her, aged twelve, of coming across photographs of Bergen-Belsen and Dachau in a bookstore in California in July 1945. "One's first encounter with the photographic inventory of ultimate horror is a kind of revelation: a negative epiphany." *On Photography* (Harmondsworth, England: Penguin Books, 1979), 19–20.

29. In Paul Gordon Lauren's *The Evolution of International Human Rights* there is a detailed discussion of this "extraordinary" influence of NGOs and individuals. See chapter 6, "A 'People's Peace': Peace and a Charter with Human Rights," 172–204. More than forty NGOs were present representing churches, trade unions, women, and ethnic minorities, and submissions came from distant groups such as the West Indies National Council, the Sino-Korean League, the Non-European United Committee of Cape Town, and the London-based Council of Christians and Jews. The NGOs present in San Francisco were very active, especially the U.S. groups, lobbying representatives and issuing press statements. For an account of the impact of an ecumenical movement of mainline Protestant churches across England, Europe, and North America on the securing of a Commission on Human Rights and the subsequent passage of the Universal Declaration of Human Rights, see John S. Nurser's *For All Peoples and All Nations*. Nurser's account brings back into human rights discourse the almost forgotten role that Protestant, Catholic, and Jewish leaders played in shaping the Universal Declaration of Human Rights. He highlights the contribution of Frederick Nolde and his associates to the drafting of what became Article 18 on religious freedom.

30. Theodor Adorno, *Negative Dialectics* (New York: Seabury Press, 1973), 365.

31. Italics mine. The Charter marks a departure from the 1919 Covenant of the League of Nations, which made no reference to human rights.
32. See the Preamble and Articles 1, 13, 55, 62, 68, 76.
33. The Latin American contribution was influenced by the Inter-American Conference on Problems of War and Peace—the Chapultepec Conference of February-March 1945—which was critical of the Dumbarton Oaks proposals and questioned the intentions of the Great Powers regarding the role of human rights in the new international organization. The conference also included NGOs and private citizens as well as official representatives of twenty-one nations, all of whom were committed to the notion of the moral validity of universal human rights. Throughout the war, there was mounting pressure for a bill of rights, coming from many sources, both within the United States and internationally.
34. Article 2:7. These Great Powers were discussing universal human rights while their own domestic situations served as a contradiction, e.g., Stalin's terror, segregation in the United States, and the British denial of rights within their empire. Many of the other states were also unwilling to limit their own sovereignty for the sake of human rights. The principles of equal rights and self-determination did not extend to an explication of the rights of indigenous peoples throughout the world.
35. See Articles 55 and 56. Lauren, in *The Evolution of International Human Rights*, 197, suggests that a "more detailed reading of *all* the provisions in the Charter revealed that the politics and diplomacy of the San Francisco Conference also had produced important qualifications, omissions, and other problems that would confront the evolution of international human rights for many years" (197).
36. The 1648 Treaty of Westphalia marked the end of the Thirty Years' War, the beginning of a constitutional system of states, and the demise of the notion of a Holy Roman Empire ruling the Christian world. In *The Shield of Achilles: War, Peace, and the Course of History* (London: Allen Lane, 2002), Philip Bobbitt reminds us that the modern form of the nation state is only over a century old and suggests a new form of "market state" is already emerging.
37. Alasdair MacIntyre, *After Virtue: A Study in Moral Theory* (London: Duckworth, 1981), 67. MacIntyre is denying the existence of human rights as an ontological category rather than "legal" rights as the product of positive law.
38. "I am quite certain that my way of justifying belief in the rights of man and the ideal of liberty, equality, fraternity is the only way with a firm foundation in truth. This does not prevent me from being in agreement on these practical convictions with people who are certain that their way of justifying them, entirely different from mine or opposed to mine, . . . is equally the only way founded upon truth." United Nations Educational, Scientific and Cultural Organization, ed., *Human Rights: Comments and Interpretations*, 10–11. Maritain, a Catholic and a Thomist, justified his belief in human rights on the basis of the natural law. He was a key figure in the drafting of the Declaration, and his own writings contributed to an acceptance of human rights discourse by the Catholic Church.

39. For an extensive account of the drafting process see Johannes Morsink's *The Universal Declaration of Human Rights*. 10. Morsink notes that although there were only eighteen nations represented on the Commission, at least four different opportunities were given for the other thirty-eight UN member nations to make contributions.

40. The first draft was known as the Draft Outline of an International Bill of Human Rights. See Morsink, *The Universal Declaration of Human Rights*, ch. 2: "The Drafting Process Explained," 1–35.

41. René Cassin is popularly described as the "Father of the Declaration," but his work on the second draft added only three completely new articles to Humphrey's draft. Morsink shows that Cassin later overstated his role in drafting the document but that he was the drafter who did most to later interpret the Declaration internationally, "almost always stressing the theme of universality" (1999: 29; 7–9; nn. 58–61, 343). See also Glendon, *A World Made New*, 65–66.

42. In his study of the Declaration, Johannes Morsink outlines details of the drafting process that link the acceptance or rejection of specific articles and phrases to these experiences of the war. Morsink discusses the rights connected with personal security, legal human rights, those linked with the procedures of democratic government, new international rights such as citizenship and asylum, and examples related to the social, economic and cultural articles of the Declaration. Morsink, *The Universal Declaration of Human Rights*, ch. 2: "World War II as Catalyst," 36–91.

43. Articles 6–12.

44. Preamble.

45. Reference to this definition is found in the preambles to the following conventions: 1949 Convention on the Suppression of Traffic of Persons; 1951 Convention on the Status of Refugees; 1952 Convention on the Political Rights of Women; 1956 Supplementary Convention on the Abolition of Slavery; 1959 Convention on the Rights of the Child. This first article is very similar to the first article of the 1789 French Declaration.

46. It is interesting to observe that the large and comprehensive *Encyclopedia of Human Rights* (New York: Taylor & Francis, 1991) has no entry on dignity. There is no reference in David Robertson, *A Dictionary of Human Rights* (London: Europe Publications, 1997), and in the *Dictionary of International Human Rights Law* (Lanham, MD: Scarecrow Press, 2004) the entry on "Dignity, Honor, Reputation" describes all three as core attributes of the human person that need protection, but there is particular emphasis on their protection against libel and slander.

47. Gabriel Marcel, "The Existential Background of Human Dignity," *The William James Lectures—Harvard*, 1961–62, 158–59.

48. Italics mine.

49. Article 3 of Humphrey's draft referred to the "willing acceptance of obligations and sacrifices demanded for the common good." It is unfortunate that this refer-

ence was omitted. The discussion of duties in the context of the drafting of the Declaration is found in Morsink, chapter 7: "Duties and Communities"; there is special reference to the late placing of Article 29 on 244–46.

50. See the preface to the 1995 British edition of Amitai Etzioni's *The Spirit of Community*, ix–xii. Etzioni says that communitarian thinking is rooted in ancient Greece and in the Hebrew and Christian scriptures. "Communitarians call to restore civic virtues, for people to live up to their responsibilities and not merely focus on their entitlements and to shore up the moral foundations of society" (ix). I am using the term in a broader sense than that used to describe the school of thought, of which Etzioni is representative, that arose in Anglo-American academic circles after the publication of John Rawls's *A Theory of Justice*.

51. The *African Charter on Human and People's Rights* has codified such duties. See Articles 27–29.

52. Johan Galtung, *Human Rights in Another Key* (Cambridge: The Polity Press), 1994.

53. See the critique of Gilles Lipovetsky's designation of our time as the epoch of *l'après devoir*, by Zigmund Baumann, *Postmodern Ethics* (Oxford: Blackwell, 1993), 2–4.

54. *Declaration*, article 29.

55. The notion of subsidiarity simply means that nothing should be done at a higher level that can be done just as well, or better, at a lower level. It points to the importance of balance between individual and small group initiative, and governmental assistance or action, without endorsing, in any way, a laissez-faire approach to economics and politics.

56. The Martens Clause, first included in the Hague Convention of 1899, affirms the applicability of "principles of international law derived from established custom, from the principles of humanity and from the dictates of the public conscience," in cases not directly covered by statutes or international agreements. See Ingrid Detter, *The Law of War*, 2nd ed. (Cambridge: Cambridge University Press, 2000), 187–88.

57. Report of the Panel on United Nations Peace Operations, August 2000, www .un.org/peace/reports/peace_operations/ [accessed August 15, 2008]. The phrase from the report, "complicity with evil," is used in the title of a book by Adam Lebor that examines the response of the UN to genocide: *"Complicity with Evil": The United Nations in the Age of Modern Genocide*. Lebor is critical of the "passive" complicity of the UN in Bosnia, Rwanda, and Darfur.

58. The Report of the Secretary-General's High-Level Panel on Threats, Challenges, and Change stressed that globalization also means globalized threats: war between States; violence within States, including large-scale human rights abuses and genocide; poverty, infectious diseases, and environmental degradation; proliferation of nuclear, radiological, chemical, and biological weapons; terrorism; and transnational organized crime. In the face of these threats, development, including combating poverty, is the first line of defence and security. *A*

More Secure World: Our Shared Responsibility, available online at www.un.org/secureworld/ [accessed August 17, 2008].

59. Falk, *Human Rights Horizons*, 9.

60. Curran, "Churches and Human Rights." George Weigel refers to a "Catholic human rights revolution of the late twentieth century," which "owes a debt of gratitude" to Leo XIII. See "The New 'New Things'" in Curran and McCormick, eds., *John Paul II and Moral Theology*, 313.

61. "On Liberalism and Religious Indifferentism," www.papalencyclicals.net/Greg16/g16mirar.htm [accessed August 17, 2008].

62. "Ultramontanism" literally means, "those who looked beyond the mountains," i.e., the Alps, to Rome. It refers to a position that resisted any attempts to engage positively with the new intellectual milieu of the nineteenth century and looked increasingly to Rome for papal guidance. It is reflected in "Integralism," which holds that nothing is "integral" unless it comes within the orbit of the Church, and "Fideism," the denial of a rational content of faith.

63. "Catholicism and Democracy: Conflict, Change, and Collaboration," in Charles E. Curran, ed., *Change in Official Catholic Moral Teachings: Readings in Moral Theology No. 13* (New York/Mahwah, NJ: Paulist Press, 2003), 20–37, at 22.

64. See John Courtney Murray's comments on these documents, "The Declaration on Religious Freedom," in Curran ed., *Change in Official Catholic Moral Teachings*, 3–12.

65. *Rerum novarum*, no. 7: www.vatican.va/holy_father/leo_xiii/encyclicals/documents/hf_l-xiii_enc_15051891_rerum-novarum_en.html [accessed August 19, 2008].

66. Ibid., nos. 51, 62.

67. Ibid., nos. 49–51.

68. In his 1942 Christmas broadcast, Pius spoke of the unspeakable horror of "the hundreds of thousands who, through no fault of their own, and solely because of their nation or race, have been condemned to death or progressive extinction," *Acta Apostolicae Sedis* 35 (1943): 9–24.

69. Pius XII is portrayed by John Cornwell as "Hitler's Pope," power hungry and anti-Semitic, in *Hitler's Pope: The Secret History of Pius XII* (New York: Viking Press, 1999). Assessments of his role during the Holocaust are written by both detractors and hagiographers. In *The Catholic Church and the Holocaust, 1930–1965*, Michael Phayer's thesis is that Pius was concerned with safeguarding Europe from Communism, avoiding a direct conflict with Nazi Germany, and protecting the city of Rome from destruction. These concerns prevented Pius from more public intervention on behalf of the Jews. Pius did, in fact, help Jews, and Henri de Lubac wrote that his own efforts to aid Jews were inspired by the pope. See *Christian Resistance to Anti-Semitism: Memories from 1940–1944*, trans. Elizabeth Englund (San Francisco: Ignatius Press, 1990). Tributes paid to Pius by Jewish leaders in the years after the war attest to the help he did give. For an insightful examination of the historical investigation of Pius's role during the war, see José

M. Sanchez, *Pius XII and the Holocaust.* Sanchez notes the fair degree of prejudgment of innocence or guilt, by authors, before starting their investigations.

The role of Pius's ecclesiology—together with the prevailing neoscholastic philosophy, which saw few points of convergence with the contemporary world—in shaping Pius's decisions must not be underestimated. In examining the conflict between the University of Freiburg theologian Engelbert Krebs and the Third Reich, Robert A. Krieg notes that Krebs developed "a theology of love of neighbour that sees the church witnessing to the coming of God's Kingdom." Krebs spoke out against National Socialism and publicly held positive views of Judaism. Kreig suggests that the greater the identification of the church with God's kingdom, the more the theologian felt that "the church must safeguard its own interests at all costs," its members, its sacramental life and institutions. Krebs and others who opposed the 1933 Concordat "held a vision of God's new creation in relation to which they condemned the Nazi leaders' motives and actions. This concluding thought stands as a hypothesis that needs to be tested in further studies of German Catholic theologians." Krieg, "The Conflict between Engelbert Krebs and the Third Reich," in Donald J. Dietrich, ed., *Christian Responses to the Holocaust: Moral and Ethical Issues* (Syracuse, NY: Syracuse University Press, 2003), 24–37, at 35, 36, 37. In referring here to Krieg's hypothesis, a direct comparison of Krebs with Pius XII is not intended, for their roles and burdens of responsibility are completely different; however, the issue of ecclesiology is a central one.

70. It is interesting to note that in 1941 Eleanor Roosevelt received a letter from the National Catholic Welfare Conference, established by the U.S. bishops to deal with concerns related to education, immigration, and social action, asking her "to push for human rights." See Morsink, *The Universal Declaration of Human Rights,* 1.

71. Hereafter referred to as Vatican II.

72. Dorr, *Option for the Poor,* 115.

73. The first session lasted from October 11 to December 8, 1962. *Pacem in terris* was promulgated on April 11, 1963. Pope John XXIII died on June 3, 1963. The second session opened on September 29, 1963, after the election of Pope Paul VI on June 21, 1963. Pope Paul announced his intention to continue the council the day after his election. Vatican II was closed on December 8, 1965.

74. The version of *Pacem in terris* used here is from Joseph Gremillion, ed., *The Gospel of Peace and Justice,* 201–41.

75. *Pacem in terris,* nos. 9–10.

76. "They [the Gentiles] show that the demands of the law are written in their hearts, while their conscience also bears witness and their conflicting thoughts accuse or even defend them." All scripture references in this book are from the *New American Bible: The Catholic Study Bible* (New York and Oxford: Oxford University Press, 1990).

77. *Pacem in terris,* nos. 142–45, at 144.

78. Ibid., nos. 11–27.

79. Inspired by *Rerum novarum,* John A. Ryan wrote an influential book titled *A Living Wage: Its Ethical and Economic Aspects* (New York: Macmillan, 1906). It was the fruit of his doctoral dissertation at the Catholic University of America, and it introduced the American Church to the importance of a right to a just wage.

80. Pope John draws from his predecessor, Pius XII, as evidenced in the large number of footnotes referring to Pius, especially his endorsement of civil-political rights in his Christmas messages of the early 1940s and the endorsement of a democratic form of government as a "postulate of human reason" in his 1944 Christmas message.

81. *Pacem in terris,* nos. 86, 89, 92, 120.

82. Ibid., nos. 30–34.

83. Ibid., no. 65. See also *Mater et magistra,* no. 119, www.vatican.va/holy_father/ john_xxiii/encyclicals/documents/hf_j-xxiii_enc_15051961_mater_en.html [accessed August 1, 2008].

84. Dorr, *Option for the Poor,* chapter 6: "Pope John XXIII—A New Direction?" 113–48, at 144.

85. Charles Curran, *Catholic Social Teaching 1891–Present: A Historical, Theological, and Ethical Analysis* (Washington, DC: Georgetown University Press, 2002), 10.

86. Murray, "Things Old and New in *Pacem in Terris,*" 614.

87. Cranston, "Pope John XXIII on Peace and the Rights of Man," 390. Cranston suggests that the intellectual force of *Pacem in terris* is comparable to that of Kant's *Zum ewige Friede.*

88. Cranston is critical of the weak treatment of the "common good" in the document, the lack of awareness of the dangerous use of the notion of the common good by totalitarian regimes, and the failure to analyze more carefully the relation between the common good and the specific human rights that it mentions. Here Cranston fails to appreciate that the principle of subsidiarity, inherited by Pope John as part of the body of teaching developed since Pope Leo XIII, is meant to prevent the common good from assuming an importance independent of the concerns of the persons in society; nor does the pope reduce the common good to the preservation of individual interests. In this article, Cranston is also critical of the pope's assimilation of economic and social rights to the same category as civil and political rights. He is concerned that if the right to a decent standard of living is seen to be an ideal rather than a genuine categorical right, there is a danger that civil and political rights may be considered *mere* ideals, and some governments may not take them seriously.

89. It must be noted that the Protestant response was not solely negative. John C. Bennett of Union Theological Seminary in New York described *Pacem in terris* as "maybe the most powerful healing word that has come from any source during the Cold War." Bennett saw the document as calling Western Christians away

from the kind of anticommunism that was often prevalent at the time. *"Pacem in terris:* Two Views," *Christianity and Crisis* 23 (May 13, 1963): 82–83.

90. Hollenbach, *Claims in Conflict*, 111.

91. Bernard Lonergan "Theology in Its New Context," in *Theology of Renewal, Vol. 1: Renewal of Religious Thought*, L. K. Shook, ed. (New York: Herder and Herder, 1968), 34–36. This shift to historical consciousness was one of the nineteenth-century trends that the Church had resisted due to the misuse of the notions of the historicity of the truth, and the question of the role of the subject in posses-sion of the truth, in order to attack the objective character of truth.

92. Emmanuel Mounier, who writes as a Christian Personalist, viewed personalism not as a system but as a perspective, method, and exigency. See *Be Not Afraid: A Denunciation of Despair* (New York: Sheed & Ward, 1962), 193.

93. *Gaudium et spes*, no. 5. (All references from the Conciliar documents are from Austin Flannery, general editor: *Vatican Council II*.)

94. Ibid., no. 3.

95. Ibid., no. 4.

96. Ibid., no. 46.

97. Ibid., no. 55.

98. Ibid., no. 10.

99. Ibid., no. 38.

100. Ibid.

101. Ibid., nos. 24, 29.

102. See no. 26. Italics are mine. Note the attribution of universality and inviolability to duties.

103. The purpose of this meeting was to look at the reality of Latin America in the light of the documents of the Second Vatican Council. There are sixteen sections in the documents, and it was the three sections on justice, peace, and poverty that offered a new perspective.

104. Segunda Conferencía General del Episcopado Latinoamericano, *La Iglesia en la Actual Transformación de América Latina a la Luz del Concilio: Conclusiones* (Mexico City: Talleres de la Imprenta Mexicana, 1970).

105. *Gaudium et spes*, no. 21.

106. Ibid., nos. 40–42.

107. Kenneth L. Grasso, "Beyond Liberalism: Human Dignity, the Free Society, and the Second Vatican Council," in *Catholicism, Liberalism, and Communitarianism: The Catholic Intellectual Tradition and the Moral Foundations of Democracy*, Ken-neth L. Grasso, Gerard V. Bradley, and Robert P. Hunt, eds. (Boston: Rowan & Littlefield, 1995), 30–33.

108. See *Gaudium et spes*, no. 74.

109. Pope John Paul II will later use the term "apostolate of human rights."

110. *Gaudium et spes*, no. 41.

111. Ibid., no. 28.

112. Hollenbach, *Claims in Conflict*, 70.

113. *Gaudium et spes*, no. 45.

114. "Amen, I say to you, what ever you did for one of these least brothers of mine, you did it for me": Matthew 25: 40, *New American Bible* (1990).

115. *Dignitatis humanae*, no. 1.

116. Although it may not be a milestone in philosophical debate, the significance of the development in *Dignitatis humanae* is acknowledged by John Rawls in one of his last essays, "The Idea of Public Reason Revisited," published together with *The Law of Peoples*, 131–80, at 166–67, no. 75. See also 142 and 170 for a positive assessment of aspects of Catholic political discourse. In that essay Rawls outlines some revisions of *Political Liberalism* (New York: Columbia University Press, 1993), revisions that were not completed prior to his death in 2002.

117. *Dignitatis humanae*, nos. 2, 6.

118. Ibid., no. 6.

119. John Witte Jr., in his book on the Calvinist contribution to the human rights tradition, shows how the early reformers discovered that the proper protection of religious rights required protection of several attendant rights both for the individual and for the religious group: the right to assemble, speak, worship, educate, parent, and the right to legal personality, corporate property, freedom of association, and freedom of press. *The Reformation of Rights*, 2.

120. Murray, "Introduction to the 'Declaration on Religious Freedom,'" 674. In Murray's work on the teaching of Leo XIII, he emphasized the idea of doctrinal evolution, continuity, and progress, so that the change in the Church's teaching on religious freedom would be more acceptable to the bishops at the Council and assuage their fears that it would contradict pre-Leonine papal teaching. A critique of Murray's fine work is outside the scope of this chapter; however, it is fair to suggest that Leo XIII would probably have held that "error has no rights" as a matter of doctrine, not dependent on historical circumstances.

121. Murray, "The Declaration on Religious Freedom," in Curran, ed., *Change in Official Catholic Moral Teachings*, 3–12, at 7.

122. In Abbott, ed., 677, no. 4. This English translation of the "Declaration on Religious Freedom" was chiefly prepared by John Courtney Murray, one of the drafters of the Latin original.

123. In *Church, State, Morality & Law*, Patrick Hannon suggests that the position of *Dignitatis humanae* regarding religious freedom could be applied to the issue of moral freedom, arguing that people "should not be made to act against their consciences nor restrained from acting according to conscience—subject to the requirements of the common good." He develops a creative and coherent argument that "the stance of Catholicism vis-à-vis freedom of moral belief and practice in civil society is analogous to its stance in the sphere of religious belief and practice" (Dublin: Gill and Macmillan, 1992), 3, 10.

124. *Address to the United Nations General Assembly*, no. 2, October 5, 1995, www.vatican.va/holy_father/john_paul_ii/ [accessed August 22, 2008].

125. Address for World Day of Peace, 1999, www.vatican.va/holy_father/john_paul_ ii/messages/peace/ [accessed August 22, 2008].

126. "Our time—a time particularly hungry for the Spirit, because it is hungry for justice, peace, love, goodness, fortitude and possibility." *Redemptor hominis*, no.18, www.vatican.va/holy_father/john_paul_ii/ [accessed August 23, 2008].

127. *Sollicitudo rei socialis*, no. 6.

128. *Redemptor hominis*, no. 19.

129. Ibid.; *Sollicitudo rei socialis*, no. 44; World Day of Peace Message, 1999.

130. This "thickening" is especially evident in *Centesimus annus*. *Sollicitudo rei socialis*, no. 15, had already outlined the "right to economic initiative."

131. *Crossing the Threshold of Hope* (London: Jonathan Cape, 1994), 200–201.

132. Ibid., 202.

133. *Sollicitudo rei socialis*, no. 38, www.vatican.va/holy_father/john_paul_ii/encyclicals/ documents/hf_jp-ii_enc_30121987_sollicitudo-rei-socialis_en.html [accessed August 2, 2008].

134. Ibid. See also no. 39.

135. Herminio Rico identifies three moments for *Dignitatis humanae*: (a) religious freedom replaces established Catholicism: Vatican II and the past to which it brought closure; (b) freedom of the Church against atheistic communism; (c) the present situation, now unfolding: new encounters of Catholicism with an evolved liberalism. See Rico, *John Paul II and the Legacy of* "*Dignitatis Humanae.*"

136. See *Centesimus annus*, no. 29, www.vatican.va/holy_father/john_paul_ii/ encyclicals/documents/hf_jp-ii_enc_01051991_centesimus-annus_en.html [accessed August 3, 2008].

137. See Reinhold Niebuhr, *Moral Man and Immoral Society: A Study in Ethics and Politics* (New York: Charles Scribner's Sons, 1932/1960).

138. *Evangelium vitae*, no. 29.

139. Ibid., no. 18.

140. Ibid., no. 19.

141. Ibid.

142. *Redemptor hominis*, no. 14.

143. An example of the diminishment of sympathy for the historically conscious methodology is found in *Evangelium vitae*, where a natural law basis is coupled with a biblical approach to fundamental themes.

144. His Thomism is enriched by engagement with phenomenological and existential insights. Andrew Woznicki, a former student of the then Karol Wojtyla at Lublin, describes his teacher's personalism: "An existential personalism, which is metaphysically explained and phenomenologically described." *A Christian Humanism: Karol Wojtyla's Existential Personalism* (New Britain, CT: Mariel Publications, 1980), 59. Stefan Swiezawski, historian of philosophy, was a colleague of Wojtyla at Lublin. He describes the distinctive character of the Lublin School of Philosophy after World War II. The experience of suffering forced

upon them profound questions of philosophical anthropology and called into question both Kantian idealism and Marxist materialism. The main canons of their approach to philosophy were "the primacy of realistic metaphysics, the central role of philosophical anthropology, and the affirmation of a rational approach to philosophy." See Introduction: "Karol Wojtyla at the Catholic University of Lublin" in *Person and Community: Selected Essays/Karol Wojytla*, trans. Theresa Sandok (New York: Peter Lang, 1993), ix–xvi, at xiii.

145. Christ "fully reveals man to himself." *Redemptor hominis*, no. 24.

146. See reference to this in *Human Rights and the Catholic Church* (London: Catholic Bishops' Conference of England and Wales, Catholic Media Office, 1998), no. 10.

147. See, e.g., *Centesimus annus*, nos. 46, 47. The change in the stance of the Catholic Church toward human rights and democracy has impacted the development of democracy in many parts of the world, particularly in the two decades after Vatican II. Samuel P. Huntington suggests that Catholicism was second only to economic development as a force for democratization during that time. In *The Third Wave: Democratization in the Late Twentieth Century* (Oklahoma City: University of Oklahoma Press, 1991), Huntington identifies three waves of democratization experienced by the modern world: The first was a century-long wave beginning in 1820, rooted in the American and French revolutions, occurring mainly in dominantly Protestant countries in North America and Europe. The second wave began after World War II and continued until the mid-1960s, during which countries such as West Germany, Italy, Austria, Japan, and Korea established democratic governments, and steps toward democracy were taken in Greece, Turkey, and many countries in Latin America, with decolonization beginning in Africa and new democracies emerging in Asia. A diversity of religions was involved. There was a period after each of the first two waves when some of the countries that had embraced democracy reverted to former undemocratic patterns of government. Huntington points to the fall of the Portuguese dictatorship in 1974 as the beginning of the third wave, which, at least in the first fifteen years, was overwhelmingly Catholic (in countries in Europe, Latin America, and Asia) due both to the Vatican II change in official teaching regarding democracy and human rights and to increasing local involvement of clergy and laity in social justice. The formation of national Episcopal conferences after Vatican II meant that in some countries, e.g., the Philippines, Poland, and Brazil, these conferences played a key role in the struggle for human rights and democracy. Huntington suggests that the Catholic impetus to democratization had largely exhausted itself by 1990. However, he overlooks the fact that the achievement of a democratic regime is not an end in itself for Catholicism, nor for any authentic Christian social ethic. Social justice remains elusive in many democratic countries, and vigilance regarding the violation of human rights cannot be weakened.

The Catholic Church in Latin America, in varying ways and to varying degrees, contributed to the redemocratization of many countries through denouncing dictatorships, protecting the persecuted, documenting the violations of human rights, legitimizing opposition, and creating "participatory spaces" for religious groups or other groups associated in some way with the mission of the Church. Even in Argentina, during the "Dirty War" (1976–83), where the bishops denounced the military regime in private but supported it in public, a courageous minority of bishops and priests, together with many other Catholics, struggled to defend human rights. (See Klaiber, *The Church, Dictatorships, and Democracy in Latin America*.) In a comparative analysis of eleven different countries, Klaiber examines the efforts of the Catholic Church to defend human rights and promote democracy. He notes that the paradox of the return to democracy, for many progressive Latin American Catholics, is that it coincided with the rise of neo-conservatism in the Church and the spread of neoliberalism (269–70).

148. Terence McGoldrick, "Episcopal Conferences Worldwide on Catholic Social Teaching," *Theological Studies* 59 (1998): 22–50. These documents are the subject of an extensive cataloguing research project at the Moral Theology Institute, University of Fribourg, Switzerland.

149. J. Bryan Hehir, "Catholicism and Democracy: Conflict, Change, and Collaboration," in Curran, ed., *Change in Official Catholic Moral Teachings*, 37.

150. Address to the Members of the General Assembly of the United Nations Organization, April 18, 2008. Available online at www.vatican.va/holy_father/benedict_xvi/ [accessed March 25, 2009].

151. Here Benedict is building on the principle established in *Pacem in terris* that the legitimacy of a government is based on its respect for the rights of their people. "Thus any government which refused to recognize human rights or acted in violation of them, would not only fail in its duty; its decrees would be wholly lacking in binding force" (61).

152. *Spes salvi*, 2007, no. 25. Available online at www.vatican.va/holy_father/benedict_xvi/ [accessed March 25, 2009].

153. *Deus caritas est*, December 25, 2005. Available online at www.vatican.va/holy_father/benedict_xvi/ [accessed March 25, 2009]. For a critique of the challenges posed by *Deus caritas est* to Catholic Aid and Development agencies, see Regan, "Justice Overshadowed by Charity?" 140–57.

154. In *A Tragic Grace: The Catholic Church and Child Sexual Abuse*, Rosetti says that a changed perspective on children, i.e., that they are human beings with inalienable rights, has helped the subject of child sexual abuse to surface in society. For a comprehensive presentation of the compatibility between the UN Convention on the Rights of the Child and the Canon Law of the Church, see Michael Smith Foster: "The Rights of the Child," in *Little Children Suffer*, Maureen Junker-Kenny and Norbert Mette, eds. *Concilium* 2 (1996): 120–27. Foster shows that the rights of children are promoted in both legal instruments. This promotion is

accomplished through the avenues of provision, protection (from threats to their personhood), and proclamation. The Holy See—the representative voice of the universal Roman Catholic Church at the UN—acceded to the United Nations Convention on the Rights of the Child in 1990, being one of the first states to do so.

155. Rosetti, *A Tragic Grace*, 49–61. He also emphasizes the ripple effect of the damage on the victim's family, the parish community, the diocese, and the whole Church.

156. Matthew 18:6–9.

157. On May 20, 2009, the Report of the Commission to Inquire into Child Abuse in Irish Institutions was published. The five-volume report concluded that physical, emotional, and sexual abuse was endemic in industrial schools, orphanages, and hospitals run by eighteen Catholic religious congregations in the twentieth century. The report is available online at www.childabusecommission.ie/ [accessed May 21, 2009].

158. "It is difficult for a 'Christian' society, in this sense, to accept full equality of rights for atheists, for people of a quite alien religion, or for those who violate what seems to be the Christian moral code (e.g., homosexuals)." Taylor, *A Catholic Modernity?* 17.

159. Don S. Browning, "The United Nations Convention on the Rights of the Child: Should it be Ratified and Why?" *Emory International Law Review* 20, no. 1 (Spring 2006): 157–83, at 173. Browning notes that modern human rights thought is largely devoid of critical grounding, and he proposes the thesis that "a lasting theory of the rights of children, families, and parents in relation to the state and the law requires a compelling religious narrative and a theory of natural rights, both subjective and objective."

160. Taylor, *A Catholic Modernity?* 26.

Chapter Two

Chapter Two

~

Theological Anthropology and Human Rights

KARL RAHNER'S CONCENTRATION ON THE HUMAN

WHERE DOES THEOLOGY FIND ITSELF on the contemporary moral landscape described by Rorty as inhabited primarily by "Kantians" and "Hegelians"? The language of human rights is problematic for theology; for certain perspectives on rights assume an adversarial view of relationships within society and can be erosive of visions and structures of communal life. An extreme "rights mentality" that views rights not as a boundary discourse in ethics but as the discourse that trumps all other ethical concerns can encourage the coexistence of disconnected subjects and the demands of narcissistic claims. A theologian may be more comfortable with a biblical vision of justice as right relationship with God, the neighbor, and the land or with a Thomistic discussion of the virtue of justice and the doctrine of the common good.

However, an overly simple appeal to biblical justice or to virtue ethics can blind us to the fact that the seeking of justice can be conflictual: It involves taking a stand or taking sides because at heart are the difficult issues of the sharing of power, the equitable and sustainable distribution of resources, the privileging of needs over wants, and the recognition of identities in contexts where they are excluded or eliminated. There are intrinsic difficulties for the theologian in engaging with human rights, for there is risk in speaking about rights, and there is also danger in not speaking of, or even silencing, the language of human rights. Whereas there are distinctively theological points raised in the critique of human rights discourse by theologians, many of the philosophical concerns about rights, discussed in chapter 1, are also shared by theologians: the question of historicity, the question of radical autonomy in a postdeontic age, and the relationship between particular cultures and universal values.

Theological Engagement with the Discourse of Human Rights

This chapter begins with a brief overview of four examples of Christian theological engagement with human rights: positive engagement, Jürgen Moltmann's appeal to "God's Right," disdain for the language of human rights, and gradual engagement by liberation theology with human rights. It will then explore some aspects of the work of Karl Rahner, whose rich theological anthropology makes a vital contribution to the contemporary discussion of the human person and helps us to understand the boundary discourse of human rights in its radical depth.

POSITIVE ENGAGEMENT

Positive theological engagement with human rights occurs in a number of different ways and in the work of both Catholic and Protestant theologians. There is some uncritical use, where the term human rights is used almost as a synonym for justice, and philosophical difficulties and inconsistencies are, to some extent, overlooked for the sake of practical aims of social justice.[1] Kieran Cronin's study of the relationship between rights and Christian ethics is an interesting exchange between analytic philosophy and Christian ethics. He suggests that Christian ethics needs to engage in the detailed analysis of rights that is found in moral philosophy and Christian jurisprudence. Cronin challenges Christian theology to be vigilant about the definition and justification of human rights, accusing some theologians of "almost naive unquestioning acceptance" of the language of human rights and of "ignoring to a great extent the analysis of the language of rights at the metaethical level."[2]

Other theologians engage with the language of human rights on the basis that these rights have Christian foundations or that there was a latent theory of human rights in Christianity from the beginning. Some scholars claim that the concept, if not the language, of human rights is found in the scriptures and that the biblical tradition offers not only a unique justification for human rights but also a distinctive understanding of their content and character.[3] Many theologians neither use the language uncritically, nor seek to render rights language theologically respectable through placing their origins in the Hebrew and Christian scriptures, but they engage creatively with the language in the interest of the larger issues of justice and the common good. Charles Villa-Vicencio uses human rights in the context of a "Theology of Re-Construction" in postapartheid South Africa. He notes that the kind of theology that is helpful in resistance "does not easily become a useful instrument in the period of reconstruction."[4] Therefore, what he calls "Nation-Building Theology" must be defined in relation to the constitutional process. He suggests that the specific task of theology is to "help locate the human rights struggle at the center of the debate on what it means to be human and therefore also at the center of social and political pursuit."[5]

David Hollenbach reflects on the engagement of Catholicism with human rights in *Claims in Conflict*. He examines the complexity of a "Christian theory of rights," acknowledging the tension between nature and grace, reason and revelation, natural law ethics and specifically Christian ethics. Hollenbach's reading of the tradition offers an understanding of the principles of justice in Catholic social teaching, which can contribute to the problem of the presence of conflict between competing rights.[6] In a later work, *The Global Face of Public Faith*, Hollenbach argues that religious communities, Christianity in particular, should be vigorous advocates of universal human rights, democratic governance, and economic development. He presents a constructive argument for movement toward consensus on a global ethic, in a world of religious and cultural pluralism, that is modest in theoretical scope but potentially significant in practice.[7] Hollenbach concludes by locating action on behalf of human rights in the human capacity for self-transcendence and the ways in which one person's capacity for self-transcendence makes a claim on another's capacity for self-transcendence.[8]

George Newlands, in *Christ and Human Rights*, attempts to bring together the centrality of human rights, "perhaps the most important geopolitical concept of the present era," with the centrality of Christ in Christian faith, focusing on a Christ of the vulnerable and the margins. He reflects on what contribution Christology can make to the theory and practice of human rights, moving from a Christology *of* human rights in the tradition of classical liberal theology to a "theology *for* human rights, grounded in Christology but explicitly articulated in relation to practical social outcomes."[9] Although Newlands does "not wish to suggest that Christology is, in essence, only a Christology of human rights," the emphasis on a transformative engagement could risk instrumentalizing Christology in the service of human rights.[10] Nonetheless, Newlands makes an important contribution to theological engagement with the discourse of human rights, reminding theologians about the importance of such engagement and reminding Christians that Jesus Christ is central to Christian reflection on rights.

A new dimension to theological engagement with human rights discourse is developing in the work of evangelical theologians in the United States. The theologian David P. Gushee argues that there is an "emerging evangelical center" that offers a new model of evangelical political engagement.[11] Gushee outlines the varied responses among Evangelical Christians to a broad range of contemporary ethical issues, including "the well-being of children and families, active efforts to address poverty and its causes, and a concern for the global environment."[12] Evangelical Christians in this emerging center engaging with questions of human rights, social justice, and environmental issues have been described by Peter Heltzel as "prophetic evangelicals" who are rooted in the deep theological convictions that motivated nineteenth-century evangelical abolitionists to fight against slavery and twentieth century evangelicals to fight for the lives of unborn children.[13] This new model of evangelical political engagement challenges what Charles Marsh terms the politicization of the gospel in the United States in the years 2000–2006, during which "the name of Jesus has been used to serve national ambitions, strengthen middle-class values, and justify war."[14]

David Gushee is also president of Evangelicals for Human Rights, an initiative established in response to human rights issues in the "war on terrorism." This group holds a broad commitment to a human rights agenda and support for human rights conventions and laws. Its members are particularly critical of Christians whose ethical blind spot prevents them from rejecting the use of torture in this "war." Secular human rights discourse is viewed by Evangelicals for Human Rights as derivative of pre-Enlightenment Christian sources, and their commitment to human rights, including the rights of suspected terrorists, is grounded in the core theological conviction that all human life is sacred. "Concern for the sanctity of life leads us to vigilant sensitivity to how human beings are treated and whether their God-given rights are being respected."[15] Their "Evangelical Declaration against Torture: Protecting Human Rights in an Age of Terror" (2007) gained significant mainstream evangelical support, thus broadening the terms of reference of the debate about torture.[16]

Gushee's moral analysis of torture is a fine example of theological engagement with a human rights issue. He begins by describing how torture violates the intrinsic dignity of the human person, made in the image of God, and then discusses the multifaceted negative consequences of torture: its mistreatment of the vulnerable and consequent violation of the demands of public justice; its dehumanization of the torturer and erosion of the character of the nation that permits it; its inordinate trust in a government that is authorized to torture.[17] Gushee laments that protorture evangelicals have succumbed to utilitarian arguments despite the "abhorrence of utilitarian thought" by conservative evangelicals. Having argued that national well-being requires a rejection of torture, Gushee concludes: "for evangelical Christians a proper understanding of our ultimate loyalty—to Jesus the tortured one—makes any support of torture unthinkable."[18] The contribution of these "prophetic evangelicals" is a reminder that Christian engagement with the discourse of human rights at the beginning of the twenty-first century is both ecumenical and theologically diverse.

THE DIVINE CLAIM: MOLTMANN'S APPEAL TO GOD'S RIGHT

Jürgen Moltmann offers a different kind of positive engagement with the language of human rights, suggesting that the specific task of Christian theology is not the repetition of what other experts have already achieved but that of "grounding fundamental human rights in God's right to—that is, his claim upon—all beings, their human dignity, their fellowship, their rule over the earth, and their future."[19] He does not exclude other religious or humanistic substantiations of human rights, but for Moltmann the notion of *Imago Dei* reflects the divine claim upon the human person. Human rights mirror God's claim upon persons because human persons are called to image God in all aspects of their lives.[20] Indivisible human rights reflect God's indivisible right to human beings, a right based on salvation history of liberation and covenant, incarnation and Paschal mystery. God's claim upon human beings was experienced in past liberation and "is experienced in concrete events of the liberation of human beings, in their covenant with God and in the rights and duties inherent in their freedom."[21]

Although divine sovereignty remains at the heart of all theological efforts to speak about justice, there are difficulties with this attempt to ground human rights in God's right. Human beings require the protection of rights because others can harm us, and the dignity of the human person, while inviolable, is nonetheless fragile. We often, implicitly or explicitly, appeal to a doctrine of analogy when speaking about qualities or attributes of God, but it does not seem appropriate to speak of "God's right" analogically. However, to say that there are difficulties with grounding human rights in God's right is not to say that there can be no theological grounding for the discussion of human rights, and it is interesting to note that Moltmann does not appeal to God's indivisible right to human beings in other places in his work where he engages with the discourse of human rights.[22]

THEOLOGICAL DISDAIN FOR HUMAN RIGHTS

In contemporary philosophical and theological discourse, there is also some disdain for the notion of rights. The word "right" is often used disparagingly, usually in reference to the right to something trivial, in order to highlight the absurdity of the demand. The disdain for rights is usually part of an overall disdain for the politics of liberal democracy and for secular concepts of justice. Positively, this perspective attempts, following Alasdair MacIntyre, to build ethics on a retrieval of the premodern tradition of the virtues, a retrieval of Aristotle, Augustine, and Aquinas. This retrieval of the language of virtue is intended to trump human rights discourse, exposing its emptiness and lack of roots. Chapter 5 will discuss more fully John Milbank's "radically orthodox" theology and the work of Stanley Hauerwas. These theologians, in very different ways, eschew positive theological engagement with human rights discourse based on what can be described as a "disdain for the secular" and a preference for a theological politics over contemporary political or liberation theologies.

LIBERATION THEOLOGY AND HUMAN RIGHTS

The engagement of liberation theology with human rights discourse is particularly interesting because it contains elements of both the positive and the negative approaches mentioned above. The relationship between liberation theology and human rights can be broadly outlined in three stages: initial rejection, gradual critique, and theological engagement. Chapter 4 will examine the gradual and eclectic use of human rights discourse by liberation theology, and the specific contribution of this theological movement, especially through its emphasis on the historicization of human rights and affirmation of the rights of the poor.

∼

This brief overview of four examples of theological engagement with human rights shows the complexity and breadth of the engagement. Theology can also learn from the ways in which other academic disciplines critically engage with this dominant moral discourse of our time. The political scientist Jack Donnelly offers a "constructivist" view of human rights, positing that at the heart of those committed to human rights is "the choice of a particular moral vision of human potentiality and the institutions for realizing that vision."[23] Theology must learn from such voices outside the walls of the *ecclesia* that articulate the hopes and aspirations, both personal and communal, that are carried in the secular discourse of human rights. Theologians who engage with the language of human rights need to listen to the critique of their colleagues who have suspicions about this engagement, but the theologians who disdain engagement also need to be aware of what philosophical assumptions they build upon and whose company they keep through the dismissal of human rights that happens outside of the theological community.

Imago Dei: *Indicative and Imperative*

In the introduction I said that the experience that is the touchstone of this book is my involvement in the work of the Credo Foundation for Justice with children who live and work on the streets of Port of Spain, Trinidad. These children are one of the most vulnerable human groups. When persons, particularly children, are denied the right to the basics of life—food, shelter, safety, and education—they are not simply denied "things" that are necessary for survival. Their human dignity—and future capacity for relationship and participation—can be fundamentally distorted by deprivation, neglect, and the various kinds of exploitation that they are exposed to in such a marginal existence.

It is a violation of the right of a child to have to scavenge for food and to have to resort to violence simply to find protection on the streets; but the more fundamental violation is that that child's capacity to trust, and therefore to give of herself or himself in relationship, is profoundly, and often irreparably, damaged. The denial of these basic rights can distort the generosity of existence for these children, damage their capacity for self-donation, and eventually can pose an actual danger to the communities on whose fringes they live. There is a profound correlation between the denial of their rights and their capacity to flourish as human beings, between their flourishing and the flourishing of the community they are part of, a correlation that is unacknowledged by theologians who remain removed from the concerns of human rights.

Human rights discourse is one way of articulating the protection of the dignity of the human person, not simply with regard to the minimal conditions necessary for that dignity, but as part of an overall concern for whatever potentially distorts or thwarts the capacity for giving and receiving, that marks the generosity of existence, which is the human vocation. The concrete language of human rights, with its talk of food and shelter, education and voting, and its prohibition of slavery and torture, arbitrary detention, and unjust discrimination, reminds us that generosity of existence is not simply a generosity of "spirit," but something that engages the "bodiliness" of Christianity.

The ultimate theological justification for engagement with human rights is the doctrine of *Imago Dei*. "God created man in his image; in the divine image he created him; male and female he created them" (Gen. 1:26–27).[24] Whereas the concept of human rights is not explicitly present in the Torah, Judaism points theology toward the concept of inalienable human dignity based on the "astonishing assertion" that God created human beings in God's image.[25] The history of theological anthropology is an attempt to come to terms with the meaning of this assertion. *Imago Dei* is evocative rather than strictly descriptive, upholding human dignity through the assertion of the likeness—and unlikeness—of the human person to God.[26]

The interpretation of Genesis 1:26–27 over the centuries has been rich and varied, focusing at different times on different dimensions of the human person that are in the image of God, dimensions such as rationality, freedom, moral capacity, creativity, relationality, and the power of self-determination. The doctrine of *Imago Dei* acts as both indicative and imperative; it implies an ethical ontology. However, in the struggle to elucidate the practical and political implications of *Imago Dei*, theology showed itself vulnerable to the same dangers as philosophical anthropology, for example, universal assertions of human dignity, which incorporated, consciously or unconsciously, careful categories of practical exclusion based on race or class or gender.

Some interpretations of the doctrine of *Imago Dei* were overly static and reflective of neither the dynamism of the biblical God nor the relatedness of the God of later Trinitarian reflection. Theologians in the twentieth century sought to interpret the doctrine in the light of a more unitary anthropology. Karl Barth's interpretation emphasizes that "God-likeness" consists not in anything the human person is or does: "He is the image of God in the fact that he is a man."[27] Barth's reflections on Creation and Covenant are influenced by Dietrich Bonhoeffer's lecture on Genesis 1:26–27, where Bonhoeffer interprets *Imago Dei* thus: "Man is like the Creator in that he is free." Bonhoeffer offers a rich reflection on freedom as something that we do not possess for ourselves. Freedom is a relationship between persons. We are free *for* worship and *for* others. This freedom exposes the illusory nature of human rule.[28]

Karl Rahner did not often use the term *Imago Dei*, but he offers a transcendentalist Thomist view of the human person akin to the doctrine of *Imago Dei*.[29] Some aspects of Rahner's theological anthropology will now be briefly explored, including the "supernatural existential," the oft-misunderstood concept of "anonymous Christianity," and his reflections on human freedom and dignity and on the mystery of human suffering. I will adopt a critically positive approach to Rahner's theology, acknowledging as well the critique of Rahner that followed in the next generation of theologians, for example in the work of his student Johann Baptist Metz, which will be discussed in chapter 3. Given the breadth of Rahner's work and the extensive body of comment and critique it has generated, the treatment here of these themes from his theological anthropology is far from exhaustive. Although Rahner is not normally brought into contemporary theological engagement with human rights, the proposal here is that his concentration on the human makes Rahner an important theological companion for a discussion of human rights.

Karl Rahner: A Concentration on the Human

Rahner did not explicitly engage with human rights discourse in his theology. The Italian journalist Giancarlo Zizola, in a 1982 interview, asked Rahner: "Are human rights theologically significant?" His response was: "Yes. We can even say that those who disregard the rights of others will one day be condemned."[30] Despite a lack of direct engagement with human rights, Rahner's theology, with its serious concern for the transcendent dimension of the human person and the realization of that transcendence in history, creates an opening for theological engagement with human rights. He offers contemporary theology a rich theological anthropology that can accompany theologians who engage with the discourse of human rights and challenge those who would dismiss that engagement.

Philosophically, Rahner continues the ontological discussion of Thomas Aquinas, forging a new direction and engaging new questions, influenced particularly by Kant and Heidegger.[31] It must be noted, however, that Rahner's theology is also influenced by his engagement with Ignatian spirituality, with its emphasis on the search for God in all things, an influence he became more conscious of in his later years.[32] His early works, *Spirit in the World* and *Hearers of the Word*, outline a place for philosophy within his theology, a theology that is not elaborated in a progressive corpus.[33] In *Spirit in the World* Rahner argues that we can know God by attending to the movement of our knowing itself toward its objects. Our thinking always reaches beyond its immediate objects toward a further horizon. Here, the movement of our knowing, and the ultimate goal toward which it reaches, can be grasped only indirectly (or transcendentally) as our thinking turns back on itself.

Rahner's theology could be described as a theology of the radical proximity of holy mystery. Everything that he writes—on the Trinity, Christology, the human person, Church, and prayer—places before us a vision of the radical proximity of holy mystery, and the implications of this radical proximity. All the Christian mysteries are concrete forms of the one mystery: "once the presupposition is made—which can however be known only by revelation—that this holy mystery also exists, and can exist, as the mystery in absolute proximity."[34]

Rahner is both praised and criticized for his attempt to speak to the subject formed by the philosophical questions of the second half of the twentieth century. He is sometimes described as being overly concerned with questions of the Enlightenment or with making Christianity relevant in the context of secularization in Europe. Although there is some truth in the interpretation of Rahner's theology as an apologetical response to growing secularization, the anthropological and ontological "turn" begins, not with the subject as merely an epistemological datum, but with the subject as the locus of God's self-communication, the subject of the generosity of God.[35] This turn to the subject is not a rejection of scripture and dogma as starting points for doing theology. Rahner challenges theology to take seriously the experience of humanity, that is, the experience of the subject of God's historical revelation. The human person, who is both historical and transcendental, reminds theology that God is to be found within human experience; God is inherent in human reality.[36] Rahner proposes a positive theology based on the fact that God speaks, not because the human being thinks. Without denying that theological shifts occur because of dialogue with philosophy, it is legitimate to begin theological discourse in a movement from the human to the Divine because the Incarnation—Logos among us—mandates and legitimates such an approach.[37]

Whereas Rahner has a particular understanding of the addressee of his theology, that person is not necessarily the same person as the subject of his theology.[38] His theology implicitly (and sometimes explicitly) speaks to the concerns of the particular European person he is addressing; however, his theological anthropology has a contribution to make to understanding the nature and vocation of the human person. He had an abiding concern with universality; God took humanity seriously, thus all persons must be taken seriously.[39] Rahner's anthropological turn highlights the mystery of the human person in her capacity for God, a theological-anthropological truth that speaks to human beings and theology beyond the borders of twentieth-century Europe, as evidenced in the influence his theology had on feminist and liberation theologians. Ignacio Ellacuría, the martyr theologian of El Salvador whose work is referred to in chapter 4, was taught by Rahner and profoundly influenced by him.[40] Ellacuría saw his own theology as a development of Rahner's theology in the context of Latin America.

With Rahner, dogmatic theology finds expression as theological anthropology. Rahner holds that the turn toward the human *necessitates* the reformulation of dogmatic theology as theological anthropology. He locates theology—*fides quaerens intellectum*—within the foundational experience of human beings but grounded on a complementary relationship between the anthropological starting point and the theological answer. His theological anthropology speaks positively and profoundly about the inner unity of human experience, and of the intimate relationship between the human person and God, but also about God who is open and responsive to, and in communication with, this human person. It is a theological anthropology that articulates an ontological possibility, an eschatological anthropology speaking of that which is unrealized but already present.[41]

Rahner acknowledges that theological anthropology can learn from the "profane anthropologies," given the multidimensional nature of the human person.[42] Theology radicalizes and thematizes the profane anthropologies by showing in what way findings point to God as the ground of the being of the human person. There is a theological dimension to all questions about the human person, thus theology helps the secular sciences to see the questions in radical depth.[43] Christianity, through anticipating God's absolute future in faith and love, "calls into question" each particular humanism. However, the Christian does not have any privileged information as to the concrete dimensions of that future and is obliged to enter into dialogue with other "fellow builders" of a common future.[44]

All things, events, persons are potentially revelatory of holy mystery; all can serve as a catalyst for movement from transcendental awareness to categorical expression of the Mystery of God. This is not a realization of the Feuerbachian task of the transformation of theology into anthropology but, rather, a reminder that to turn toward the human person is to discover the place where mystery is engraved in the world. For Rahner, the question of how the Eternally Incomprehensible God could be the meaning of human life is a "universal" question of meaning.

Rahner argued, presuming the Kantian critique of metaphysics, that what we can know about the mystery of God we know by being irreversibly turned toward the world. The human person is bound to this world, but the other side of this worldliness is the human hunger for meaning. This hunger is evidenced in the ability to place everything under question, in the endless desire to know, and in a passion for knowledge and reality that drives this human questioner toward the unlimited and the incomprehensible. Thus, the human person, ever confronted with mystery, moves endlessly into mystery without abandoning the world. Because the human person is a dynamism toward mystery, the "fulfillment of human nature is the consummation of its orientation towards the abiding mystery."[45]

What, then, are the characteristics of Rahner's "person"? From his earliest writings, Rahner described the person as simultaneously spiritual and material, as embodied spirit in a material world.[46] He identifies the human person as a "Hearer of the Word," the possessor of *potentia obedientialis*—a term derived from Aquinas—referring to the fundamental capacity for grace in the human person.[47] The human person is finite spirit, a self-present subject, who goes out of herself. The person is a questioner, a being with infinite horizons, that is, an infinitely open questioner. The early Rahner uses very Heideggerian terminology,[48] especially in his definition of transcendence as absolute openness to being.[49] The question must be raised as to whether or not Rahner is captive to a generalized ontology (as characteristic of some twentieth-century theology) that locates him in a philosophical conceptual world that renders theology "neutral" through focusing on a "generalized," rather than particular, God. Such a risk is present in Rahner's earlier works, but his writings on Christology and the Trinity challenge this notion of the captivity of his ontology. The generalized ontology of absolute openness to being is followed, in Rahner's theology, by a greater emphasis on "mystery" than on "being."

In *Foundations of Christian Faith*, Rahner summarizes his earlier work, describing the human person as (a) Hearer of the Message (the potential Word of God), (b) someone who finds himself in the presence of absolute mystery, and (c) a being "radically threatened by guilt." As finite spirit, the human person is dynamic and in every encounter with the finite is moved toward the infinite. "The infinite horizon of human questioning is experienced as an horizon which recedes further and further the more answers man can discover."[50] He then offers the definition, which is at the heart of his theological anthropology, "Man as the Event of God's Free and Forgiving Self-Communication."[51] God's self-communication is God's self-donation, not a word *about* God, but God giving Godself. God's self-communication in the human person is an existential-ontological reality.

Even in the early Rahner, the person was not simply an abstraction; space and time were not considered "adjunct" to the essential human condition, "spacetime is his interior specific constitution."[52] Like Thomas Aquinas, Rahner sees the human person as a dynamism of knowledge and love; the religious dimension of the human person is seen in both these aspects of human subjectivity. Rahner takes Thomas's unitary anthropology, the intrinsic relation between body and soul, and echoes the same concern for integration in terms of history and transcendence. The "hearer" is someone historical. Transcendence is the condition of possibility for history, and history is the concrete mediation of transcendence.

Although there is some validity to the criticism of an individualistic bias in Rahner's anthropology, his theology is nonetheless profoundly open to interpersonal and social concerns. Relatedness is seen to be essential to the human being. In his earlier works Rahner writes that there is no individuality without community and no community other than the intersubjectivity of individuals. Subjectivity stands in a tripartite context: the relation of the subject to herself, to God, and to other persons. Rahner notes that these relations do not simply exist in parallel relationship but are "mutually conditioning one another, in every act of the subject endowed with intellect and freedom, whatever form this act may assume."[53] Relatedness is part of the transcendental dimension of the person. The encounter with another is an experience of numinosity, for all persons are potentially revelatory. All serve as a catalyst for movement from transcendental awareness to categorical expression of absolute mystery, but all are revelatory in themselves and not simply a means toward the beatific vision. Human persons are community builders; person and community are correlative, and the possibility of being-generous-in-community has its source in the Triune God.[54]

Human Capacity for God: Supernatural Existential

Rahner attempts to elucidate the transcendental orientation of the human person, the human capacity (or aptitude[55]) for God, using the term "supernatural existential." It is a theological hypothesis used to encapsulate a religious ontology that is essential to his theology, a hypothesis for which he does not provide an exact definition. By using the adjective "supernatural" for the existential, Rahner did not intend to remove it from the ontological realm but to indicate the graced character of human reality, grounded in creation and redemption. His use of "existential" is Heideggerian: a permanent determination penetrating all elements of human existence, which reveals its meaning and structures, characterizing the human being before she engages in any free action.[56] God's self-communication in the human person is an existential-ontological reality. God's free love affects the deepest interior of the human being.

The background for Rahner's articulation of the orientation of the human person to a supernatural end in terms of the "supernatural existential" is his engagement with the French-based *Nouvelle Théologie*.[57] This "New Theology" sought to overcome the extrinsicism inherent in the neoscholastic approach to nature and grace, an approach that, in a desire to protect the gratuitousness of grace, defined the relationship between nature and grace negatively, that is, as being no more intense than freedom from contradiction.[58] In reaction to neoscholasticism, some aspects of this *Nouvelle Théologie* may have tended toward intrinsicism, or the collapsing of grace into nature. Rahner holds that human receptivity to the Word of God and the generosity of God's grace cannot be portrayed simply as nonrepugnance or mere passive receptivity. He attempted to walk a *via media* in terms of the relationship between nature and grace, avoiding the extremes of pure extrinsicism and pure intrinsicism. Although the original context in which Rahner coined the term "supernatural existential" changed, he did not significantly change his position on this theological hypothesis.[59]

God created in human persons the potential and possibility of ontological unity with the Trinity. This a priori vocation is a potential and a possibility contingent on the free and loving response of the person. "The capacity for the God of self-bestowing personal love is the central and abiding 'existential' of man as he really is."[60] Rahner holds that this God of self-bestowing personal love and God's invitation to generosity are effective, not at some marginal dimension of the human person, but in his or her deepest interior.

The supernatural existential begets in the human person an immanent orientation toward union with the Trinity, even prior to that person hearing the Gospel proclaimed. Without denying that "faith comes from hearing," the "hearer" is already graced and the gospel is a graced word that is spoken to the person whose auditory capacity is graced, so grace calls upon grace to respond. The Rahnerian perspective reminds us that the experience of transcendence is neither rare nor transient but present in everyday life as the condition of possibility, the origin and goal of all meaningful human activity: knowing, willing, loving, deciding, and hoping.

This radical capacity of nature for grace—supernatural existential—means that nothing is "merely" human, for the human person is a unity of nature and supernatural existential. The concept of "pure nature" is a remainder concept (*Restbegriff*). Rahner holds that there is no human being who is not graced. "*Every* person must be understood as the event of a supernatural self-communication of God, although not in the sense that every person necessarily accepts in freedom God's self-communication to man."[61] Our capacity for God is a capacity to receive what is communicated. This capacity is ontologically grounded. The recipient is called to mirror this self-giving to others; the human person is called to live out this capacity for generosity, a capacity that is ontologically grounded, to be responded to in freedom.

However, Rahner does not sufficiently acknowledge what might "damage" the supernatural existential; he seems to assume that the only possible obstacle might be guilt, or the lure of atheism. He offers some glimpses of what that divine self-communication might mean in terms of human fragility, but in general he does not so much deny the shadow sides of human existence as subsume them in the broad category of experience.[62] The somewhat convoluted Rahnerian terminology of "supernatural existential" is an articulation of human transcendentality: the call to life with God, as a permanent reality of human existence and an ethical evocation of concern for the fullness of loving and giving to which the human person is called by virtue of that call. The theological-anthropological view of the luminosity of the human person is both indicative and imperative, both ontology and ethics. The transcendentality of the "other" makes a claim on my transcendentality. The capacity for God, and the generosity of existence that flows from that capacity, necessitates a concern with all that can distort that capacity and that generosity. Concern with the promotion of human rights can be one way of articulating a deeper concern, that is, with protecting the transcendental capacity of the human person and seeing in that capacity a call that evokes concrete historical responsibility.

Human Goodness: The "Anonymous Christian"

For Rahner, the fullest expression of personhood and freedom for those with explicit Christian faith is found in Jesus Christ. The Incarnation is the very center of the Christian reality: "only here is the mystery of participation in the divine nature accorded us; and the mystery of the Church is only the extension of the mystery of Christ."[63] Through his transcendent Christology, Rahner seeks to make the claims of Christian faith that Jesus is absolute Savior intelligible for reasons intrinsic to the human being as such.

Using the language of twentieth-century philosophy, he proposes that there is something in the human being that makes this claim reasonable, that is, a basic desire for God. The human being is a question that desires completeness; in all our finite experiences we desire the Infinite. Rahner uses the term "searching Christology" to indicate that in human reality (at least where implicit faith exists) there is an implicit fundamental search for the "absolute saviour," a search that culminates in the encounter with Jesus of Nazareth.[64] We have a searching hope that life will make sense. This human experience of searching hope is implicit, a priori, that is, transcendental Revelation. Our yearning and desire for the absolute, for total Love and Justice, is God's Spirit. The Holy Spirit is a priori, has been always in and over human existence, and abides as searching memory. The Holy Spirit is divine immanence in the world, the condition that makes Christ—the historical savior—possible.

Christians claim that Jesus is the historic event that will give meaning to the searching hope of humanity. In Jesus, implicit Transcendence becomes explicit, a mediation to consciousness in history, that is, a categorical Revelation. In Jesus we see a concrete human person, who suffered, died, and is gathered up into eternal life. He experiences the victory over loss, pain, suffering, and death that we all hope for; thus implicit hope becomes explicit in history. What human beings truly are has been revealed historically and unsurpassably in Jesus Christ. Jesus is *the* exegete of the human person. Jesus is also God's self-donation visible in time, space, and culture. Through the Incarnation, God becomes an existential human being; God takes on otherness, an otherness that allows for human participation in the self-donation of the Divine. Humanity is the ontological and existential result of Christ's *kenosis*. God's free love affects human persons at their deepest core, inviting participation into the generosity of existence that marks the Trinitarian life.

Rahner attempts to articulate the relationship between two Christian beliefs, the universal salvific will of God and the necessity of faith in Christ. In relation to the question of possible union with Christ by grace for those who are not formally Christian, Rahner developed his famous and oft-misunderstood concept of "Anonymous Christianity."[65] It was conceived by Rahner primarily in response to a pastoral question regarding the persistence of so much unbelief. "Anonymous Christianity," also a development of the supernatural existential, is an attempt to articulate an understanding of someone who accepts God's gracious self-offer transcendentally in and through implicit faith.[66]

Using the term "anonymous Christian," Rahner holds that all persons are "Christian," that is, caught up in God's universal saving grace, by the fact that they exist, regardless of whether or not they are baptized. He stresses that it is the clear expression of Vatican II that "someone who has no concrete, historical contact with the explicit preaching of Christianity can nevertheless be a justified person who lives in the grace of Jesus Christ."[67] Rahner uses the term "anonymous" because this relationship remains nameless. It applies both to members of other faiths and to those people who consider themselves "atheists"; the former, those who have religious faith that is not Christian, are not simply believers in a false religion, for these can be the historical and social mediations of grace, and the latter, who live in fidelity to their conscience, can mediate grace in ways that are not explicitly religious. All people are intrinsically related to the Church because they are related to Christ.[68] The dilemma of the "good pagan" becomes, in Rahner, the positive assertion of the anonymous Christian.[69] What this comes to mean in practice, with regard to the expressly Christian revelation, is that the human person already accepts this revelation when he really accepts himself completely, for it already "speaks" in him: "Prior to the explicitness of official ecclesiastical faith this acceptance can be present in an implicit form whereby a person undertakes and lives the duty of each day in the quiet sincerity of patience, in devotion to his material duties and the demands made upon him by persons under his care."[70]

Anyone who has accepted his or her own humanity, "and all the more so, of course, the humanity of others," has said "yes" to Christ—even if he or she does not know it—because "in him God has accepted man."[71] It is striking how ordinary and mundane the acceptance, which is deemed Christ-like, is:

> If God's self-communication is an ultimate and radicalising modifica-
> tion of that very transcendentality of ours by which we are subjects,
> and if we are such subjects of unlimited transcendentality in the most
> ordinary affairs of our everyday existence, in our secular dealings with
> any and every individual reality, then this means in principle that the
> original experience of God even in his self-communication can be
> so universal, so unthematic and so "unreligious" that it takes place,
> unnamed but really, wherever we are living out our existence.[72]

Hans Urs von Balthasar, Rahner's most famous critic, maintained that Rahner's theology of grace contributed to a relativization of biblical revelation and the Church, and the loss of genuine Christian witness, of martyrdom.[73] Balthasar charged that the concept of the "anonymous Christian" made a simi-lar error to German idealism, in that it attempted to deduce the reality of the absolute from the openness of the human spirit to the absolute. He saw Rahner as allowing theology to be subsumed within an alien philosophical system, and thus reducing the historical Christ-event to the manifestation of God's salvific will in history, rather than as *the* definitive event of salvation.

A common criticism of the anonymous Christian concept is that it is disre-spectful of people of other religious faiths who would not wish to self-identify as Christians and to atheists who would not want to self-identify as "religious"; however, this criticism would apply only if Rahner's conceptualization of the anonymous Christian is other-directed, that is, at those of other religious faiths and at atheists, as imposed self-understanding.[74]

Rahner's anonymous Christianity must be read in the light of his searching reflections on the mystery of human existence and his central theological asser-tion of the radical proximity of absolute mystery. Metz offers a pithy articula-tion when he says that in talking about anonymous Christianity, Rahner was trying to communicate a sense of the breadth of God and the narrowness of the Church.[75] Thus this thesis of anonymous Christianity, although problematic, is not so much a patronizing categorization of the "other" nor a refusal to acknowledge real religious pluralism but a way in which Christians can understand the goodness of others and the fecundity of grace.[76] Salvation is achieved in *all* dimensions of human existence: when someone follows his or her conscience, or loves in a responsible way, when a person serves others selflessly, even in an instance when the human person does not interpret these actions in a "consciously" religious way.[77]

Rahner's reflections on the anonymous Christian enlarge our understanding of the goodness of others and the fecundity of God's grace. Rather than reducing or relativizing biblical revelation, as von Balthasar charges, these reflections deepen our understanding of the mystery of the incarnation and implicate all of human goodness in that mystery. They point us to the recognition of Christ in those who, without necessarily grounding their ethics in a theological anthropology, courageously and generously work for the promotion and protection of human rights, even to the point of giving up their own lives in defense of the poorest and most vulnerable of our world.

It was argued earlier that Rahner does not sufficiently acknowledge what might "damage" the supernatural existential and that he subsumes the shadow sides of human experience in the broad category of human experience. Likewise it must be noted that Rahner's emphasis on the fecundity of grace leaves the shadows of the world unmentioned. His "high" theology of grace needs to be nuanced by the ways in which grace is under threat by what Leonardo Boff describes as "dis-grace": "i.e., lack of encounter, refusal to dialogue, and closing in upon oneself." Grace and dis-grace exist as two possibilities of freedom; Boff locates this in the mystery of creation, "an absolute mystery to which reason does not have access."[78] Human beings live in this paradox of grace and dis-grace—evidenced by both the grace of courageous ethical or theological humanitarian action *and* the dis-grace of horrendous violations of human rights—a paradox that is not sufficiently acknowledged by Rahner.

Human Freedom

The Catholic Church came to an acceptance of human rights through its acknowledgment of the right to religious freedom in *Dignitatis humanae* (1965), as was outlined in chapter 1. This freedom is concerned with safeguarding that which is most precious in the human person, the capacity for transcendence, for living out the orientation to God, which is the human vocation. Human rights are one mechanism for protecting the human person and her or his vocation. Where does Rahner situate his exploration of the notion of freedom? In *Hearers of the Word*, Rahner views human freedom "primarily as freedom vis-à-vis particular goods."[79] Later, his theological reflections on freedom locate the mystery of freedom at the heart of human subjectivity. It is the essence of the human person and intimately connected to Rahner's understanding of salvation.

Rahner sees this freedom, an essential quality of the human person, as operative on two levels. The human person has a freedom of choice wherein every act of freedom is a freedom with regard to a finite object or possibility in the world. A deeper level of human freedom consists in the ability of human persons to "make" themselves, to actualize themselves. Both levels of human freedom are aspects of the one dynamic of human freedom. All finite choices, all small acts of choice, are dimensions of that freedom wherein self-actualization is at stake.

Freedom is, therefore, a matter of self-actualization, of "making oneself" in response to God.[80] Freedom is also self-surrender; the paradox of freedom is that it increases as one lives in dependency on God, for it is "graced" freedom. Freedom is the capacity to decide about oneself in one's totality; it is not so much the power to decide one thing or another, but the power to decide about oneself and to actualize oneself.[81] Freedom as self-actualization before God through affirmation or negation of Holy Mystery is not a gnostic freedom, nor a disembodied and decontextualized freedom, but a "freedom in and through history and in time and space."[82] It is a situated freedom, which calls forth responsible action. Freedom is thus the "event of something eternal": "Since we ourselves are still coming to be in freedom, we do not exist with and behold this eternity, but in our passage through the multiplicity of the temporal we are performing this event of freedom, we are forming the eternity which we ourselves are and are becoming."[83]

Because we are a unity of body and soul, history and transcendence, our self-actualizing freedom is not lived out in disconnected acts of choice, in a multiplicity of detached finite decisions. Freedom concerns the human person as a single reality, and therefore our finite choices are ways in which we generously engage the paradox of self-possession and self-disposal, of self-realization, and self-surrender. In terms of theological ethics, this points to our "fundamental option." Rahner situates discussion of the fundamental option in the context of transcendental anthropology, seeing this option operative at the level of transcendental freedom, whereas categorical freedom is the arena of particular concrete choices.[84] The human person is not just the subject who acts (or is acted upon), but also the subject who becomes: The "fundamental option" refers to the exercise of freedom in its most basic sense, as the responsibility for "making oneself," the dynamic of personalizing or depersonalizing through actions performed and choices made.

The centrality of grace saves Rahner's theology from simply echoing the Kantian assertion of the ultimate freedom to determine oneself, but it borders on the Kantian because of its undeveloped (rather than unacknowledged) historicity. However, Rahner does acknowledge that his focus on the mystery of freedom "does not mean that it is not necessary to fight for the concrete possibilities of such freedom in society and the Church."[85]

Despite the emphasis on the situated character of personalizing freedom in and through history, time, and space, and despite the acknowledgment of the dialectical unity of freedom and manipulation (legitimate and sinful) in society and Church and the need to fight for the concrete realization of freedom in both of these spheres, Rahner does not pay sufficient attention to the constraints that people experience in the living out of this capacity for self-determination.[86] Jennifer Beste examines Rahner's theological anthropology and his theory of the fundamental option in the light of insights from contemporary trauma theory, asking if it is possible for us to harm one another to such an extent that our capacity to respond to God's grace is severely diminished or even altogether destroyed.[87]

This is a question that resonates with the concerns of this book about embodied and embedded human damage and the theological challenges born of recognizing that. In the light of the terrible trauma of sexual abuse and incest, Beste evaluates Rahner's claim that all persons, with the aid of God's grace, have sufficient freedom to effect a fundamental option. She describes the severely fragmented self that results from trauma, fragmentation that impedes the development of an effective sense of agency, distorting the relationship with God. She argues that "a more adequate Rahnerian account of freedom and grace, one that takes seriously incest victims' experiences of both traumatization and recovery," must include two claims supported by the conclusions of trauma therapy: (a) the acknowledgment of the "sober *possibility*" that interpersonal harm can severely, and perhaps irreparably, impair human freedom to effect a fundamental option; and (b) the insufficiency of the idea of God's grace being "directly infused" into human persons, thus focusing on the mediation of divine grace through "loving, interpersonal relations."[88]

Beste posits that, given Rahner's commitment to the role of human experience in theology and his argument that theology must take seriously the insights of the other sciences, if "confronted with contemporary trauma studies [Rahner] would probably have taken steps to qualify his theology to avoid the danger of blaming trauma victims for their compulsive traumatic reenactments."[89] She develops a revised Rahnerian theology of freedom and grace in the light of what can be learned from trauma victims about the realization of human freedom.

Rahner offers us a profound theology of human freedom, locating the mystery of freedom at the heart of human subjectivity. It points to the freedom to "make oneself" in response to God's call, a situated freedom that calls forth responsible action. However, he does not adequately stress that we live out this graced freedom as wounded persons in a broken world.

Human Experience and the Experience of God

Rahner's reflections on freedom as self-actualization are illumined by his reflections on the relationship between the experience of the self and the experience of God. When Rahner uses the term "experience," he is aware of its potential "abstractness," and he states that what he intends is a sense of concretized and historical experience, unique in each person and involving the totality of that person's existence, of which the search for conscious knowledge is only a part. He forges an intimate link—an equivalence—between the personal history of the experience of self and the personal history of the experience of God. The unity of both these experiences is the condition that makes it possible to recognize the unity between the love of God and love of neighbor "which is of fundamental importance for any right understanding of Christianity."[90] Rahner's understanding of the term "experience" as concrete and historical, unique in each person and involving the totality of that person's existence, together with his linking of the experience of self with the experience of God, opens a way for theological consideration of the religious significance of the experience of women, the poor, and other overlooked persons and groups.[91]

Rahner holds that in the history of the experience of self, the experience of loss of identity is also "a loss of experience of God or the refusal to accept the abiding experience of God."[92] Recognizing the difficulties with language of "loss" of identity, and with the proviso that what is lost still always remains present in its own way, Rahner nonetheless holds that loss in one area marks a loss in the other. The experience of loss of identity, which for Rahner is also a loss of experience of God, tends to be interpreted in terms of the denial or lack of acceptance of the mystery of one's life. However, his point about the relationship between the two forms of loss speaks to us of "the loss which is not loss," but something which is never properly found, the damaged possibility of the vulnerable child through, for example, deprivation, neglect, exploitation, and abuse. This is a more grievous loss, for there is no memory or standard by which to "measure" oneself. Chapter 3 will address the "loss" that results from the impact of the trauma of torture on human persons and communities.

If we take seriously Rahner's position on the intimate link between the experience of the self and the experience of God, to be concerned about the provision and protection of human rights, defined here as a boundary discourse of human flourishing, is also to be concerned about the capacity of the person to relate to and flourish in relationship with the radically proximate holy mystery, and the relationships with others that flow from this dynamic.

Human Dignity

The concept of human dignity is foundational for any discussion of the human person and human rights. Rahner makes an important contribution to this discussion. He addresses the question of human dignity through the theme of freedom as a necessary condition for this dignity: Human dignity is both the goal and the judge of human freedom. Rahner sees dignity as signifying that a person has by her very nature a "determined objective position within the manifoldness and heterogeneity of being which demands respect and protection as well as realization both in its relations to others and in itself."[93]

This dignity is given as part of the essential structure of being and is also given as a task to be accomplished. Dignity, thus, is dynamically ontological, as capacity and task. Although preestablished, it can exist as something denied, but it cannot be rendered nonexistent. Its nature, for Rahner, is to be discerned with the help of reason and revelation. The essential dignity of the human person consists in being open and receptive to the love and communication of the divine, particularly that communication that takes place in Jesus Christ. However, Rahner does not relegate this to an exclusively internal realm, but rather, he holds that human dignity formally embraces the person as embodied, gendered, and historicized, embracing the internal, external, and relational dimensions of human personality. The human person, "incarnate and mundane," consists of a plurality of existential and interrelated existential dimensions.

Rahner recognizes that human dignity is vulnerable to threats, from within and from without and that there is a relationship between these internal and external threats. He explores the threats from within in relation to dignity as a task imposed on the person who can dispose of himself in freedom. The preestablished nature of the essential dignity of the person cannot be erased, but it can be contradicted and degraded; freedom holds before the person the choice of degradation of human dignity or "preserving it by the grace of God and converting it into achieved dignity."[94]

Recognizing that the ultimate degradation of human dignity can arise "only through the free decision of man from within," he nonetheless believes influences from without can threaten every dimension of the person and her or his dignity: "Every 'external' event can be significant and menacing for the ultimate salvation of the person and is, therefore, subject to the law of the dignity of the human person, who as such can be degraded by some intervention from without."[95]

As the result of these internal and external threats, the human person finds herself either in a state of guilt or in a state of redemption insofar as she has had any free control at all over herself. "The human person by its nature and dignity demands an unconditional respect which is independent of any freely exercised determination of an end and value, i.e., is absolute" (by "absolute," Rahner means "unconditional").[96] Absolute dignity is another way of articulating the sacredness of human life. It also points to the dignity of receptivity, an aspect of dignity that some rights discourse, with an overemphasis on autonomy and independence, seems to ignore. Each person—unconditionally—has eternal destiny, is always an end, and can never be sacrificed as a means. This is more than a Kantian rejection of means-end rationality; it is also a pointer to the relationship between absolute dignity and absolute mystery.

Freedom and its concrete actualizations are integral components of the absolute dignity of the human person before God and in the community of other persons. It is our capacity to determine who we shall be before God and with others. It is a relational dignity, and Rahner suggests that it can only be "perfected" to the extent that one is open in love and service for others.[97]

Rahner does not elucidate the nature of the threats to human dignity from without; nor does he reflect upon our responsibility when the dignity of others is under threat. A concern for the theological dignity of humankind necessitates a concern with that dignity as it is historicized and particularized and with the concrete threats to that dignity.[98] Rahner does not directly address this concern, but he does offer a vision of the relationship between human efforts on behalf of dignity and the Christian understanding of salvation. Wherever this preestablished human dignity is either preserved or realized, "even in its natural dimensions," even where there is no consciousness of the source of this dignity, even if it is not explicitly accepted as redemption, there is redemption by the grace of Christ.

Human dignity is not only preserved within "the visible framework of Christianity." Rahner uses the unusual metaphor of "God's secret" to describe the mystery of God's graceful donations. This secret prevents us from making "any equivocal judgment in the concrete, individual case about whether grace has been given and thus the vocation and dignity of man has been preserved."[99] Rahner here brings the thesis of anonymous Christianity into the question of the recognition, protection, and promotion of human dignity.

Human Suffering

The evasion of transcendence is a constant theme of Rahner's theology. "Out of fear of the mysterious" the human person "can take flight to the familiar and the everyday."[100] However, he does not often address the question of suffering. Is this an evasion of another kind? Is there a connection between the evasion of transcendence and the evasion of suffering?

Rahner's engagement with suffering can be characterized by "silence." What is the nature of this response to suffering? Why the seeming hesitation or "refusal?" Metz maintains that it is related to Rahner's fundamental theological respect for the suffering of humanity. Rahner did not engage in theodicy, nor did he ask how we could speak of God in the light of the Holocaust.[101] Through an examination of the instances where he does address the question of suffering, it could be said that his is not a silence born of complicity, nor one of avoidance, nor one of justification, but a silence born of the incomprehensibility of God. Rahner had a sense that to speak too prescriptively of human suffering is to try to explain, and to try to explain is to reduce, and to reduce is to dishonor those who have suffered.

Rahner addresses the question most directly in the essay, "Why Does God Allow Us to Suffer?"[102] It is interesting that he chooses a title that reflects the most poignant of questions with which the human person grapples. At the end of the essay Rahner quotes Romano Guardini on his deathbed. Guardini said that his last judgment would also involve him asking God the question which no theology, no dogma, no theodicy could answer: "Why, God, these fearful detours on the way to salvation, the suffering of the innocent, why sin?"[103] Rahner analyzes four "explanations" of suffering, four attempts at a Theistic answer: (a) "Suffering as a Natural Side in an Evolving World"; (b) "Suffering as an Effect of Creaturely, Sinful Freedom"; (c) "Suffering as a Situation of Trial and Meaning"; and (d) "Suffering as a Pointer to Another, Eternal Life."[104]

Rahner moves toward an answer by suggesting that the incomprehensibility of suffering is part of the incomprehensibility of God. He displays sensitivity to human pain, an awareness that playing down the pain in world history is a betrayal of human dignity, and a cheapening of what people have endured. Although there is explicit mention of the gas chambers of Auschwitz and the child victims of napalm in Vietnam, his writing on suffering does remain abstract, because of his focus on the mysterious dimension of suffering.[105] And even though we do recognize the complexity of the relationship between Heidegger's philosophy and Rahner's theology, and that Heidegger's influence is more evident in early Rahner, the question must be asked about the extent to which the Heideggerian view of death affected Rahner's treatment of human suffering. There is a congruence between his focus on the incomprehensibility of God and the incomprehensibility of suffering and there is an honesty in his desire not to retreat into either theodicy or talk of a "suffering God." Nevertheless, the Heideggerian influence in Rahner's reading of death may have contributed to his somewhat generalized approach to suffering.

In the section where he tackles "Suffering as a Situation of Trial and Maturing," Rahner comes close to acknowledging the destructive effects of human suffering: "Suffering which is destructive in its effects, despite all good will to endure it in a human and Christian way, which simply demands too much from a person, warps and damages his character, leaves him preoccupied solely with satisfying the most primitive needs of existence, makes him stupid or wicked. In desperation it might almost be said that suffering as a means of Christian maturing is something that can be endured only by a noble mind untouched by any real distress, practising spiritual massage in an ivory tower."[106]

However, Rahner does not connect this perspective on suffering with the supernatural existential, nor with what he writes on threats to human dignity from within and from without. He does not make the connection between suffering and the impact it has on the human capacity to mirror God's generosity. Metz points to Rahner's insistence on respecting the "non-transferrable negative mystery" of human suffering as an attempt to resist all efforts to dilute the negativity of human suffering, seeing discourse about a "suffering God" as potentially an attempt by theology "to reconcile itself with God behind the back of the history of human suffering."[107] Metz summarizes Rahner's position as "Suffering Unto God"; however, Rahner does avoid the question of the preventable aspects of suffering, particularly the suffering that comes from injustice and violence.

Rahner's vision of the human person as constitutively oriented toward mystery includes the embrace of suffering within this orientation. If we follow the logic of his emphasis on the radical proximity of holy mystery, then that radical proximity is no less radically proximate in suffering. Rahner does not speak about a suffering God, both out of respect for mystery and to avoid doing theology behind the back of human suffering. Liberation theology will later offer the sound of theology speaking, not behind the back of human suffering, but with the voices of the crucified peoples.

Conclusion

Karl Rahner is not normally brought into contemporary theological engagement with the discourse of human rights as he does not offer the kind of theological engagement with rights that the theologians mentioned at the beginning of the chapter do. However through exploring his theological anthropology, the concepts of "supernatural existential" and "anonymous Christian," his reflections on human freedom and dignity, and on the mystery of human suffering, we have seen that Rahner offers a transcendentalist Thomist version of *Imago Dei*, which makes an important contribution to understanding the mystery of the human person both in her transcendence and in her historicity.

Rahner's theological anthropology needs engagement with the boundary discourse of human rights so that it does not speak too easily about the capacity of the human person to live out graced freedom in response to the radical proximity of holy mystery. Theological engagement with the boundary discourse of human rights finds that Rahner's concentration on the human makes him an important theological companion for such engagement, a companion who leads us to perceive human rights issues of provision and protection in their radical depth, linking human rights with the ultimate luminosity of the human person.

Notes

1. This "uncritical use" tends to occur in the area of practical theology. It is also evident in some discussion of human rights that is not strictly theological but appeals loosely to religious language. Robert Drinan's book, *The Mobilization of Shame*, is primarily an introduction to international human rights. Drinan, professor of law at Georgetown University, is critical of the human rights record of the United States, but he writes a book for the "believer" in human rights and uses loose religious parallels, for example, "The value and beauty of the idea of a worldwide set of human rights accepted by everyone is a concept that, *almost like the gospel*, suddenly becomes appealing to groups or nations for reasons that are not entirely predictable or explainable" (74, italics mine).

2. Cronin, *Rights and Christian Ethics*, xviii–xix, 16. Cronin does not sufficiently explore the theological aspects of the relationship between rights and Christian ethics.

3. See, for example, Christopher D. Marshall's *Crowned with Glory and Honor*.

4. Villa-Vicencio, *Theology of Reconstruction*, 34.

5. Ibid., 128.

6. Hollenbach, *Claims in Conflict*; also David Hollenbach, *The Common Good and Christian Ethics* (Cambridge: Cambridge University Press, 2002).

7. Hollenbach, *Global Face of Public Faith*, chap. 12, "Faiths, Cultures, and Global Ethics," 231–59.

8. Ibid., 246–48.

9. Newlands, *Christ and Human Rights*, 50.

10. Ibid., 21.

11. Gushee, *Future of Faith in American Politics*. Gushee was also the principal drafter of both the Evangelical Climate Initiative (2006) and the Evangelical Declaration Against Torture (2007), available online www.evangelicalsforhumanrights.org [accessed September 1, 2009].

12. Gushee, *Future of Faith in American Politics*, 103.

13. Peter Goodwin Heltzel, "Prophetic Evangelicals: Toward a Politics of Hope," in Jeffrey W. Robbins and Neal Magee, eds., *The Sleeping Giant Has Awoken: The New Politics of Religion in the United States* (New York/London: Continuum, 2008), 25–40, at 25.

14. Marsh, *Wayward Christian Soldiers*, 1, 77.

15. www.evangelicalsforhumanrights.org.

16. In response to President Obama's executive order banning torture on his first full day in office, Evangelicals for Human Rights stated: "Congress passed laws during the Bush years that in some cases need to be repudiated through new legislation. Executive orders are a powerful tool but they can be reversed by new presidents or under new circumstances. We need new laws, and we also need a comprehensive review of what was done to people in our name since September 11. We need a religious and moral accounting, not just a legal one." See "Evangelicals for Human

Rights Celebrates Executive Orders Reversing Detention Policies; Three-Year Campaign Meets Key Goal," January 22, 2009, www.evangelicalsforhumanrights .org/storage/mhead/documents/ehr_press_release_after_executive_order.pdf [accessed December 1, 2009].

17. Gushee, *The Future of Faith in American Politics*, chap. 5, "Torture and Human Rights," 121–39, especially 129–38. Gushee acknowledges the lateness of his own theological reflection on torture. "I became involved in addressing the torture issue only after a request from the editors of *Christianity Today* in late 2005. I regret that I had not really focused on the issue before that time" (121).

18. Ibid., 139.

19. Moltmann, *On Human Dignity*, 20.

20. Moltmann builds on Emile Brunner's articulation of the right of God: "The *jus divinum* is not in the first place the right which God gives, but the right which God has, and this right alone is absolute." Jürgen Moltmann, *Christianity and Civilization* II (London: Nisbet, 1948), 112.

21. Moltmann, *On Human Dignity*, 23.

22. Moltmann, "Human Rights, the Rights of Humanity and the Rights of Nature," in Küng and Moltmann, eds., *Ethics of World Religions and Human Rights*, 120–135.

23. Donnelly, *The Concept of Human Rights*, 31.

24. *New American Bible* (1990).

25. Judaism holds that every human being has an inalienable dignity and bases this claim on the two themes of creation and covenant: "The one is the astonishing assertion that God created human beings in God's own 'image.' . . . An even more daring belief, God's incomparable greatness and goodness being kept in mind, is the central Hebrew religious perception that God has brought humankind into active partnership with God, the relationship symbolized by the ancient Semitic legal term 'covenant.'" Eugene B. Borowitz, "The Torah, Written and Oral, and Human Rights: Foundations and Deficiencies," in *Ethics of World Religions and Human Rights*, Küng and Moltmann, eds., 26.

26. Some commentators, e.g., Irenaeus, make a distinction between "image" and "likeness"; however, this can be interpreted as an example of Hebrew parallelism.

27. Karl Barth, *Church Dogmatics, Vol. III: The Doctrine of Creation*, 1 (Edinburgh: T&T Clark, 1958), 184.

28. Dietrich Bonhoeffer, *Creation and Fall: A Theological Interpretation of Genesis 1–3* (London: SCM Press, 1959), 33–38, at 35.

29. A CD-ROM search of Rahner's twenty-three-volume *Theological Investigations* found only three references to the specific term *Imago Dei* (electronic text published by Mary Immaculate College, Limerick, to mark the centenary of Rahner's birth in 2004).

30. Rahner, "The Future of the World and of the Church," in *Faith in a Wintry Season: Conversations and Interviews with Karl Rahner in the Last Years of His Life*, Paul Imhof and Hubert Biallowons, eds., trans. Harvey D. Egan (New York:

Crossroad, 1990), 159. This is the only direct reference I could find to Rahner addressing the question of the theological significance of human rights.

31. Rahner presumed the Kantian critique of metaphysics, arguing that what we know of the divine we know by being irreversibly turned toward the world. He uses Kantian terminology to articulate not a philosophical concern with establishing a foundation of human knowing but a theological concern with the possibility of the act of faith. He engaged the realism of Thomas Aquinas through the Kantian transcendental question, pushing beyond the Kantian borders of the phenomenal world to explore the a priori conditions of human (categorical) knowledge of reality in a preconceptual, athematic "knowledge" of Being itself. This a priori grasp of Being becomes the a priori grasp of God. Rahner was insistent that modern philosophy, and hence theology, must not seek to reverse the transcendental anthropological direction of Descartes and Kant, a direction continued into modern phenomenology and existentialism. He held this transcendental anthropological direction to be indispensable in modern Christian philosophy and theology. It is precisely this setting forth of the intrinsic importance of transcendental anthropology that opens Rahner to the type of criticism articulated by Fergus Kerr. In *Theology after Wittgenstein*, Kerr sets forth the thesis that far from having to incorporate the view of the self inherited from Descartes and Kant, modern theology has been saturated with their assumptions. Kerr points to theologians such as Eberhard Jüngel, who have a completely different assessment of the significance of the turn to the subject in modern theology.

32. In a study of the relationship between Rahner's theology and the Ignatian spiritual tradition, Philip Endean suggests that it was only in the 1970s that Rahner became "consciously convinced" of how Ignatius had influenced him, an influence—particularly through the *Spiritual Exercises*—that Rahner considered more important than any other philosophical or theological influences. Endean holds that his study "relativizes" the importance of Rahner's early philosophical works and "confirms how unhelpful it is to see Rahner's theological achievement as merely the outgrowth of *Spirit in the World*." He concludes that although there "are grounds for doubting the elderly Rahner's assertions about how Ignatius was the most significant influence on his theology," Rahner certainly lived and matured in a community shaped by the Ignatian tradition. Philip Endean, *Karl Rahner and Ignatian Spirituality* (Oxford: Oxford University Press, 2001), 4, 7, 241.

33. Rahner describes his early works, *Spirit in the World* and *Hearers of the Word*, as the "rather lopsided works of my youth." He asks not to be stereotyped by them. See Rahner, "Grace as the Heart of Human Existence," in Imhof and Biallowons, eds., *Faith in a Wintry Season*, 22.

34. Rahner, "The Concept of Mystery in Catholic Theology," in *Theological Investigations*, vol. 4 (London: Darton, Longman & Todd, 1966), 36–73, at 72.

35. Fergus Kerr accuses Rahner of being obsessed with epistemological prelimi-
naries and preoccupied with the cognitive subject. He suggests that this results
in Rahner's "most characteristic theological profundities" being "embedded in
an extremely mentalist-individualist epistemology of unmistakably Cartesian
provenance." Kerr, *Theology after Wittgenstein*, 14.
36. Including scripture and dogma.
37. After the Enlightenment, the anthropological approach in theology was initiated,
particularly in the writings of Friedrich Schleiermacher, whose *The Christian
Faith* (1821) marks the first significant synthesis of Enlightenment and Christian
theology. Schleiermacher is known as the "father of modern theology."
38. "The average person who comes to theology today, and this includes not only
those who are preparing for priesthood, does not feel secure in a faith which is
taken for granted and is supported by a homogeneous religious milieu common
to everyone." Rahner, *Foundations of Christian Faith*, 5.
39. Metz describes Rahner's ecclesial axiom: "All persons who are not excluded in
advance because they are irrational or of evil will, must be heard, must absolutely
be heard and taken extremely seriously." Metz, *A Passion for God*, 113.
40. Ellacuría was a student of Rahner's in Innsbruck in 1958–62.
41. Is it a theological anthropology or an anthropological theology? Perhaps it is more
accurately called an "anthropological theology," because the human person is the
starting point, but not the terminus, of his theological exploration. Whatever
its description, and despite the many valid criticisms that are made of Rahner's
theology, *the* horizon against which all questions arise is God as holy mystery;
the graced (if not sufficiently mindful of evil) vision of persons and reality stands
out against this horizon. The turn to the subject is *not* the turn from the source
of that subject.
42. Rahner holds that there are many sciences, including psychology and sociology,
that contribute something to an understanding of the human person, but these
all have the tendency to formalize everything in humans and to lead back to
abstract structures so that the individual concrete human person disappears. See
"The Theological Dimension of the Question about Man." Rahner, *Theological
Investigations*, vol. 17 (London: Darton, Longman & Todd, 1981), 53–70.
43. Ibid., 57–60.
44. Rahner, "Christian Humanism," *Theological Investigations*, vol. 9 (London: Darton, Longman & Todd, 1972), 187–204, at 202.
45. Rahner, "Concept of Mystery in Catholic Theology," 49.
46. Rahner, *Spirit in the World* (London: Sheed & Ward, 1968).
47. He offers a general definition: "The capacity of the creature, obediently accepting the disposition and action of God, to receive a determination for which the
creature is not 'in potency' in such a way that this determination is 'due' to it.
The potency is not such that if not actualized by the determination in question it
would be frustrated, and hence could not have been constituted by a wise creator

unless this determination were to be added." Rahner, *Sacramentum Mundi*, vol. V (London: Burns & Oates, 1970), 65.

48. Heidegger's influence is felt most strongly in the early Rahner, especially in the themes of being, time, dread, fear, and history. This influence is very obvious in *Hearers of the Word*, where there are echoes of Heidegger's *Being and Time*, but the use of Heideggerian language lessens in Rahner's later works. Heidegger influenced Rahner's existential ontology, but Rahner would disagree with Heidegger's position on the end of metaphysics. However, whatever the direct textual influence of Heidegger's philosophy on his theology, Rahner viewed Heidegger as his most important teacher, especially in the way Heidegger taught students to read and question texts in a new way, "to see new connections that would not immediately strike the ordinary person . . . to question anew so much in the tradition considered self-evident." Rahner, *I Remember: An Autobiographical Interview with Meinold Krauss* (New York/London: Crossroad/SCM, 1985), 45.

49. "Man is absolute openness to being in general, or, in a word, man is spirit. Transcendentality with regard to being in general is the basic constitution of man. And so we enunciate the first proposition of our metaphysical anthropology." Rahner, *Hearers of the Word*, 53.

50. Rahner, *Foundations of Christian Faith*, 32.

51. Ibid., 116–37.

52. Rahner, *Hearers of the Word*, 133.

53. Rahner, "Experience of Self and Experience of God," in *Theological Investigations*, vol. 13 (London: Darton, Longman & Todd, 1975), 122–32, at 128.

54. The interrelationship of the doctrine of the Trinity and theological anthropology is a constant concern of Rahner. He laments the isolation of the doctrine of the Trinity in "piety and textbook theology" that occurred as a result of neoscholasticism. See Rahner, *The Trinity*, trans. Joseph Donceel (New York: Crossroad Publishing, 2002).

55. Metz suggests that Rahner's term *"Begabung"* can be translated as "aptitude," "talent," "skill," or "gift." See Metz, *A Passion for God*, 195, n. 2.

56. Rahner, *Being and Time*, trans. John Macquarrie and Edward Robinson (Oxford: Blackwell, 1967), 32–40, 44, 78–90. One permanent determination—existential—of the human person, for Heidegger, is that he or she is a being-towards-death.

57. Rahner first used the term "supernatural existential" in the 1950 debate about *nouvelle théologie*: See "Eine Antwort" in *Orientierung* 14 (1950), 141–45; English translation: "Concerning the Relationship between Nature and Grace," *Theological Investigations*, vol. 1 (London: Darton, Longman & Todd, 1961), 297–317. Developed in Europe after the Second World War, this "new theology," represented by Yves Congar, Henri De Lubac, and Marie-Dominique Chenu, was viewed with suspicion by Rome, which saw it as linked with modernism's dilution of the gratuity of grace and the supernatural order and the undermining of the official teaching authority of the Catholic Church. Although the work of the

nouvelle théologie was rejected by Pope Pius XII in his encyclical *Humani generis* (1950), the insights of these theologians were eventually validated by the Second Vatican Council, at which they served as *periti*.

58. The neoscholastic extrinsicism, with its view of the nature-grace relationship as two parallels, saw grace as a superaddition to a nature that already had its own integrity. Extrinsicism, in general, neglects the subjective and fails to grasp that that particular knowing is transcendent.

59. See David Coffey, "The Whole Rahner on the Supernatural Existential," *Theological Studies* 65 (2004): 95–118.

60. Rahner, "Concerning the Relationship between Nature and Grace," 312.

61. Rahner, *Foundations of Christian Faith*, 127–28.

62. "It is in the 'paradoxical' utterances that we have the clearest view of God's attitude as personal and existential. . . . He does not communicate himself to those who are metaphysically close to him, the wise, the strong, the successful, the ontologically compact, but to the foolish of the world, the weak, the failures, the inwardly brittle and empty." Rahner, "*Theos* in the New Testament," *Theological Investigations*, vol. 1, 116.

63. Rahner, "On the Theology of Incarnation," *Theological Investigations*, vol. 4, 105.

64. See Rahner, *Foundations of Christian Faith*, 295–98.

65. See Rahner, "Membership of the Church According to the Teaching of Pius XII's Encyclical *Mystici corporis Christi*," *Theological Investigations*, vol. 2 (London: Darton, Longman & Todd, 1963), 1–88. "Anonymous Christianity" is the subject of several articles by Rahner and is mentioned in sixteen of the volumes of *Theological Investigations*.

66. Rahner was influenced by Henri de Lubac, who argued that the Fathers of the Church and the principles of Thomas Aquinas upheld the universality of the grace of Christ (*Catholicisme: Les aspects sociaux du dogme*, 1938). The question of accounting theologically for the salvation of "non-Christians" was also raised by Karl Barth. Barth suggested that the task of the Christian community sent into the world included concern, not just with "an actual but certainly with a virtual or potential Christian, with a *christianus designatus*, with a *christianus in spe*." Barth, *Church Dogmatics IV, 3: The Doctrine of Reconciliation* (Edinburgh: T&T Clark, 1962), 810.

67. Rahner, *Foundations of Christian Faith*, 176.

68. Rahner, "Christianity and the Non-Christian Religions," in *Theological Investigations*, vol. 5 (London: Darton, Longman & Todd, 1966), 115–34; Rahner, "On the Importance of the Non-Christian Religions for Salvation," in *Theological Investigations*, vol. 18 (London: Darton, Longman & Todd, 1984), 288–95; Rahner, "Atheism and Implicit Christianity," in *Theological Investigations*, vol. 9 (London: Darton, Longman & Todd, 1972), 145–64.

69. "For the Augustinian explanation that in the good behaviour of the unbeliever his virtuous conduct is only apparent and superficial, Rahner would substitute

the explanation that it is his unbelief which is only apparent, and that the efficacy in history of God's will that all men be saved can be presumed to prevail over the belief that all men have sinned." John Mahoney, *The Making of Moral Theology: A Study of the Roman Catholic Tradition* (Oxford: Clarendon Press, 1987), 100–101.

70. Rahner, "Anonymous Christians," *Theological Investigations*, vol. 6, 390–98, at 394.

71. Rahner, *Foundations of Christian Faith*, 228.

72. Ibid., 132.

73. In *Love Alone: The Way of Revelation*, trans. Alexander Dru (London: Burns & Oates, 1968), von Balthasar, without specifically referring to Rahner, critiques the anthropological starting point in theology. He later launched a direct attack on Rahner's theology in *The Moment of Christian Witness*, trans. Richard Beckley (Glen Rock, NJ: Newman Press, 1969). Eamonn Conway, in *The Anonymous Christian—A Relativised Christianity? An Evaluation of Hans Urs von Balthasar's Criticisms of Karl Rahner's Theory of the Anonymous Christian* (Frankfurt am Main: Peter Lang, 1993), examines von Balthasar's criticisms of the "anonymous Christian" theory up to and after the Second Vatican Council and evaluates the criticisms in the light of Rahner's teaching as a whole. Conway refutes the charges that Rahner's theology, central to which is the theory of the anonymous Christian, constitutes a reduction or relativization of the Christian mystery born of Biblical revelation. He concludes his evaluation of von Balthasar's criticisms by showing the complementary nature of von Balthasar's understanding of Christian anthropology and Rahner's transcendental theology.

74. An overview of various criticisms of the "anonymous Christian" theory is to be found in Karen Kilby's *Karl Rahner: Theology and Philosophy*. Kilby distinguishes between criticisms that charge Rahner with not doing justice to Christianity and those that charge him with undermining other religions and systems of belief. See chap. 7: "The theory of the anonymous Christian," 115–26. It must be noted that the failure to differentiate between its origins in response to a pastoral question and subsequent use of the concept in interreligious dialogue also leaves it vulnerable to criticism.

75. Metz, *A Passion for God*, 113. Some years earlier, Metz raised a concern that the doctrine of transcendental faith that grounds this thesis was marked by "an élitist gnoseology." See Metz, *Faith in History and Society*, 159–60. Rahner's response to the difficulties raised by his thesis of "Anonymous Christianity" can be found in "Observations on the Problem of the 'Anonymous Christian,'" in *Theological Investigations*, vol. 14 (London: Darton, Longman & Todd, 1976), 280–94. "By way of preliminary it may be pointed out that a distinction should be drawn between the question of what constitutes the best possible terminology from every point of view, and the further question of the actual reality signified by the phrases 'anonymous Christian' or 'anonymous Christianity' (281)." Rahner,

while valuing his own terms, was open to whatever "terminology best suits the purpose" (292).

76. Yet John Milbank, in *Theology and Social Theory*, charges Rahner with "naturalizing the supernatural," with contributing to ethics the "astonishingly shallow" idea that "Christian belief provides only 'motivations' for rational ethical behaviour," and with leading political and liberation theology to a "version of integralism [that] can only make the social the real site of salvation by a dialectical baptism of secular society" (220–23, 229–32). Milbank is critical of Rahner for directing his renewal of Aquinas toward "a mediating theology, a universal humanism, a *rapprochement* with the Enlightenment and an autonomous secular order" (207). Milbank does not do justice to Rahner's theology, and his charge of a Rahnerian naturalizing of the supernatural overlooks the centrality of the mystery of God in Rahner's theology and his emphasis on transcendence as a way of being in the world and in history.

77. Rahner, "Christian Humanism," in *Theological Investigations*, vol. 9, 187–204, at 189.

78. Leonardo Boff, *Liberating Grace* (Maryknoll, NY: Orbis, 1979), 4.

79. Ron Highfield outlines the development in Rahner's theology of freedom. He critically examines Rahner's notion of sin as a free and definitive "no" to God, suggesting that it creates insurmountable inconsistencies in his doctrine of sin and points to foundational inadequacies in his theological system, problems that, Highfield suggests, are rooted in Rahner's practice of endowing engraced human nature with divine-like attributes. "Instead of listening to scriptural and dogmatic texts for their understanding of human freedom, Rahner runs past them, attributing to the human being a divine-like freedom." Highfield, "The Freedom to Say 'No'? Karl Rahner's Doctrine of Sin," in *Theological Studies* 56 (1995): 485–505. Although I have some reservations about the completeness of Highfield's conclusions, his concern about Rahner's notion of freedom relates to our concern that Rahner does not adequately consider the paradox of grace and dis-grace that marks human existence.

80. Commentators note that Rahner uses a variety of German terms for this notion of "self-actualization" (*selbsttat*), a variety not always obvious in English translations: self-realization (*selbstverwirklichung*), self-fulfillment (*selbstvollendung*), self-performance (*selbstvollzug*), self-disposal or self-determination (*selbstverfugung*), self-responsibility (*selbstverantwortung*), self-possession (*selbstbesitz*). See David Lowry, *The Prophetic Element in the Church: As Conceived in the Theology of Karl Rahner* (Lanham, MD; London: University Press of America, 1990), 91–92.

81. Rahner, *Foundations of Christian Faith*, 38.

82. Ibid., 94–95.

83. Ibid., 96.

84. Bernard Häring grounds the theory of the fundamental option in the biblical notions of covenant and heart. Häring holds that to agree to live in covenant

with God is a basic act of faith, the most self-committing act we can ever make. This act of faith is the fundamental option. But we live in a broken world where that innermost orientation of our heart is challenged and threatened. Häring demonstrates a greater sensitivity than Rahner to the obstacles, determinants, and influences that have the potential to affect our living out of self-actualizing freedom. See Häring's *Free and Faithful in Christ, Vol. I: General Moral Theology* (Middlegreen, Slough: St. Paul Publications, 1978).

85. Rahner, *Meditations on Freedom and the Spirit* (London: Burns & Oates, 1977), 36.

86. Ibid., 48–62. Rahner notes that sinful manipulation can exist in both Church and society.

87. Beste, *God and the Victim.* In the previous chapter our discussion about the impact of the cases of child sexual abuse within the Catholic Church pointed to the failure of the Church to take seriously its own ethic and its commitment to human rights. It could also be suggested that the Church failed to ask the kind of question that Rahner also seems not to have asked about the impact of interpersonal damage on our capacity to respond to God's grace.

88. Ibid., 93.

89. Ibid.

90. Rahner, "Experience of Self and Experience of God," in *Theological Investigations,* vol. 13, 122–32, at 126.

91. For a feminist engagement with Rahner's essay "Experience of Self and Experience of God," see Elizabeth A. Johnson's *She Who Is: The Mystery of God in Feminist Theological Discourse* (New York: Crossroad, 1993), 65–67.

92. Rahner, "Experience of Self and Experience of God," 132.

93. Rahner, "The Dignity and Freedom of Man," in *Theological Investigations,* vol. 2, 235–63, at 235–36. Rahner made a significant contribution to the revised theory of Natural Law, particularly through his enlargement of what must be considered when analyzing human nature and his view of that nature as *potentia obedientalis.*

94. Ibid., 242.

95. Ibid.

96. Ibid., 245.

97. This stress on the relational dimension of human dignity is just one example from Rahner's theology that counters Fergus Kerr's charge that the transcendental experience Rahner wants for the human person "obscures and excludes the membership of a community and a tradition that gives rise to subjectivity in the first place." Kerr, *Theology after Wittgenstein,* 8. See also Rahner's reference to the social nature of the human person: "The question of salvation cannot be answered by bypassing man's historicity and his social nature." Rahner, *Foundations of Christian Faith,* 40.

98. In response to criticisms by Johannes Metz and Peter Eicher that his theology is too transcendental and neglectful of the encounter with the concrete God of

history, Rahner said that his theology "at least held open . . . in principle, and in no sense denied" the perspectives that these theologians would adopt. "I don't regard my theology as universal and as having general and final validity." See Rahner, "The Importance of Thomas Aquinas," interview with Jan van den Eijnden, May 1982, Imhof and Biallowons, eds., *Faith in a Wintry Season*, 51. Fergus Kerr acknowledges Rahner's role in working out the implications of recognizing the historicity of theology: "Again and again he returns to the difficult problem of reconciling the claims of truth with the recognition of the dependence of knowledge on context or system or culture." Kerr, "Rahner Retrospective II: The Historicity of Theology," *New Blackfriars* 61 (July/August 1980): 331–41, at 340. However, Rahner does not always acknowledge the complexity of historicity, and this leads to the difficulties that Metz and Eicher outline. Rahner's concern with historicity and historical development is most evident in his involvement in issues regarding the renewal of the Church both during and after Vatican II.

99. Rahner, "The Dignity and Freedom of Man," 244.

100. Rahner, *Foundations of Christian Faith*, 32.

101. The following revealing comment by Rahner is quoted in Endean (2001), 110: "Think back to the time of the Third Reich. I think there were relatively few priests whom you can really prove to have clearly transgressed moral principles in their dealings with the ideology prevailing at the time, with the persecuted Jews, etc. But can you then say with equal clarity that we all always really did the right thing (and I don't except myself here)? That much is certainly not clear to me." From *Der Anspruch Gottes und der Einzelne* (1959), 534–35.

102. Rahner, "Why Does God Allow Us to Suffer?" in *Theological Investigations*, vol. 19 (London: Darton, Longman & Todd, 1983), 194–208.

103. Ibid., 207–8.

104. Ibid., 197–205.

105. In *Foundations of Christian Faith* (270–74), Rahner has a Heideggerian tone when he writes his anthropological reflections on death and the finality of human existence. His tendency to emphasize death as the fulfillment of life, with *less* emphasis on death as a result of sin, may reflect the influence of Heidegger's existential ontology.

106. Rahner, "Why Does God Allow Us to Suffer?" 203.

107. Metz, *A Passion for God*, 118–19.

Chapter Three

≈

Human Rights in Time

REALISM BETWEEN MEMORY AND HOPE

T HIS CHAPTER SITUATES HUMAN RIGHTS as a "realist" discourse in time, located between the memory of suffering and hope for the future. It begins with a brief exploration of the concept of memory, particularly the efforts to develop what Paul Ricoeur calls a culture of *just memory*. The contribution of *Recuperación de la Memoría Historica*, produced by the Human Rights Office of the Catholic Archdiocese of Guatemala, to our understanding of the impact of human rights violations, not just on individuals—damaging thereby both victims and perpetrators—but also on the fabric of community, will be examined. The "interruption" of theological discourse by the stark realism of the Holocaust is explored in the work of Johann Baptist Metz, as are the challenges of this interruption for Christian theology.

Memory

Memory is constitutive of the human person. Biologically we are memory, our DNA inherited from a complex set of ancestral cells. Memory is usually associated with the area of cognitive psychology explaining how we learn and retain information and experiences. However, there are biological, psychological, spiritual, cultural, and political dimensions to human memory; and despite many explanatory models of memory, it is difficult to describe exactly how this constitutive dimension works. From Plato, Plotinus, and Augustine we see that memory is an ancient philosophical and theological concern. However, the Enlightenment rupture of anamnestic rationality from scientific rationality haunts the placing of human suffering in modern philosophical and theological discourse. The shadow side of the Enlightenment sanitized memory, for everything was considered explainable and capable of being rationally ordered. This led to an underestimation of the powers of memory and imagination.

The Holocaust returned the memory of suffering to the foreground of European and Anglo-American philosophical and theological consciousness. In making this observation, I am also aware that there are other memories of suffering that question the claims of European humanism and Enlightenment liberty—one of the most obvious being the Atlantic slave trade—memories that are embedded in Africa, the Caribbean, North America as well as Latin America but that were either invisible or marginal to Western philosophical and theological concerns. The memory of suffering is a raw and volatile subject, and the recent truth-seeking initiatives in postconflict situations point to the difficulties inherent both in the excess of memory and in the denial of memory.

The Ethics of Memory

The significance of memory is acknowledged by Paul Ricoeur who points to memory as having two relations to the past, a relation of "knowledge" and a relation of "action." It is within the relation of action, of *re-membering*, that we face the ethical in terms of the use and abuse of memory. Ricoeur describes the ethics of memory as operating at three levels: the pathological-therapeutic level, the pragmatic level, and the properly ethical-political level.[1]

At the pathological-therapeutic level we face the scars and wounds of memory. Ricoeur draws from two Freudian ideas regarding memory: memory as work, that is, working through the past in order to move from repetition to remembrance, and memory as the movement from melancholia to authentic mourning. Both excess of memory and denial of memory, in different ways, trap the scars and wounds of memory in repetition and melancholia, thus weakening the possibility of reconciliation. Ricoeur describes the Freudian work of memory as "travail" and suggests that we keep in mind this concept of the "work of memory." However, the philosopher does not connect the work that is "travail" with the travail that leads to birth.

Ricoeur notes that it is at the pragmatic level that the abuses of memory are more noticeable. The praxis of an ethic of memory is enabled through the use of narrative. He attributes to narrative an educative function. Ricoeur is mindful of the need for a hermeneutic of critical suspicion so that narratives are not idealized. He acknowledges that the narrative of a foundational event for some can be a wound in the memory of another. Narrative needs the hermeneutic of suspicion that comes from those who bear the wounds of the story, those unnamed within it, those at the margins, or the guests and strangers who hear it in a different way. This hermeneutic of suspicion creates the possibility for a "telling otherwise" that can move us from past to future.[2]

At the ethical-political level, the duty to remember (*devoir de memoir*) moves toward a construction of the future. Ricoeur notes that this duty of remembrance is necessary for three reasons: first, in order to prevent the destructive tendency of time from eroding the traces; second, to allow the possibility of forgiveness as liberation from the burdens of the past; and third, to remember our heritage, especially that dimension which consists in the memory of suffering, the traces of a parallel history of victimization that would counter the tendency of history to celebrate the victors.[3]

Ricoeur addresses the possibility of a duty to forget and remarks that there is no symmetrical relationship between the duty to forget and the duty to remember because "the duty to remember is a duty to teach, whereas the duty to forget is a duty to go beyond anger and hatred. The two aims are not comparable."[4] He concludes by pointing to the necessity of developing "a culture of *just memory*."

Trials and Truth Commissions: Just Memory?

How is Ricoeur's culture of "just memory" achieved? Is it through an emphasis on judicial remembering and forensic truth seeking? We live in a post-Nuremberg age, where trials for human rights violations can seem merely the implementation of the law of the victors, fraught, therefore, with the weaknesses of politicization and selectivity. Recognizing that the court should not be the locus for every exploration of truth and the difficulties of developing authentic judicial means for the pursuit of justice, particularly after periods of violence and repression, trials can create a space "between vengeance and forgiveness" wherein the question of individual responsibility in the context of mass atrocities is raised, credible public records of these events are created, and, in the case of the International Criminal Court, limits placed on state sovereignty in the case of gross violations of human rights.[5]

The concerns of formal justice are primarily those of the defendant or perpetrator, and of the state; such a legitimate legal process is crucial for democracy. However, the voices and concerns of victims do not play a prominent role in the drama of formal justice. Since the 1970s, and influenced by the increasing dominance of human rights as both a moral discourse and an international movement, other methods of recovering memory after periods of war and oppression have been explored. Of particular interest is the establishment of over twenty "truth commissions" in various parts of the world, reflecting a wide range of political circumstances and historical contexts. These truth commissions are not intended to be a substitute for trials, but they have a "breadth and flexibility" helpful in confronting a painful past, and remembering the complexities of tragic and oppressive situations.[6] The exhumation of the graves of victims of violations and the help of forensic anthropology means that even the dead can "speak" in the process of remembering. Truth commissions do not constitute a simple choice between truth and justice, and while the word "reconciliation" was part of the South African commission, it did not preclude the right of victims to press criminal charges or to seek restitution.[7]

The difficulty with designating "truth" as the object of such commissions is that it can burden the process with an expected product defined by a misplaced sense of the "objective." A truth commission is often not so much about finding an unknown truth as it is about public acknowledgment of what is already known but not acknowledged. Moral repair and social reconstruction cannot proceed without such acknowledgment. Those who have been silenced can speak publicly to those who silenced and to those who chose neutrality in the context of that silencing.[8]

Truth commissions expose the pain of human rights violations and the impact of this pain on human beings. Elaine Scarry describes physical pain as having the ability to destroy language. Interrogation and other forms of discourse that accompany torture aid this destruction of language. Scarry stresses the political consequences of deliberately inflicted pain, particularly in cases of war and torture and points to the importance of actions of creativity that can challenge the "unmaking" of the person and their world that is the aim of such violations. The telling of painful stories by—and on behalf of—victims of war and torture constitutes a way of recovering from what Scarry sees as a reversion to the state of sounds and cries anterior to language. It allows pain to rehabilitate language and to find a voice. Of course, the telling of painful stories is not an easy or universally applicable process; some people who have been tortured find that the pain is, in fact, unspeakable.

Scarry, examining the phenomenon of torture in many countries, notes that not only does the person who is being tortured revert to the cries and screams anterior to language, but former political prisoners recall that the persons inflicting the pain also revert to a prelanguage of uncaring noises.[9] To allow the narration of the story of the victim, particularly someone who has suffered isolation and torture, is to offer a retort to the torturer who reinforces the physical brutality with the reminder that no one either knows or cares.

A different reading of those linguistically anterior cries is offered by Nadezhda Mandlestan, wife of the Russian poet Osip Mandelstan who endured vicious interrogation and internal exile during the Stalinist era. She suggests that to cry and scream is the way a human person leaves "a trace," a "pitiful sound" that is "a concentrated expression of the last vestige of human dignity."[10] In affirming Scarry's view of the way in which pain can unmake the world, the intention is not to minimize the importance of lament as a more primal and perennial category, which redeems the sounds and cries from the hands of torturers and welcomes these sounds back into the discourse of the community.

In a truth commission, victims are allowed to tell their story without courtroom cross-examination and the strict proceduralism of trials. As we saw, Ricoeur attributes to narrative an educative function, which enables the praxis of an ethic of memory. Narrative thus can unveil the real meaning and human impact of terms such as "violations of human rights." It is a potentially misleading term, giving the impression that somehow abstract moral or legal rights are violated. It is human persons—in theological terms, those who are *Imago Dei*—who are violated and damaged when human rights are ignored. Without a kind of rationalistic sanitization, the stories of victims (and perpetrators) can begin to express adequately the pain and humiliation of torture, the pathos of exclusion, the agony of hunger or homelessness, or the symbiotic dehumanization that occurs in the process of dehumanizing and damaging others. Statistics and calculations are very important, for without them violations can be minimized; but narrative puts the human persons, *Imago Dei*, at the heart of the pursuit of justice.

However, even where the stories are told without interruption or cross-examination, they may only hint at the true level of the damage. In the case of the South African commission, a disproportionate number of those who came to testify were women, most of whom did not speak for themselves as victims, but for other family members, such as husbands and sons. The level of shame and violation felt by women at sexual humiliation meant that they hid aspects of the narrative; this led the commissioner to create a forum specifically for the women's own experience. Such underreporting of abuse suffered by women in conflict situations has been a feature of truth commissions. Sexual violence against women remains a routine part of armed conflict and silence about sexual abuse in the domestic realm was often matched by silence about such abuse in the political realm. In June 2008 the United Nations Security Council voted unanimously in favor of a resolution classifying rape as a weapon of war, affirming its intention, when establishing and renewing state-specific sanction regimes, to consider imposing "targeted and graduated" measures against warring factions who had committed rape against women and girls.[11]

The stories of children who suffer in war and conflict create special difficulties with regard to eliciting evidence, for example, the risk of public exposure of minors or the danger of retraumatizing children who were forced to take part in human rights violations. Richard Rorty's image of the remnant child, placed at the very beginning of this book, seems to presuppose an innocent child victim devoid of dignity, but his reflection does not address the terrible poignancy of the children of war who are simultaneously victims and perpetrators of violence.[12]

There are, of course, many difficulties with truth commissions, not least the issues of the possibility of finding the truth about complex situations, and of knowing how much truth to tell. Memories of even benign events can differ among those who were present, so it is inevitable that the reconstruction of situations of human rights violations will have various "truths" articulated by victims, perpetrators, and bystanders. Acknowledgment is more difficult in situations where gross violations have been committed by both sides in a conflict, for example, in the Balkans. However, the recording of the "truth" of traumatic times is helpful in preventing future potentially revisionist readings of history that would seek to obliterate memory, especially the memory of suffering.

Other difficulties include the issue of naming perpetrators, the question of the role of the international community in arming local conflicts, and the fact that without subpoena powers individual narratives of suffering are not related to official government, military, and police documents.[13] Discernment is needed about the timing and methodology of truth commissions, and funding is a major issue.[14] Conflicting expectations about what these commissions will achieve can impact the degree of satisfaction and healing experienced by people. Some victims and communities may even experience retraumatization, as wounds that had begun to heal are reopened. Without adequate support after giving evidence at these commissions, victims and communities can be left in trauma as the investigators move on to consider other atrocities.

The truth commissions of recent decades have articulated a variety of aims including punishment, establishment of truth, repair of wounds in society, memorialization of victims, and future prevention of human rights abuses. All such commissions envisage a process that contributes toward moral reconstruction; and the overall aim is justice, in which truth telling, healing and reconciliation play a significant role. Despite their limitations and disappointments, truth commissions are now an important element in the process of transitional justice in a newly founded or regained democracy.[15]

In combination with other cultural and religious ways of articulating suffering and healing wounds, truth commissions represent the desire to find a way out of damage and trauma, and they provide a tentative way forward that helps to reconcile memory and hope. They also contribute to the institutionalization of human rights locally and globally. Although truth commissions and similar processes must be read within their particular historical and political contexts, they are not simply about the travail toward just memory of distant places under rogue regimes. They have something to teach more stable societies and established democracies, for they weave together the personal and the political, social justice at its micro and macro levels, serving as a reminder that justice is not simply a "general" problem but is embodied in, and the damage of injustice embedded in, particular persons and communities.

These attempts at transitional justice show how horror is played out and constitute an evolving way of dealing with the embeddedness of damage in human persons and communities. It is sometimes suggested that the focus of a truth commission is therapeutic.[16] However, these commissions are not meant to represent the triumph of the therapeutic over the political, nor to suggest that human rights are founded on the basis of the degree of suffering endured. Their purpose is to highlight—however tentatively—the connections between the recognition that human rights violations damage human persons and the future building of community and consolidation of democracy.

In the context of a discussion on the virtues, Thomas Aquinas explores the relationship between truth and justice, asking: "Is truth a part of justice?" Telling the truth, Aquinas concludes, is indeed part of the virtue of justice, for we owe the truth to one another. Truth, as constitutive of justice, is other-directed and essential for social life.[17] A truth commission might perhaps be perceived by Aquinas as one way of giving his or her due to the victim, and the Thomistic emphasis on the connection between social relations and justice would relate the effect of the individual falsehood in social relations to that of the social falsehood in human sociality and community.

Although we must be cognizant that travail toward just memory is not fully completed when the silence is broken, the lies exposed, and the reports all signed, the efforts of those who participate in truth commissions must be recognized and, in particular, what Archbishop Desmond Tutu describes as the "magnanimity" of the victims.[18] The South African Commission and other such processes, while fraught with difficulties, are not just attempts to hear and acknowledge the pain experienced by so many people; they also exemplify communities attempting moral repair not achievable by legal means alone and seeking a flourishing that is beyond "formal" justice.

Toward Just Memory: A Guatemalan Case Study

We now turn to examine the *Recuperación de la Memoria Historica* (REMHI), the Recovery of Historical Memory Project, produced by the Human Rights Office of the Catholic Archdiocese of Guatemala.[19] It is an attempt at bleakly realistic narrating of the specific faces of injustice in human rights violations as well as the exploration of the reality of loss and damage to persons and communities, victims, and perpetrators. REMHI exemplifies the praxis of an ethic toward what Ricoeur described as "just memory."

Although the actual report is devoid of explicitly theological language, REMHI is a document of pastoral theology in that it is an expression of the human rights ministry of the Church and part of its social mission. This theological orientation is obvious both in the presentation speech of Bishop Juan Gerardi and in the introductory remarks by Archbishop Prospero Penados Del Barrio. The vision of REMHI is grounded in an implicit anamnestic and eschatological theology, that is, a theology of recovering the memory of the suffering of those whose human rights were violated for the purpose of developing a new and different society.

The Church was aware that healing and reconciliation were not possible until the whole truth of the violence and oppression in Guatemala was uncovered. There was also acknowledgment that for genuine transformation, each sector of society, including the leadership of the Church, must "engage in a process of reflection that reaches into the far corners of the collective conscience"[20] for any failure of commission or omission that did not protect people from the horror and must embark on the "task of breaking the silence that thousands of war victims have kept for years."[21]

REMHI exemplified the commitment of the Church to human rights, to a pastoral ministry serving the dignity of people, in particular the Mayan peoples who had constituted over eighty percent of the victims, and to memory as an instrument for the construction of a new Guatemala. Thus the theological vision involved denunciation of evil and annunciation of alternatives. It was not simply a political project, or an ecclesiastical effort to match the secular call for the truth of history, but a project carried out in the light of faith, a praxis of ongoing revelation of "the face of God, the presence of the Lord. In all these events, it is God who is speaking to us."[22] In many ways the report is also a martyrology, a memorialization of those who bore the image of the crucified Christ in Guatemala.

The project was strengthened by the Church's strong rural networks and its active presence in the midst of the poor and indigenous Guatemalan majority. It also had authenticity in the eyes of these victims as they had seen that, at least since the 1970s, the Church had engaged in a preferential option for the poor and, because of this, had also suffered oppression. REMHI was not a judicial body and therefore did not have ultimate responsibility for apportioning guilt or innocence; however the data collected, the memory recovered in this report, was incorporated into the *Memoria del Silencio* report of the official Guatemalan "truth commission."[23] REMHI adopted a pastoral approach: It went to the people, allowing those who could not afford to come to a hearing in the city to participate in the recovering of memory. The report acknowledges that the testimonies collected represent a significant but partial sample of the human rights violations that took place in Guatemala for that thirty-six-year period, focusing mainly on the most violent period of the early 1980s and the fact that most of the victims were rural, indigenous people.[24]

The methodology consisted of open-ended interviews based on seven basic questions: Who was the victim? What happened? Who did it? Why did it happen? What did you do to cope with the situation? What effect did the event have on you and the community? What needs to be done so that it doesn't happen again?

The first question was developed into a conversation about the person, which allowed the witnesses to enflesh the bare bones of the name and age of a victim, into a fuller picture of his or her personality, thus breaking down undifferentiated references to victims of human rights violations into identifiable human beings located in families and communities. This questioning marked the first effort in Guatemala to gather together all the perspectives that might contribute toward a just memory of the civil war. The interview techniques allowed the narratives of the victim to emerge in a way that also offered emotional and psychological support to those giving testimony.

The particular process used by REMHI also facilitated the articulation of suffering that is not encapsulated in a list of rights violations, for example, the effect on a community as it is forced to participate in mutilation of corpses. It brought to light the forced disappearances, often used by the Guatemalan intelligence services and described elsewhere as the "most blatant form of atrocity by deception."[25] If the deliberate infliction of physical pain unmakes the world and results in a loss of language, a disappearance is the ultimate unmaking, for it deprives the grieving of the proper lament that is the point of departure for the narrative that may be creative of just memory.

The report also helped uncover a genocidal policy directed against the Mayan Indians and the systematic sexual abuse of women that was a planned part of this, although, as in so many other situations of conflict, the women, when giving testimony did not refer directly to their experiences as women.[26] Rape was used as a bartering tool, as an exchange for the survival of the woman or that of her children. Children conceived by rape were often shunned "as a form of community resistance."[27]

Half of the recorded massacres included the collective murder of children, and pregnant women were particular targets, with extreme cruelty shown toward the children in their wombs. The unborn victims of the war do not appear in the statistics, but the narratives of their elimination and the fact that children appear as direct or indirect victims in most of the testimonies point to the genocidal desire to destroy the community.[28] Children were forcibly recruited by the military, thus drawn into complicity with the brutality. Those who lived in hiding could neither run nor play, with the consequent effects on their development as children. However, despite the "militarization of childhood," REMHI also pointed to the remarkable survival skills of children and the instincts that often led them to flee from danger. These positive signs indicated that with proper support and help to preserve the memory of their families, these children could reclaim their sense of identity and become relatively well adjusted.

The oppressive and brutal military machine sought to permeate the entire social fabric through a psychology of terror and a network of agents and informers, damaging the social fabric of communities, particularly in rural areas. The report identifies community destruction, destruction of nature (which in Mayan culture is akin to an assault on the community), and distrust and internal breakdown as the most common effects of the political violence. The criminalization of any form of community leadership that did not succumb to military control led to a breakdown of traditional authority and, consequently, to an erosion of many Mayan ways of conflict resolution, which tended to be reparative and restorative rather than punitive. Household goods and tools were destroyed in an effort to eradicate people's means of survival. The report even describes the assault on the Mayan "colors of identity," their highly symbolic traditional woven costumes. These were not only damaged in the destruction of everyday life, but it became dangerous to wear them because they would have identified the allegiance of the wearer and the community.[29] There are even examples of military "model villages" where peasants were supervised in a regimented existence.

Violence against religion and culture was part of the assault on the social fabric. Places of worship and Mayan sacred sites were destroyed; in some cases, churches were occupied by the military, which used them as detention centers. Catholicism was considered subversive by the army, and many people lived in fear of expressing their faith. "With the exception of some Protestant churches that stood by the affected populations, influential evangelical sects increasingly found that the repression had created a religious vacuum."[30] The military saw these small churches as a way of controlling the population and as a channel for their own "narrative" of the violence in the country, a narrative that blamed the victims themselves for the violations that were visited upon them.

REMHI focuses on the social aspects of torture, which was conceived as an assault on the collective identity. One in six of the massacres analyzed by the report took place on a special day for the community. Massacres were not spontaneous outbreaks of violence but premeditated attacks on days when the community would be gathered together, for example, on a market day or on days that held symbolic significance, such as Christmas Day.[31]

As well as the torture of those who disappeared, there was a policy of "exemplary torture," even of children, as a means of deepening the terror in communities. I emphasize the importance of seeing the communal impact of the violations of rights, the complicated implicatedness of other people in the violations, and the damage caused to the social fabric. Both victim and torturer are systemically related to others, who are thus drawn into the evil and suffering. Those who assert that human rights discourse is simply concerned with the protection of atomized individuals overlook the communal dimensions of these violations, a dimension that is well understood by perpetrators of human rights violations.

Although the voices of victims dominate REMHI, it also includes testimonies from a small but significant number of perpetrators who came forward themselves to the volunteers. These were men who were haunted by the memories of what they had seen and done. During most of the period of conflict in Guatemala, young men were forcibly recruited into the military. The officers were almost exclusively from the Ladinos—the traditionally dominant nonindigenous Guatemalans—who had trained in military academies and Special Forces schools, including the infamous U.S. Army School of the Americas.[32] In contrast, most of the soldiers were from the poorer classes and many were Mayan. No names were attached to the testimonies of perpetrators who came forward, but their stories are obviously those of lower-ranking soldiers and forcibly recruited civilians, stories that give insight into how a system of terror trains people to torture and murder. The report also includes extensive research into the intelligence behind the violence, a complex military and police apparatus that permeated the entire social fabric. REMHI gives names of military and intelligence leaders, and the names of torturers are included in the testimonies of the victims; such naming was one of the aims of the Church's commission. In general, the silence of the intellectual authors of the human rights violations remains unbroken, and many of the military still believe that these violations were necessary methods in a necessary war.

Avishai Margalit suggests that the paradigmatic case of a "moral witness" is one who has experienced the suffering, a sufferer rather than an observer.[33] This exclusive definition of a moral witness could be broadened to include the perpetrators. If all human beings are moral agents (victims, perpetrators, and those victim-perpetrators/perpetrator-victims caught in a terrible and ambiguous space in situations of repression), then surely all moral agents can offer moral witness of some kind. The witness to evil of the torturer and murderer is still the voice of a moral agent.

Although the prime concern of truth commissions is to allow the voices of the victims—both dead and alive—to echo in a way that breaks the silence about their suffering, the voices of the perpetrators remain part of the moral fabric. It is clear that many perpetrators of human rights violations do not see themselves as damaged by what they have done to others, but the Guatemalan report offers an insight into those who may have had some such awareness. REMHI describes how each of the perpetrators who came forward voluntarily cried before he spoke, marking perhaps a redemptive reversion from the torturer's prelanguage of uncaring noises, described by victims of torture, to the cry that marks movement toward the authentic mourning necessary for just memory. They also spoke about the horrors they claim to have witnessed, revealing unwillingness to self-identify as the perpetrators in the narrative, which, together with the anterior crying, suggests a guilt that may, perhaps, issue in remorse.[34]

The section of the report titled "The Methodology of Horror" outlines an appalling education in violence, forced obedience, and complicity in murder, and a training devoid of respect for the dignity and lives of the soldiers themselves, engendering in them the contempt for human life that facilitated the widespread atrocities and the "celebrations" that followed these atrocities.[35] One of the frightening aspects of this section is the description of the trained interrogator or torturer, not as a psychopath, but as someone with particular insight into a wide variety of fields such as science, the arts, religion, and community customs. The insight of the torturer gives him access to the "core inconsistencies," enabling him "to consciously delve into the complex world of what is inaptly termed 'Human Being.'"[36] The oppression and violence are facilitated by a paradox: the paradox of training in dehumanization that coexists with the training of torturers who are "expert" in understanding the human person for the purpose of the infliction of pain and the destruction of community.[37]

With REMHI, the Church brought a perspective on human rights that was far from individualistic but sought to uncover the social aspects of torture and reveal the impact of these violations on communities. Human rights violations are never simply an assault, either by commission or by omission, upon the dignity of an atomized individual. The generosity of existence of the entire community, that is, the capacity to give and receive toward greater flourishing, is profoundly affected. Sociality itself is damaged, for sociality is vulnerable because it does not exist in some abstract and pure form.

Trauma bruises the capacity of the person to trust. Jean Améry, who endured brutal Gestapo interrogation, comments on those who, without the experience of being beaten, suggest that with the first blow the human person loses his or her dignity. Améry holds that what is lost is "trust in the world," the certainty that this person "by reason of written or unwritten social contracts—will respect my physical . . . and metaphysical being." He concludes that those who have succumbed to torture "can no longer feel at home in the world . . . trust in the world which already collapsed in part at the first blow, but in the end, under torture, fully, will not be regained."[38] The relationship between the "physical and metaphysical" dimensions of the human person, between internal and external damage, is a factor that is not taken seriously by theologians who dismiss engagement with human rights.

That bruising of trust affects close relationships, the community in which the violations of human rights happen, and especially those whose role it is to record the trauma. Even the people who have to type accounts of human rights violations at truth commissions become "sponges of trauma," absorbing the horror but without the "comfort" of seeing the person and the resilience with which people were often able to tell their story of suffering, thus leading to a secondary traumatization.[39] The effects of systemic political repression on victims and on society as a whole lead therapists to emphasize that torture is a social and political, not a medical, problem.

Unless these dimensions of torture are acknowledged, there will be no cure for what therapists see as the life-long and intergenerational effects for victims, perpetrators, and societies.[40] Both the damage and the repair occur at individual and social levels. Reflecting on repair in the context of Chile after the dictatorship, therapists stress the need for restoration of responsiveness at both the individual and collective levels: "the capacity for being *moved* ethically must be recovered."[41] The capacity of torture to damage the generosity of existence of persons and communities is expressed by therapists in descriptions of the destruction of intersubjectivity. Therapists also speak of the necessity for nurturing again the capacity for idealism that has often been left for dead in the person. The results of this research by therapists into the impact of gross violations of human rights on individuals and communities concur with the argument of this book that rights protect the conditions in which virtue and the capacity to live ethically are nurtured.

However, the REMHI report is not one of unmitigated horror, for despite the riskiness of solidarity, there is the witness of many people who courageously sought to help others in the midst of the violent repression, "repeated examples of solidarity and profound altruism."[42] The resistance of women is specifically identified, both their relentless searching for the "disappeared" and the groundbreaking role they played in advocacy for respect for human rights during and after the violence.[43] The majority of the testimonies were in Mayan languages, breaking the silence in languages that had not been considered part of Guatemalan identity, allowing the possibility of a "telling otherwise," which Ricoeur suggested can move us from past to future. REMHI recognized both the eschatological focus of the travail for just memory and the riskiness of such remembering: "The path has been, and continues to be, full of risks, but the construction of the Kingdom of the Lord is risky, and can only be built by those who have the strength to confront those risks."[44]

Two days after presenting the report, Bishop Gerardi, head of the Human Rights Office of the Archdiocese of Guatemala, was murdered.[45] The travail for just memory in postconflict situations can be a dangerous activity, but to avoid it is to risk dangerous forgetfulness.

> accidental observers
> give doubtful figures
> accompanied by the shameful word "about"
> and yet in these matters
> accuracy is essential
> we must not be wrong
> even by a single one
> we are despite everything
> the guardians of our brothers
> ignorance about those who have disappeared
> undermines the reality of the world.[46]

Theology toward Just Memory: The Haunted Tardiness of Johann Baptist Metz

We turn now to the theology of Johann Baptist Metz, not because his work contains sustained theological engagement with the discourse of human rights but because it engages interrelated themes and concerns located at the intersection of that discourse and contemporary theology: The necessity of a practical and political theology toward *just memory* finds expression in Metz's work, and his theology struggles with the implications of the Holocaust for Christian theology. Reflecting on Metz's theology toward just memory, especially the memory of those who suffered in the Holocaust, I am aware that the naming of the catastrophe with this unified term "Holocaust" is indeed problematic. The philosopher Gillian Rose, for example, suggests that to use this term to describe the Nazi genocide is to over-unify and sacralize it.[47] Thus, we proceed

with this exploration of Metz's work, conscious of the risks of facile symboliza-
tion and the limitations of linguistic signification of the *Shoah*.

Metz's theology serves as a bridge between the transcendentalist Thomism
of Rahner and the liberation theology that emerges out of Latin America.
Before examining the particular challenge that Metz offers theology, we briefly
outline the development of his theology. There are three stages that mark a
gradual movement from transcendental theology to political theology, without
completely abandoning the commitments of transcendental theology to the
turn to the subject and to *dialogue with the secular*. After Metz moves into political theology, there is a distinct fissure born of his facing up to the silence of
European theology in the face of the Holocaust. This fissure became clear at a
particular point in the late 1970s, but I contend that it was slowly breaking into
his theology through his exploration of the categories of memory, narrative,
and solidarity in history.

The Influence of Karl Rahner

In the first stage of his theology (1950–63), Metz engages with transcendental
Thomism and the influence of his teacher Karl Rahner is obvious as Metz
appropriates the turn to the subject and confronts the issue of secularization.
His 1961 doctoral dissertation in theology was written after editing the second edition of Rahner's *Spirit in the World*. Metz's theology was thereafter in
a dialectical relationship with Rahner's theology, a dialecticism that should
not be overlooked in order to avoid an interpretation of his theology as merely
"corrective" of Rahner's.[48] Reflecting back on his work in later years, Metz has
stated that he owed everything he could do theologically to Rahner,[49] saying
that it is "almost impossible" to overestimate the mark that Rahner made on
his theology: "Understanding theology as a way of life derives entirely from
Rahner."[50]

Metz's theology began by engaging with Rahner's transcendental method,
an engagement in which Metz already showed evidence of his own particular
concerns, and although his work moves in a different direction, he continues
to draw from Rahner while exposing the transcendental method to the painful
questions with which Rahner's theology does not directly engage. He is critical
of what he perceives to be Rahner's "idealist" attempt to explain the historical identity of Christianity, that is, by means of speculative thought, without
reference to memory or future, grounded in an abstract present. Although

Metz's theology would later undergo a profound interruption, he continues to be a passionate defender of modernity's turn to the subject and, although also sensitive to the critique of postmodern philosophy, continues to assert the values of the Enlightenment, which are potentially liberative.

Both Rahner and Metz are conscious, in different ways, of doing theology "after-Kant"; the former responds primarily to the Kantian epistemological challenge, the latter to the Kantian ethical challenge. Rahner drew from Kant's transcendental teaching and his question about the conditions for the possibility of knowledge, seeking in his transcendental Thomism to respond to Kant's challenge to religion as found in the *First Critique*.[51] The political theology later espoused by Metz draws from Kant's teaching about the primacy of practical reason and the subsequent primacy of praxis in philosophy.[52] At the beginning of his career, Metz engaged with Aquinas and Heidegger, writing his doctoral dissertation for philosophy on "Heidegger and the Problem of Metaphysics." However, he contends that his relationship to Heidegger "was and still is divided."[53] Metz suggested that the influence of Heidegger's existentialist anthropology on Rahner forged a compatibility between theology and modernity but that the price of this compatibility was the privatization of theology. Metz later entered into dialogue with members of the Frankfurt School, thinkers who were both atheist-Marxist and Jewish. His seminal work, *Faith in History and Society*, contains more references to Theodor Adorno, Walter Benjamin, and Ernst Bloch than to Aquinas and Heidegger.[54]

For Rahner—following Heidegger—the limit situation that one must embrace for authentic existence is the reality of one's own death. For Metz, the key to authentic existence is the embrace of the suffering and death of the other. Metz upholds Rahner's commitment to articulate "faith seeking understanding" in the context of post-Kantian modernity while gradually subjecting that tradition to a hermeneutic of suspicion in terms of the loss of the "dangerous" character of Christian narrative and dogmas. Metz drew out Rahner's basic thesis of theology as anthropology in a more explicitly historically, socially, and politically structured way. He moved the general historical sensitivity of Rahner to theological engagement with specific historical moments, particularly the challenges of Marxism, the Holocaust, and the "Third World," challenges that he felt could not be handled adequately by either neoscholastic or transcendentalist-idealist theology.[55]

Political Theology

The years 1963–70 approximately mark the second stage of Metz's work and many of the essays in *Faith in History and Society* date from this period. In *Theology of the World* (1968), Metz first uses the provocative term "political theology," saying that he realizes that the "theology of the world must be political theology."[56] He is aware of the ambiguity of the term and the burden of specific historical connotations that it carries resulting from its association with the controversial and anti-Semitic legal scholar Carl Schmitt.[57] Metz's position on political theology at this stage can be summarized as follows: (a) political theology is primarily corrective of an extreme privatizing trend in theology; (b) political theology is secondarily constructive in terms of the meaning of eschatology for the contemporary world; (c) at the heart is a new relationship between theory and praxis; and (d) the Church is also subject to critique.[58]

In *Faith in History and Society*, Metz defines political theology as a practical fundamental theology whose prime categories are "praxis" and the "subject." Political theology binds fundamental theology to continual interruption by praxis. He holds that a middle-class concept of praxis has largely replaced the authentically Christian concept of freedom and praxis. In this middle-class replication the dialectical tension between theory and praxis has been lost, and praxis has been rendered subordinate to the primacy of theory or ideas.[59] Metz describes Christian faith as "a praxis in history and society that is to be understood as hope in solidarity in the God of Jesus as a God of the living and the dead who calls all people to be subjects in his presence. Christians justify themselves in this essentially apocalyptical praxis (of imitation) in their historical struggle for their fellow human beings."[60]

Unlike Rahner, Metz's political theology was, from the beginning, oriented toward Kant's teaching about the primacy of practical reason and also to the dialectics of theory and praxis in Marxism. Metz does not go the Marxian route of the total mediation of theory through praxis, but he holds to the dialectical nonidentity position. He is not systematic in his treatment of praxis and was aware that his early work did not distinguish clearly enough between individual moral praxis and social praxis because of his conflation of the teachings of Kant and Marx on praxis.[61] Nonetheless, Metz raises again the important questions of the "practical" for theology, reminding us that God is a practical question and the heart of theological concern should be that all human persons become subjects. He also reminds us that to be practical is to be sociopolitical and that practice is only practice in history.

Metz writes of the "pathic structure of human praxis" consisting not simply in action but also in suffering.[62] Above all, he describes Christian faith as a praxis in history and society, an apocalyptic praxis of hope in solidarity with the God of Jesus who is God of both the living and the dead and who calls all human persons to be subjects in his presence. This praxis for social change—in solidarity with the suffering—is simultaneously related to hermeneutics, for the concern is not simply with comprehending the conditions of knowledge, but also with the practical modification of these conditions. Metz acknowledges that his own students had cautioned him about the limits of a purely theoretical "critical theology," queried the consistency of his view of the unity of theory and praxis, and that these students went on to develop further the Marxian concept of praxis.

In an interview much later than the publication of his early work on political theology, Metz offers an insight into his understanding of "post-idealist theology," saying that such theology is "practical" because "in formulating its concepts it can never do without the wisdom that is gained in the doing."[63] Perhaps it is more accurate to say that, for Metz, it is the wisdom that is gained in suffering that marks the practical in his theology. His practical fundamental theology, social-political theological anthropology, is constituted by three basic and interconnected categories: memory–narrative–solidarity.[64] Metz intensifies his concern with these categories from 1970 onward, marking a third stage in the development of his work, a stage that is marked not just by the intensification of his political theology but also by the profound interruption of this theology.

Memory: Dangerous Memory

A Klee painting named *Angelus Novus* shows an angel looking as though he is about to move away from something he is fixedly contemplating. His eyes are staring, his mouth is open, his wings are spread. His face is turned towards the past. Where we perceive a chain of events, he sees a single catastrophe which keeps piling wreckage upon wreckage and hurls it in front of his feet. The angel would like to stay, awaken the dead, and make whole what has been smashed.

But a storm is blowing from Paradise; it has got caught in his wings with such violence that the angel can no longer close them. This storm irresistibly propels him into the future to which his back is turned, while the pile of debris before him grows skyward. This storm is what we call progress.

—Walter Benjamin, *Illuminations*

These are the words of the Marxist philosopher Walter Benjamin whose work is etched with Jewish theological themes, in particular Messianic themes. Benjamin's work gave expression to the way in which human suffering in history shattered historicist, cultural, and universalist philosophies. The paradox of progress is the human wreckage that it leaves in its wake: "There is no document of civilization that is not at the same time a document of barbarism."[65] Benjamin displays an awareness of the way in which this wreckage interrupts; he wants to blast open this continuum of human history so that the wreckage of human suffering is exposed and in this exposure history becomes vulnerable to the Messianic event, the redemptive rupture.

Together with his critique of historicism and fascism, Benjamin shows a great sensitivity to the challenge of interruption provided by suffering and the catastrophe that loomed ahead of him in his own life. The tardy articulation by theologians of the relation of wreckage to theology appears all the more poignant given the urgent clarity of Benjamin's perspective. From Benjamin, Metz drew the category of memory as a way of reconstituting history and the consciousness of the human subject, on the grounds of remembering the tragic suffering in history.

The most significant contribution of Metz to political theology is to place the concept of memory at its heart. Memory becomes the link between tradition and eschatology *via* historical praxis. Metz suggests that the first function of theology is to protect the narrating memory of salvation in our scientific world—and not only to protect memory but also to restore it as a genuine cognitive category and an authentic dimension of reason. The interrelationship of memory with narrative and solidarity protects memory from reduction to either romanticized past or totalitarian future.

Despite the Enlightenment prejudice against the memory of suffering, Metz points to memory as a constitutive category in the histories of both philosophy and theology. Philosophically, Metz traces it from Plato's doctrine of anamnesis to the Cartesian notion of innate ideas via Thomas Aquinas's notion of an a priori light of reason. In terms of theology, Metz shows that, in the biblical tradition, the process of salvation breaks into history at concrete points, for example, the Exodus; the life, death, and resurrection of Jesus. It was his encounter with Judaism that led Metz to rethink the biblical foundations of Christianity and to contrast the ahistoricity of Greek categories with historically grounded biblical thought.

It is the remembrance of the victims of history, whose story is the underside of all history, that will give to memory its critical and liberating power. Metz perceives the critical and practical purposes of such memory as grounded in liturgy. Christian liturgy celebrates the Paschal Mystery in its entirety, the whole of the mystery of Christ, his life, death, and resurrection. Metz does indicate that he is aware of the criticism that he obscures the resurrection. He emphasizes resurrection mediated by way of the memory of suffering.[66] However he does not sufficiently acknowledge that the suffering of Christ is rooted in his preaching and praxis and cannot be determined in isolation from the whole of the Christ event.

Memory operates as both a category of the salvation of identity and a category of liberation.[67] It becomes a source of opposition and imaginative resistance to any form of refusal of the subjectivity of the human person. Precisely because of its oppositional potential, "the destruction of memory is a typical measure of totalitarian rule."[68] Slavery and colonization thrive on the obliteration of memory, and resistance to these is fed by memory's subversive power. However, it is not simply the totalitarian rulers who screen out the importance of suffering. Metz holds that we all tend to avoid an understanding of history *ex memoria passionis* as a history of the vanquished.[69]

The Christian memory of suffering is an anticipatory memory in that it anticipates a future for the suffering and oppressed. It offers political life a new moral imagination challenging politics toward "uncalculating partisanship on behalf of the weak and unrepresented."[70] Metz sees the Christian memory of suffering as ferment for a new political life together with other "subversive innovative factors in society."[71] Walter Benjamin, who emphasized the memory of tragedy in history, also values the historian who has "the gift of fanning the spark of hope in the past," an emphasis in Benjamin that is overlooked by Metz.[72]

John Milbank, whose alternative—"radically orthodox"—reading of theology after Kant is discussed in chapter 5, questions the lack of an appeal in

Metz's theology to the memory of saints and holy communities whose lives, as well as their modes of death, were provocations to justice and not simply the endurance of suffering.[73] It is clear that a moral imagination forged only by suffering in itself is inadequate. The hopeful memory of proactive justice, of good politics, of resisters and rescuers—not just of victims—is also essential for subversion and innovation. The Paschal Mystery calls us not only to the memory of suffering but also to the memory of loving rescue, of just resistance, and peace.

There can be a forgetfulness of this dimension of memory. The memory of martyrs is essential, but these other kinds of memory can also be subversive and potentially solidaristic. Remembering love and honor, bravery and solidarity, can forge the moral imagination as much as the memory of suffering, although these other memories can be diluted without the memory of suffering. We draw not only from exhumed graves of mass atrocities, but also, as George Eliot so beautifully reminds us, from the realization that "things are not so ill with you and me as they might have been, [is] half owing to the number who lived faithfully a hidden life, and rest in unvisited tombs."[74]

Throughout his writings Metz emphasizes the deeply rooted prejudice against the memory of suffering in the Enlightenment model of reason. In later years Metz seeks to outline the amenability of anamnestic reason—a reason endowed with memory—to the Enlightenment and modernity through the a priori of suffering.[75] Of course, it is precisely this attempt at amenability that Milbank is most critical of, seeing Metz as trying to show this a priori of suffering as belonging to the "universal foundations" of a sense of justice.[76] It could be suggested that the exploration of memory and justice in truth commissions, discussed earlier in this chapter, provides an example of the merging of anamnestic reason and the juridical rationality of the politics of human rights.

Metz's desire for anamnestic amenability with Enlightenment reason does not neglect the concrete *Memoria Passionis et Resurrectionis* of Christ. Christians are mandated to *anamnesis*, to un-forgetfulness: Do this in *memoria* of me. It is precisely the participation in this un-forgetfulness that nourishes the Eucharistic community and strengthens them in their receptivity toward suffering and those who suffer. For Metz, the Bread of Life is the food of mourning—mourning defined as the opposite of apathy—the nourishment of the capacity to be hospitable to the sufferer. Metz's reflections on the category of memory with the constant reference to the remembrance of the victims of history and its linking of liturgical anamnesis with hospitality to those who suffer must lead one to question if the memory of the victims of the Holocaust was seeping through, unacknowledged, in Metz's theology.

Narrative: Dangerous Stories

What is a dangerous story? It is a story that tells the history of suffering that draws the listener into the struggle of suffering people, into an involvement that is transformative, and that reveals the way in which the shadows of history have been suppressed. Dangerous stories uphold the negative as a category of salvation. Although Metz frequently quotes a passage from Marcuse on the dangerous perceptions that can dawn upon us through remembrance of the past, his notion of "danger" is also formed by Christian apocalyptical literature.[77] Quoting both from the scriptural promise of persecution and the extracanonical writings of Origen, Metz writes of the danger of closeness to Jesus, danger that is avoided by "bourgeois," "domestic" religion. This bourgeois manifestation of Christianity has negated the "dangerous" prophetic dimensions, thus undermining the power of Christianity to confront injustice.

Narrative brings memories to life, has the potential to stimulate empathy, and to create community. The logos of the cross and resurrection has a narrative structure and Christianity from the beginning has been a community of remembering and narrating with practical intention; thus narrative is not an arbitrary choice as a theological category. Metz wants to stress its cognitive primacy in theology, together with its capacity to highlight the unity that exists in the histories of salvation and suffering. Whereas Metz shares the general concerns of narrative theologians about universalist and foundationalist approaches to political theology, his emphasis is on the danger of the narratives, narratives grounded in the story of suffering, a story that must be forever interrupted.

In his reflections on the category of narrative, Metz quotes Adorno's caution about human forgetfulness of past suffering, directly engaging someone whose philosophy was profoundly shaped by the Holocaust. Metz's engagement with the writings of the Frankfurt School, for whom the Holocaust was *the* symptom of liberalism's dialectical self-transformation into barbarism, must have confronted Metz at some intellectual level with the catastrophe. The direct reference to Adorno in Metz's reflections on narrative, although not leading him to name the story of human suffering that was the Holocaust, must surely point to the gradual breaking in of the Holocaust into Metz's theology. "Forgetting is inhuman because man's accumulated suffering is forgotten—the historical trace of things, words, colours, and sounds is always the trace of past suffering"[78]

Solidarity: Dangerous Responsibility

The pursuit of political-historical solidarity is, for Metz, the practical realization of the liberating power of the memory of suffering. Without some movement toward solidarity, narrative and memory (even the memory of suffering) remain idealist and abstract categories of theology. Metz defined the religious task as that of standing up for all people as subjects in the face of violent oppression and a weakening of solidarity.[79] He is aware that solidarity can be caricatured and narrowly interpreted: Heideggerian solidarity with the "world weary intellectual"; the proletarial solidarity of Marxism; the personalist rendering of solidarity in terms of the "I–Thou" relationship; or the exchange-based solidarity of bourgeois capitalism forged not by concern for the suffering of the other but by mutual self-interest.

The ebbing of a sense of responsibility had led to a weakening of the sense of being a subject in solidarity with others. Metz, immersed in Christian apocalyptical consciousness, stresses that such consciousness demands a practical solidarity with the least of the brothers and sisters, a demand that "is clear from the apocalyptical chapters at the end of the Gospel of St. Matthew."[80] Metz holds that the theological category of solidarity reveals its mystical and universal aspect above all in its memory of solidarity with the dead.[81] John Milbank's interpretation of this anamnestic solidarity as a refusal to leave the dead as dead overlooks the two-fold nature of the solidarity inherent in a practical fundamental theology, that is, its mystical and universal aspect, and its political and particular aspect.[82] "This double structure protects the universal aspect of solidarity from apathy and its partisan nature from hatred and forgetfulness."[83] Christian solidarity is meant to issue forth a counteralliance that is expressed in the partisanship of the imitation of Christ. The emphasis is on the partisan nature of solidarity, and Metz is critical of reductionistic views of solidarity, which exclude concrete and practical solidarity.[84]

Solidarity points both to the hopeful, future-directed character and to the social nature of the human being. It is a commitment to the human person, to his or her subjectivity, a commitment to the otherness of the sufferer and the nonidentity of what other sufferers have endured.

Solidarity is thus a tensive stance; it is not a presumption of simple identity with, nor is it a diluting of, suffering. At the conclusion of chapter 1 it was suggested that the secular discourse of human rights continually pushes what Charles Taylor calls the "impulse of solidarity" beyond the frontiers of Christendom, or indeed, beyond the frontiers of any communal entity that strives to define dignity, equality, and justice in self-referential terms.[85] Metz offers a view of solidarity and of Christianity that sees that "impulse of solidarity" as possible from within, in collaboration with other solidaristic forces in society, based on the memory of suffering.

According to Metz, the guiding question for Christian solidarity is: What happens to others, especially those who suffer?[86] Yet, for all the reference to solidarity with the dead, the dead of the concentration camps and battles of the Second World War remain unnamed. These essays give the impression of a man wrestling with demons who dares not mention them for fear they may need to be named and exorcized.[87]

Metz's *Faith in History and Society* contains three references to Judaism, two of which are to the history of persecution of the Jews: "Christology without an apocalyptical vision becomes no more than an ideology of conquest and triumph. Surely those whose apocalyptic tradition was so triumphantly suppressed by Christianity—the Jews—must have experienced this most painfully."[88]

However, despite this very direct reference to the history of Jewish suffering and to Christian culpability for that suppression, Metz does not "interrupt" his theology with specific reference to the Holocaust. At the end of *Faith in History and Society*, in his concluding reflections on solidarity, Metz bypasses the dead of the Holocaust to look back at the failure of the nineteenth-century German church to enter into solidarity with the working classes and the implications of that failure for the contemporary German church. Although he stresses solidarity with those who suffered and died as an essential aspect of Christian solidarity, the name of Auschwitz is never mentioned in the book, even though he is quite obviously haunted by the Holocaust, particularly in his reflections on the memory of suffering. For this reason, I suggest that a close reading of his categories of memory, narrative, and solidarity indicates the appropriateness of describing Metz's theological response to the Holocaust as marked by a "haunted tardiness."

Auschwitz: An Interruption That Orients

It took a long time before I grasped the fact that Auschwitz was a
deadly attack on everything that we Christians hold sacred.

—Metz quoted in Ekkehard Schuster and Reinhold
Baschert-Kimmig, *Hope against Hope*

Although Metz's theology is marked by a gradual emphasis on the memory
of suffering and a strong critique of the sacrifice of the human subject to the
power of technical rationality,[89] he took many years to explicitly acknowledge
the reality that the Holocaust implicated both the German Enlightenment
and the theology in which he himself had been formed as a theologian.[90] It was
only in 1978 that Metz specifically mentioned Auschwitz, and he acknowledges
his "belated horror."[91] At this time, both the Holocaust and the histories of
the suffering in the "Third World," especially Latin America, interrupt Metz's
writings in concrete and specific elucidation of the themes with which he had
been engaging in the previous two decades.[92] This marks a fissure, and could
possibly be described as a fourth stage, in his theology. Notwithstanding this
lack of direct engagement and his own acknowledgment of his "belated horror,"
I hold that a close reading of his categories of memory, narrative, and solidarity
indicates the haunting of Metz by the concerns of the Holocaust.

The silence of most Christian theologians in the face of and in response
to the Holocaust remains as a lingering rebuke to Christian theology and a
permanent wound in the context of Jewish-Christian relations. The difficulty of
imagining the evil that had occurred, and the subsequent conceptual difficulty
of adequately responding to it, must have contributed to this silence, for the
Holocaust calls into question the categories on which philosophy and theology
were founded. The Holocaust is not only an interruption in the emancipatory
project of the Enlightenment, but also an interruption in the intelligibility of
God's purposes in history. The focus here is primarily on the Jewish victims
of the Holocaust because of the genocidal policy directed against the Jews by
the Nazis and because of Christian implicatedness in anti-Semitism. But the
memory of the suffering of the Holocaust includes remembering victims who
were members of other groups targeted by the Nazis for political, racial, or

religious reasons: gypsies, Poles, Russians and other Slavs, political dissidents and members of national resistance movements, homosexuals, people with disabilities, and Jehovah's Witnesses.[93]

"Auschwitz"—used by Metz to symbolize the whole of the Holocaust—is a "dangerous memory" that became the test-case for Metz's postidealistic political theology. He suggests that Auschwitz is the paradigmatic case of an interruption in history: "For me nowhere in the twentieth century does the absolute prohibition against making comparisons—and by such comparisons neutralizing the catastrophe—show itself so clearly and unavoidably as it does in that which we signify with the word *Auschwitz.*"[94]

Because of its very incomparability, Metz suggests that Auschwitz marks the end of the modern era and therefore constitutes a paradigm shift in theology. What Metz does not adequately examine is the difference between comparing, which runs the risk of neutralizing, and relating the Holocaust to other catastrophes and suffering that "interrupt" human history. It is difficult to situate the uniqueness of the Holocaust without setting up a system where suffering is measured and competition among victims is characterized by exchange value. To borrow a phrase from the Irish poet Micheal O'Siadhail, there is "no Richter scale of tragedy" no "calculus of pain."[95]

I suggest that the term "unprecedented" is more helpful in trying to elucidate the radical negation of the Holocaust. Each radical disruption of *Imago Dei* is unique; to suggest that the Holocaust is "unprecedented" is not to imply a hierarchy of suffering and victimhood. The unprecedented nature of the Holocaust is tentatively captured in the voice of a character in Bernice Ruben's novel *Brothers*, who describes its "sublime and obscene efficiency":

> Mass murder when not a minute is lost. Mass burial where nothing is wasted. Human skin for reading-lamps. Human flesh for soap. Human hair for pillows. Man's teeth for investment. No waste. It is a system meticulous in every detail, long pre-meditated, planned and co-ordinated, administered with the most sophisticated and satanic technology. It is an artistry of murder that achieves a certain beauty in its symmetry. That is the core of its obscenity. That is why it is different.[96]

The importance of understanding and articulating the unprecedentedness of Auschwitz, without relegating other victims as inferior sufferers, is highlighted by the fact that part of the revisionist remembering of the Holocaust consists in questioning its uniqueness. How can its incomparability be presented in a nonstatic way, that is, in a way that does not "compare" scales of suffering but that nonetheless allows the memory to reconstitute present response to and preparedness for catastrophe?

Theology has to make an about face, "a turn which will bring us face to face with the suffering and the victims. And this theology is political theology."[97] What is important for Metz is that this political theology is not one that is concerned with systems but, rather, with subjects. It is a theology of subjects with practical foundation.

This turning to face the suffering and victims evokes the most difficult and perennially challenging God-question, the theodicy question. Metz suggests that it must be theodicy in a political key, embued with a strict universal solidarity that gathers all those who have suffered, living and dead, and that on such a solidarity, the fate of human beings rests. Whereas the whisper of a concern with theodicy is found in his earlier writings, this concern becomes a dominant issue in Metz's theology in the 1980s, together with a more negative assessment of the direction of modernity.[98]

Metz reflects on the expulsion of God from the center of history in the modern theories of history and freedom, an expulsion that replaced the *Deus Salvator* with *homo emancipator* as the universal subject of history. However, this did not eliminate the "incriminating presence of the history of suffering"[99]; suffering simply became more efficient as emancipative theories of history replaced the history of redemption. In place of theodicy, an analogous "anthropodicy" began to develop. The historical responsibility of *homo emancipator* must be muted through exonerating mechanisms such as placing the responsibility in historical processes, in a universal Hegelian "world spirit," or in "nature."

The shadow side of human historical damage can be transferred outside of *homo emancipator*, who can then claim credit for progress and success. Metz's central insight is that any emancipation cast as a universal historical totality is dangerously abstract and contradictory.[100] He does not see the problem of evil as something that theology must solve but rather as a question that must be continually and systematically raised, not allowing the question to be "transferred to human jurisdiction."[101] Anthropodicy brings no greater clarity and inevitably leads to the question of whether one can speak at all of the human "subject." Ultimately, the question of the Holocaust is a matter for both jurisdictions, the responsibility of both God and of humanity.

Criticism of the lateness of the interruption of theology by the Holocaust is compounded by criticisms from the next generation of German theologians of the nature and focus of that interruption. Metz belongs to what is known as the "Hitler Youth Generation," that is, those who moved from childhood to early adulthood toward the end of the war. The next generation of German theologians, who are engaged in what might be termed "theology after *after Auschwitz*," are critical of theologians like Metz and Moltmann. Both of these theologians were soldiers in the final months of the war. This experience affected their theological response, which, as part of the discursive context of "cultural amnesia" in postwar Germany, viewed Germans primarily as victims of the war. Notwithstanding the suggestion here that Metz's response can be characterized as a haunted tardiness, the Holocaust generally emerges only later in the careers of the "after Auschwitz" theologians. Björn Krondorfer, one of these new generation theologians, further criticizes the work of Metz and Moltmann, saying that the Holocaust is faced by them as an intellectual and moral, rather than personal, challenge.[102] Metz thus identifies himself as a *Christian* theologian but not as a *German* Christian theologian and "fails to differentiate between perspectives of victims and victimisers."[103]

In one of the few biographical references to his experience of the war, Metz narrates his forced conscription into the army and subsequent traumatic experience of finding the dead bodies of his company of young soldiers:

> Towards the end of the Second World War, at the age of sixteen, I was snatched out of school and conscripted into the army. After a hasty training in the barracks of Wurzburg I arrived at the front, which at that time had already advanced over the Rhine into Bavaria. My company consisted solely of young people, well over a hundred of them. One evening the company commander sent me with a message to battalion headquarters. I wandered during the night through shattered, burning villages and farmsteads, and when next morning I returned to my company I found only the dead: dead bodies, overwhelmed by a combined fighter-bomber and tank attack. I could only look into the still, dead faces of all those with whom on the previous day I had shared the anxieties of childhood and the joys of youth. I cannot remember anything but a silent cry. I can still see myself there today, and my childhood dreams have collapsed before that memory.[104]

This account gives an insight into the trauma experienced by Metz as a barely out of childhood soldier. It also locates him within the "cultural amnesia" context, which viewed Germans primarily as victims of the war, not only in his description of the dead young men "overwhelmed by a combined fighter-bomber and tank attack," but also in the reference to his night journey through "shattered, burning villages." His childhood dreams "collapsed" before that memory, a memory that abides. This reference to the memory that abides indicates a real experience of trauma for him as a young man, but it also raises a painful question about the selective nature of his memory of suffering.

Challenge: A Future Based on the Memory of Suffering

The emphasis on the memory of suffering in Metz—akin to Ricoeur's parallel history of victimization—does not consist of a simple hagiography of victimhood, nor does it fulfill a Nietzschean prophecy of the collective triumph of victims over the free and the noble. The excess of memory in many societies and cultures facilitates the oppressed becoming oppressors, and the violence of victims become perpetrators remains a thorny area in discussions of ethical responsibility.[105] Victims of human rights violations and injustice may not always be absolutely correct in their perception of injustice, but there can be no comprehension of injustice without the hearing of their voices. There can be no constructive discussion of *eudaimonia* or of human flourishing that does not give due consideration to injustice, violation, and damage. It is not about a *polis* of the wretched governed by the authority of those who suffer but the recognition that decisions made in the *polis* without taking the experience of suffering into account are not only unjust, but are politically dangerous.

Metz describes political universalism, the universalism of human rights, as a procedural universalism, a universalism of the rules of the game that are supposed to ensure agreement among persons and within humanity.[106] He suggests that the authority of those who suffer is the one authority that has not been superseded by any of the critiques formulated on modernity's ground. For Metz, any politics that aims to be universal must reckon with this authority. There can be no political culture that does not respect this authority, and the articulation of that suffering is essential for the universal claims inherent in the politics of human rights. Respect for, and the articulation of, the suffering of the other is vital for building forms of political action based on solidarity and ensuring a politics that does not become totalitarian.

In the face of suspicion of, and disdain for, the universal, Metz suggests that it is the particular challenge of theologians to be the "last universalists."[107] Indeed, Metz describes theologians as being obligated to universality, even at the risk of being considered passé, for the future of our world "depends on some sort of preserved universalism."[108] He is not a naïve universalist. His work contrasts a historico-theology of redemption with "emancipation" used as a "universalist, quasihistorical, philosophical category" in the modern history of freedom.[109]

Metz is not rallying theology to the triumph of the Christian metanarrative, nor pushing a universalism that swallows difference and plurality, but is calling forth a universalism of responsibility based on the memory of suffering: the suffering of others, of the stranger, and even of the enemy. For Metz, this emphasis on the suffering of the other constitutes a negative universalism, which can be formulated "without myth or ideology on modernity's ground."[110] Metz sees a "universal" in this a priori of suffering. He suggests that the history of suffering unites all people like a "second nature."[111] It excludes the possibility of freedom and peace at the expense of the suppressed history of suffering others. The universality of responsibility as bridge between the negative universalism of suffering and a positive conception of justice remains undeveloped in Metz.

Metz posits that the political power of the memory of suffering is evident, positively and negatively, but he continues to hold that there is only one absolutely universal category, the *memoria passionis*, a dangerous memory that calls into question our "tightly sealed identities."[112] His idea of the "second (human) nature" based on the history of suffering points to a "negative" reading of natural law, a path toward natural law that takes the *via negativa* of absence, pain, and suffering. There is a sense in which much of what is articulated in terms of concern for human rights and their violation in the contemporary world reflects this "second nature." Human rights discourse becomes a common, albeit imperfect, discourse for expressing indignation at violations of human dignity, born of a sense that suffering is a common experience that points to a positive constructive commonality, the articulation of which is often more difficult than indignation.

Silence and Interruptive Realism

Elie Wiesel says that it was only ten years after Auschwitz that he passed "through the doors of silence into literature,"[113] but there can be no equivalence between the silence of the surviving victims and the silence of theology in the face of the Holocaust. Metz places before the theologian the question of silence and its meaning. Silence of itself has many "voices." Silence can be powerful in solidarity, in refusal to verbally mirror abusive or prejudicial speech, in listening to painful experience, in drawing toward the mystical *via negativa*, and in mute accompaniment to suffering that is beyond words.

But silence in response to cries for help and solidarity, silence in the face of obvious violence and dehumanization, places it potentially in the category of refusal. It is the silence of refusal that judges theologians and philosophers. If the silence is reflective of Cicero's second kind of injustice whereby "when injury is being inflicted upon others, they fail to deflect it even though they could," then theologians are vulnerable to Plato's words about philosophers who, "hindered in their devotion to learning," abandon those whom they ought to protect.[114]

Sometimes silence is simply born of being rendered inarticulate in the face of horror and damage, or the fear of being wrong that must inevitably accompany any attempt to speak of wisdom in terms that are concrete and practical. However, given the incremental nature of the assault on the Jews by the Nazi regime, in the forms of exclusion, boycotting, segregation, and attack, given the gradual erosion of their basic rights and the pattern of dehumanization, the silence before and during the Holocaust is even more troubling than that afterwards. The United Nations Declaration of Human Rights, fragile and flawed as it is, broke into legal philosophy and into public discourse about morality. Why then was theology "interrupted" so much later? The issues raised by theological silence as refusal point to the need for issues such as human suffering and embedded damage to be placed at the heart of fundamental theology, considered as core theological themes and not reserved to the area of applied ethics or practical theology, a reserve that is challenged by liberation theology.

Metz's reflections on the interruptive nature of the Holocaust move theology from the Rahnerian tendency toward "idealism," which does not directly engage with specific painful questions, to a bleaker realism that interrupts theological discourse, what will be termed here "interruptive realism." The concept of interruptive realism is not sufficient in itself, for it presupposes theology only as response to that which interrupts. One can conclude from Metz that theology must be ever open to interruption, but what is it that places the theologian in a stance of preparedness for interruption? Interruption cannot be structured into a theological program.

Although philosophical and theological discussion about human rights seems to be the purview of liberal thinkers, and discussion about virtue articulated in the territory of communitarians and the "radically orthodox," Metz's later theology challenges theologians, not just to the practical and the political, but to the cultivation of a *habitus operativus bonus* of vigilance toward suffering. Bernard Häring describes vigilance, one of the eschatological virtues, as corresponding to the biblical concept of *kairos, hora,* "signs of the times."[115] Metz's theology challenges theologians to develop a vigilance toward suffering, a prudential sensitivity to the faces of injustice and violations of human dignity, and a practical wisdom that includes the capacity to discern the moral significance of concrete situations and the skill of knowing when to risk for justice or friendship.

Conclusion

Metz favors the essay format in which a number of themes are repeatedly explored, thus contributing to the impression of a fragmentary, and somewhat repetitive, corpus. At times, his use of language appears provocative rather than critical. Although very conscious of being situated in the context of postwar/late-twentieth-century Germany, Metz also seems constrained by his ecclesial and academic situations, unable to think his way through the provocative nature of his theology into constructive work. The movement from provocation to construction, and from general critique to specific action, seems to elude him. His emphasis on theology as negative critique and *memoria* has been criticized for contributing to the separation of theology from constructive historical projects, a separation that does not serve present victims of injustice.[116] Metz does not offer, like Hans Urs von Balthasar, a preestablished program, but perhaps that is because he is trying to programmatize what could not be programmatized. The wreckage of history is not easily ordered, and human suffering seeps through any attempt at precise philosophical or theological calculation. Political theology remains ambiguous and risky territory.[117]

Although Metz does not work out a systematic political theology, and there is an imbalance in his work in terms of favoring apocalyptic eschatology to the neglect of creation and redemption, he does succeed in placing the concerns of transcendentalist-idealist theology firmly within history. He attempts to translate Rahner's transcendental method into practical terms. The internal tensions in theology between the grasping of eternal mystery and movement with history find an inadequate but nonetheless important contribution in Metz's challenge to take history seriously and to forge a new relationship between theory and praxis. His theology—unfulfilled program that it is—thus bridges the concerns of transcendentalist theology and those of the next major theological movement of the twentieth century, liberation theology, to which we will turn in chapter 4.

Metz's insistence on the necessity of a practical and political theology toward just memory challenges theologians to take seriously the authority of those who suffer, to nurture the dangerous memory of suffering, to tell the dangerous stories of suffering that undermine idealized narratives, and to enter into practical solidarity with "the least" and with all those who suffer. With his philosophical companion Walter Benjamin, Metz offers a critical perspective on the dialectical heritage of the Enlightenment, one that challenges those who would abandon the ideals of universal human rights for political pragmatism or postmodern perspectivalism. With Benjamin, he also challenges any understanding of human progress that eliminates the contribution of religious hope. Above all, he challenges Christian theologians to face the Jews, to look backward to "Auschwitz" so that we may face them in the present and, in that facing, learn something of preventing catastrophe. He reminds us of the distinctive Christian anamnesis, the mandate to un-forgetfulness and a Eucharist that nourishes us for receptivity toward those who suffer: "We remember the future of our freedom in the memory of his suffering."[118]

As we engage in travail toward just memory in seeking what might be described as an Aristotelian mean between remembering and forgetting, at the conclusion of the Gospel of John we are presented with an image that points to the already but not yet possibility of a rhyme between history and hope.[119] It is the image of the Risen Christ who carries both wounds and hope for a cure, reminding us of both the materiality of memory and the possibility of redemption in embedded damage (John 20:19–29).

Notes

1. Paul Ricoeur, "Memory and Forgetting," in *Questioning Ethics: Contemporary Debates in Philosophy*, Richard Kearney and Mark Dooley, eds. (London: Routledge, 1999), 5–11.
2. Ibid., 9.
3. Ibid., 10–11.

4. Ibid., 11. See also Ricoeur, "Memory-Forgetfulness-History," ZiF: *Mitteilungen*, Universitat Bielefeld 2 (1995), 3–12. Here Ricoeur discusses the issue of forgetfulness in the context of integrating traumatic memories from the totalitarian era.

5. Minow, *Between Vengeance and Forgiveness*, 48–50.

6. See Hayner, *Unspeakable Truths*, 16.

7. The South African Truth and Reconciliation Commission (TRC) is sometimes criticized for privileging reconciliation over truth. André Du Toit noted that the objectives of the TRC shifted as different actors and constituencies came on the scene. As religious leaders played a greater role in the work of the Commission, "the influence of religious style and symbolism supplanted political and human rights concerns." See Steiner, ed., *Truth Commissions*, 18. Du Toit noted that because people needed to open their wounds and yet accept the fact that this would not lead to the punishment of perpetrators, "the religious theme of forgiveness helps people to make sense of this situation" (Steiner, ed., *Truth Commissions*, 51). Archbishop Desmond Tutu said that a more reasonable goal for the TRC would be to *promote*—not *achieve*—national unity and reconciliation; see Tutu, *No Future without Forgiveness* (London: Rider, 1999), 126–27.

   The structure of the TRC consisted of the Amnesty Committee, which focused on perpetrators, and the rest of the Commission, which focused on victims. The decisions of the Amnesty Committee were binding on both the Commission and the government. Amnesty was offered in exchange for admission of guilt—not necessarily entailing apology or remorse—only for full disclosure of politically motivated crimes committed between 1960 and 1994. These conditions were not acceptable to all victims and their families, and there is no doubt but that some of the over 9,000 people who applied for amnesty admitted guilt only in order to avoid prosecution. However, the TRC, as a measure of transitional justice in a transitional democracy, also contributed to a new South African judicial system and Constitution. It was preceded by open debate, it modeled respect for all victims, its proceedings were transparent, and it marked an effort to engage the apartheid leaders in a conversation about ethical responsibility. It also included special hearings to examine the role of the judiciary, the health system, the media, and business under apartheid. Although these hearings did not focus on the responsibility of specific individuals, they mark the only effort to address the structural dimensions of apartheid. The neglect of the structural dimensions has been criticized as leading to too narrow a definition of victims, focusing more on the damage of death, torture, and violence and not on the way in which apartheid structured exclusion, discrimination, and deprivation into every part of the social fabric, damaging people and communities, stymieing—but never destroying—the efforts at human flourishing within the majority population. An overly narrow definition of "victim" was inevitably mirrored by an overly narrow definition of "perpetrator," thus excluding from such a definition the many more who were beneficiaries of the apartheid system.

John de Gruchy suggests that the TRC led to a shift from "a social contract based on compromise to a more covenantal form of democracy [that was]
cemented by the introduction of institutional structures" that would embody and
support national reconciliation, hence "the adoption of one of the most democratic constitutions in the world," a Constitutional Court to protect it, and both
a Human Rights Commission and a Gender Commission. de Gruchy, *Reconciliation: Restoring Justice* (London: SCM Press, 2002), 187.

8. The broadcasting of the TRC on South African radio and television meant that
it placed the reality and horror of the damage of apartheid before white people
who chose to ignore or support apartheid, and who benefited from the damaging
structures and systems. The victim-perpetrator focus of the TRC was broadcast
live, thus indirectly drawing bystanders and beneficiaries into the process, even
if unwillingly.

9. Scarry, *The Body in Pain*, 56.

10. Nadezhda Mandlestan, *Hope against Hope: A Memoir*, trans. Max Hayward
(New York: Penguin Books, 1970), 48.

11. Press Release, June 19, 2008. www.un.org/News/Press/docs//2008/sc9364.doc
.htm [accessed November 25, 2008].

12. Rorty, "Postmodernist Bourgeois Liberalism," 201.

13. The South African commission, unlike earlier commissions, had subpoena powers and thus could access official records.

14. See Hayner, *Unspeakable Truths* (chap. 4), on the issues of timing and
methodology.

15. A political transition after a period of violence and repression when a legacy of
human rights violations may have to be confronted and accountability examined.
Transitional justice has arisen in various contexts such as denazification, decom-
munization, and dejuntafication. The purpose of mechanisms of transitional
justice is not merely retrospective but forms part of the ongoing formation of
civil society.

16. Rowan Williams describes the South African Commission as "an attempt at a
massive exercise in national therapy." *Lost Icons* (London/New York: Continuum,
2003), 148.

17. See discussion in *Summa Theologia*, trans. Fathers of the English Dominican
Province (Allen, TX: Christian Classics, 1981), IIa IIae, q. 109, a 3.

18. Tutu, *No Future without Forgiveness*, 76. The Archbishop refers specifically to the
fact that many victims did not desire revenge despite having suffered so much.
A similar comment on the "generosity" and the "near transcendental principle
of forgiveness" of the victims at the South African Commission is made by the
Nigerian playwright Wole Soyinka in *The Politics of Memory: Truth, Healing and
Social Justice*, Ifi Amadiume and Abdullahi A. An-Na'im, eds. (London: Zed
Books, 2000), 25. However, it must be noted that Tutu has been criticized for
his focus on the ability of black people to forgive.

19. The acronym REMHI is used here to refer to the project in its entirety, as process and end product. REMHI was supported by the pastoral teams of eleven dioceses and by many other people. The report is titled *Guatemala: Nunca Más!* The four-volume report—1,400 pages—was released on April 24, 1998. References here are from the abridged English edition (Maryknoll, NY/London: Orbis Books/CIIR, 1999), henceforth *Nunca Más*.

20. In his introductory remarks to *Nunca Más*, Archbishop Penados Del Barrio referred to the Joint Pastoral Letter of July 1995, *Urge la Verdadera Paz*, no. 18. See *Nunca Más*, xxix.

21. Bishop Gerardi, *Nunca Más*, xxiv.

22. Ibid., xxiii.

23. Known by the Spanish acronym CEH, the *Comisión de Esclarecimiento Histórico* (Commission for Historical Clarification), was instituted at the Oslo Accord in 1994 and given the mandate of investigating the human rights violations of the thirty-six-year Civil War and of recommending measures to promote peace. The resulting document, *Guatemala: Memoria del Silencio*, was published in 1999 (Guatemala: United Nations).

24. "Few of the testimonies concern violence in eastern Guatemala in the 1960s or urban violence in the 1970s. Therefore, the firsthand data compiled do not portray the true scope of the violence during those periods." *Nunca Más*, 289.

25. Hayner, *Unspeakable Truths*, 27.

26. *Nunca Más*, 76–80.

27. Ibid., 37.

28. This brutality toward children and pregnant women led the CEH to conclude that acts of genocide were committed against particular Mayan communities. The postwar National Reconciliation Law made provisions for amnesties, but genocide was not included in this; thus, the possibility of prosecution exists.

29. For a full account see *Nunca Más*, chap. 3: "The Assault on Community," 40–50.

30. Ibid., 47.

31. Ibid., chap. 9: "The Methodology of Horror," 126–74.

32. Many Guatemalan military officers were trained at the U.S. Army School of the Americas, renamed in January 2001 the Western Hemisphere Institute for Security Cooperation. Latin American military officers have been trained at this institution for almost sixty years.

33. Margalit, *Ethics of Memory*, 150.

34. As noted earlier, there was no requirement of remorse from those who came forward for amnesty at the South African Commission. Not only was there no such requirement, but there was no indication of any, even nascent, remorse from some perpetrators.

35. *Nunca Más*, Part Two: "The Methodology of Horror," 105–77.

36. "Ejerito de Guatemala," quoted in *Nunca Más*, 132.

37. Primo Lévi describes the "silent Nazi diaspora" that taught the "art of persecution and torture to the military and political men of a dozen countries, on the shores

of the Mediterranean, the Atlantic and Pacific." Quoted by Jonathan Glover in *Humanity: A Moral History of the Twentieth Century* (London: Jonathan Cape, 1999), 39.

38. Jean Améry, *At the Mind's Limit: Contemplations by a Survivor on Auschwitz and Its Realities* (Bloomington, IN: Indiana University Press, 1980), "Torture," 21–40.

39. Thulani Grenville-Grey, the mental health expert at the South African Truth and Reconciliation Commission, used this phrase to describe the effect on Commission staff, many of whom, because of absorbing the horror and pain, began to experience the same symptoms as the victims. Worst affected were the clerical staff, who had to process more statements than the Commission members who took the statements from the witnesses. For a first-hand account of the traumatic effects on an Afrikaner journalist of attending the TRC see Krog, *Country of My Skull*.

40. See Yael Danieli, "Preliminary Reflections from a Psychological Perspective," in *Transitional Justice, Vol. I: General Considerations*, Neil J. Kritz, ed. (Washington, DC: U.S. Institute for Peace Press, 1995), 572–82.

41. David Becker and team at the Latin American Institute of Mental Health and Human Rights (ILAS), Santiago, Chile. See "Therapy with Victims of Political Repression in Chile: The Challenge of Social Reparation," in *Transitional Justice, Vol. I*, 583–90, at 590.

42. *Nunca Más*, 45.

43. Ibid., "Women's Resistance," 81–84.

44. Bishop Gerardi, April 24, 1998, the day of the presentation of the REMHI report. See *Monseñor Juan Gerardi: Testigo Fiel de Dios, Mártir de la Verdad y de la Paz* (Guatemala de la Asunción: Conferencia Episcopal de Guatemala, 1999).

45. Rather than suppressing the report, the murder of Bishop Gerardi drew attention, both in Guatemala and internationally, to the voices and violations recorded in *Nunca Más*. Francisco Goldman, in *The Art of Political Murder: Who Killed the Bishop?* (New York: Grove Press, 2007), tells the story of the strange circumstances surrounding the death of Bishop Gerardi, the ruthless forces behind both the murder and the suppression of the truth about it, and the courage of a group of human rights workers who bravely struggled toward just memory.

46. From Zbigniew Herbert, "Mr. Cogito on the Need for Precision," in *Report from the Besieged City and Other Poems*, trans. John Carpenter and Bogdana Carpenter (New York: Ecco Press, 1985), 64–67. This poem refers to the Polish discussion after World War II as to whether five and a half or six million Poles perished in the war.

47. See Rose, *Mourning Becomes the Law*, 27–28.

48. J. Matthew Ashley holds that Metz's theology is a "genuine and provocative alternative in its own right." See Ashley, *Interruptions*, 135.

49. "I had the good fortune to learn that Catholic theology which in my eyes was the best of that time, and to it I owe everything that I can do theologically myself. I

mean the theology taught by Karl Rahner." Metz and Moltmann, *Faith and the Future*, 40.

50. Schuster and Boschert-Kimmig, *Hope against Hope*, 19.

51. Immanuel Kant, *Critique of Pure Reason*, trans. F. Max Muller (New York: Doubleday, 1966).

52. Immanuel Kant, *Critique of Practical Reason*, Mary Gregor, ed. (Cambridge: Cambridge University Press, 1997).

53. Metz acknowledges the usefulness of Heidegger's ontology of time for theology, specifically his program for the temporalization of metaphysics. See Schuster and Boschert-Kimmig, *Hope against Hope*, 27–29.

54. Metz, *Faith in History and Society*. First published in German as *Glaube in Geschichte und Gesellschaft* (Mainz: Matthias-Grünewald-Verlag, 1977).

55. See Metz, *A Passion for God*, chap. 2: "On the Way to a Postidealist Theology," 30–53.

56. Johann Baptist Metz, *Theology of the World* (London: Burns & Oates, 1969), 96. Charles Davis, *Theology and Political Society* (Cambridge: Cambridge University Press, 1980), 13, suggests that Metz's first public use of the term and concept of political theology was at a 1966 symposium in Chicago, but I have not been able to confirm this.

57. Carl Schmitt (1888–1985) was a brilliant but controversial legal scholar and jurist who was complicit with the National Socialist regime in 1933–36. He coined the term in his 1922 book *Politische Theologie. Vier Kapitel zur Lehre von der Souveränität*. See Carl Schmitt, *Political Theology: Four Chapters on the Concept of Sovereignty*, edited and translated by George Schwab (Chicago: University of Chicago Press, 2005).

58. See Metz, *Theology of the World*: ch. 5: "The Church and the World in the Light of a 'Political Theology,'" 107–24. See also the article by Metz on "Political Theology" in *Sacramentum Mundi, Vol. V,* Karl Rahner, ed. (London: Burns & Oates, 1970), 34–38.

59. Metz, *Faith in History and Society*, 28.

60. Ibid., 111.

61. Ibid., 53.

62. Ibid., 57.

63. Schuster and Baschert-Kimmig, *Hope against Hope*, 12.

64. Metz states that he uses the word category "in the widest sense." He stresses the close connection among the three categories. "It is only if they are taken together that memory, narrative and solidarity can be regarded as the basic categories of a practical fundamental theology. Memory and narrative only have a practical character when they are considered together with solidarity, and solidarity has no specifically cognitive status without memory and narrative." Metz, *Faith in History and Society*, 183. Metz also describes his treatment of these three categories as not fully elaborated and systematized. In many ways, this comment on his own earlier work is reflective of his treatment of themes throughout his writings.

65. Benjamin, *Illuminations,* "Theses on the Philosophy of History," 248.
66. *Faith in History and Society,* 113.
67. Ibid., 67, 184.
68. Ibid., 110.
69. Ibid., 111.
70. Ibid., 117–118.
71. Ibid., 118.
72. Benjamin, *Illuminations,* "Theses on the Philosophy of History," 247.
73. See Milbank, *Theology & Social Theory,* chap. 8: "Founding the Supernatural: Political and Liberation Theology in the Context of Modern Catholic Thought," 206–55.
74. George Eliot, *Middlemarch* (London: Penguin, 1994), 795.
75. See Metz, *A Passion for God* n. 25, 142–3.
76. Milbank, *Theology and Social Theory,* 239.
77. "Remembrance of the past may give rise to dangerous insights, and the established society seems to be apprehensive of the subversive contents of memory. Remembrance is a mode of dissociation from the given facts, a mode of 'mediation' which breaks, for short moments, the omnipresent power of the given facts. Memory recalls the terror and hope that passed." Herbert Marcuse, *One Dimensional Man: Studies in the Ideology of Advanced Industrial Society* (London: Sphere Books, 1968). See Metz, *Faith in History and Society,* 193–94.
78. Metz, *Faith in History and Society,* 214. Metz is quoting from Adorno's "Thesen über Tradition," *Ohne Leitbild,* 34ff.
79. Metz, *Faith in History and Society,* 47.
80. See Ibid., 177.
81. See Ibid., 232, on solidarity extended to the conquered and forgotten dead.
82. Milbank, *Theology and Social Theory,* 239.
83. Metz, *Faith in History and Society,* 232.
84. Ibid., 232.
85. Taylor suggests that there was a necessary breach with the culture of Christendom in order for this impulse of solidarity to transcend the frontiers of Christendom itself. Taylor, *A Catholic Modernity?* 26.
86. Metz, *Faith in History and Society,* 232.
87. In 1975 Eva Fleischner wrote: "To our knowledge, only Hans Küng, among Germany's major theologians, has dealt with Jewish problems. The subject is totally absent from the works of J. Metz and W. Kasper, and occupies a minimal place in the writings and thought of Karl Rahner." *Judaism in German Christian Theology since 1945: Christianity and Israel Considered in Terms of Mission* (Metuchen, NJ: Scarecrow Press, 1975), 36. The analysis of Metz's work in terms of "haunted tardiness" nuances Fleischner's statement about the total absence of "Jewish problems" from Metz's work, but her observation confirms that Auschwitz did, eventually, mark a profound interruption in Metz's theology.
88. Metz, *Faith in History and Society,* 176.

89. This critique is at the heart of *Faith in History and Society*.

90. The idea of the Holocaust as an "orienting event" comes from Irving Greenberg. Greenberg identifies the Exodus as the basic orienting experience for Judaism; for Christians, it is the life, death and resurrection of Christ. Greenberg holds that the Holocaust is a contemporary "orienting event" because of the radical change it brought about in fundamental perceptions of both Exodus and Easter. Greenberg, "Cloud of Smoke, Pillar of Fire: Judaism, Christianity, and Modernity after the Holocaust," in *Auschwitz: Beginning of a New Era*, edited by Eva Fleischner (New York: Ktav, 1977), 7–55.

91. Schuster and Baschert-Kimmig, *Hope against Hope*, 47. He connects this—not by way of excuse—with what he perceives to be the fading of eschatology and apocalypticism in Christology.

92. Metz wrote a document in 1975 for a synod of the German Catholic dioceses on the position of the Catholic Church in relation to the extermination of the Jews by the Nazis: "Unsere Hoffnung. Ein Bekenntnis zum Glauben in dieser Zeit." The conclusion was that with the exception of certain individuals and groups, the Catholic Church was overly concerned with its own protection and turned its back on the Jews. The writing of this document may have consolidated Metz's specific response to the Holocaust. Available online at www.jcrelations.net/de [accessed September 14, 2009].

93. In *After Tragedy and Triumph: Modern Jewish Thought and the American Experience* (Cambridge: Cambridge University Press, 2009), Michael Berenbaum discusses the question of non-Jewish victims of the Holocaust. Berenbaum argues that "only by discussing all of the Nazi's victims can the uniqueness of Jewish suffering be convincingly conveyed as a matter of fact rather than a statement of faith" (17). See chap. 2, "The Uniqueness and Universality of the Holocaust," 17–32.

94. Schuster and Baschert-Kimmig, *Hope against Hope*, 35.

95. Micheal O'Siadhail, *The Gossamer Wall: Poems in Witness to the Holocaust* (Newcastle: Bloodaxe Books, 2002), "Signatures," 22. In this poem, O'Siadhail asks: "Surely all tragedies are both singular and one?" (21). He explores this question with reference to a variety of human tragedies from the Soviet gulags to the slave trade and the Irish famine coffin ships. Acknowledging that Holocaust victims included Gypsies, homosexuals, and others deemed "sub-human" by the Nazis, O'Siadhail concludes the poem with reference to the particularly Jewish nature of the genocide: "And the one strain singled out for elimination/This breed apart/ A whole apparatus of hate / Bent on wiping a people from Europe's face."

96. Bernice Ruben, *Brothers* (London: Hamish Hamilton, 1983), 360–61. I am grateful to Anita Lasker-Wallfisch—who herself survived both Auschwitz (as a cellist in the women's orchestra there) and Belsen—for pointing me to this novel in response to my question regarding the difficulty of discussing the incomparable or unprecedented nature of the Holocaust. For an extensive treatment of the uniqueness of the Holocaust as an epistemological event see Steven T. Katz's

The Holocaust in Historical Context (Vol. I): The Holocaust and Mass Death before the Modern Age (New York: Oxford University Press, 1994). Katz argues that the Holocaust is unique because it is the only case of genocide in history but emphasizes that he is comparing historical events, not the quantity or quality of human suffering involved.

97. Metz, "Theology in the New Paradigm: Political Theology," in Hans Küng and David Tracy, eds., *Paradigm Change in Theology: A Symposium for the Future* (Edinburgh: T&T Clark, 1989), 362.

98. See his essay on the dialectic of emancipation and redemption, Metz, *Faith in History and Society*, 119–35.

99. Ibid., 124.

100. Ibid., 127–28.

101. Quoted in Ashley, *Interruptions*, 125.

102. An interesting overview of the generational differences between the "after Auschwitz" theologians and theologians born after the 1950s is found in Krondorfer's article "Theological Innocence and Family History in the Land of Perpetrators: German Theologians after the Shoah."

103. Ibid., 72.

104. Moltmann, *How I Have Changed*, 31.

105. For an examination of this theme in the context of the Rwandan Genocide see Mahmood Mamdani, *When Victims Become Killers: Colonialism, Nativism, and the Genocide in Rwanda* (Princeton, NJ: Princeton University Press, 2001). Mamdani maintains that most academic writing has focused too heavily on the genocide as a state project and ignores its subaltern and "popular" character. How does one explain mass participation in genocide? He states that his main objective in writing the book "is to make the popular agency in the Rwandan genocide thinkable" (8).

106. Metz, *A Passion for God*, 144.

107. "The Last Universalists," in *The Future of Theology: Essays in Honor of Jürgen Moltmann*, Miroslav Volf, Carmen Krieg, and Thomas Kucharz, eds. (Grand Rapids, MI: Eerdmans, 1996), 47–51.

108. Ibid., 51.

109. Metz, *Faith in History and Society*, 120.

110. See Metz, *A Passion for God*, n. 19, 198.

111. Metz, *Faith in History and Society*, 105.

112. Schuster and Baschert-Kimmig, *Hope against Hope*, 33–34.

113. Ibid., 60.

114. See Cicero's discussion of two types of injustice, *On Duties* (Cambridge: Cambridge University Press, 1991), Book I, 22–30.

115. Bernard Häring, *Free and Faithful in Christ*: Vol. 1, *General Moral Theology* (Middlegreen, Slough: St. Paul Publications, 1978), 206.

116. Ivan Petrella, one of a new generation of liberationist scholars, presents an overly harsh criticism of Metz's approach to political theology in *The Future of Liberation*

Theology: An Argument and Manifesto. Petrella charges Metz with reacting to the particular German experience wherein theology was used "to disguise blood-thirsty idolatry in divine garb" and universalizing that experience into a general opposition to any link between theology and historical projects. The result, Petrella holds, is that Metz's understanding of theology could enable theology to serve an unjust status quo; ibid., 127–28.

117. It is only somewhat of a caricature to say that one is condemned for abstraction if one offers such a perspective without a concrete program; and one is condemned for proposing concrete strategies in response to particular historical situations because discussion of concrete strategy risks the fragility of contingency.

118. Metz, *Faith in History and Society,* 111.

119. This idea of hope and history rhyming is drawn from Seamus Heaney's play, *The Cure at Troy: A Version of Sophocles' Philoctetes* (London: Faber and Faber, 1990). Heaney explores the tension between holding onto the wound and hope for a cure, portraying the dangers of Sophocles' theme of honor and the potential festering of a wound of memory. Heaney brings together the history of the Trojan War and the violence, on both sides, in modern Ireland. "History says, *Don't hope/On this side of the grave/*But then, once in a lifetime/The longed-for tidal wave/Of justice can rise up/And hope and history rhyme/So hope for a great sea-change/On the far side of revenge/Believe that a further shore/Is reachable from here" (77).

Chapter Four

~

Liberation Theology
and Human Rights

FROM INTERRUPTIVE REALISM TO
THE CENTRALITY OF *LA REALIDAD*

THIS CHAPTER IS NEITHER AN OVERVIEW of liberation theology nor an exposition of particular liberation theologians but an exploration of the engagement of liberation theology with human rights discourse and the contribution it makes to this discourse through its focus on the preferential option for the poor and the historical realization of the rights of the poor.[1] My approach to liberation theology is both sympathetic and critical, conscious of the poles of idealization and dismissal that often characterize responses to this theology.

This sympathetic and critical perspective is forged not only by intellectual engagement with the texts, but also by witnessing the influence of this theology in poor Christian communities, and the particular impact of visiting Centro Romero in Universidad Centroamericana (UCA) in San Salvador, a university center dedicated to the memory of the martyrs of El Salvador and the university's own martyrs. This center makes one aware of the dangers of either romanticizing or dismissing what has been a costly theology for many named and anonymous martyrs. Liberation theology is marked by an urgency that is not generally characteristic of theological discourse. At times this urgency begets stridency that I recognize as a serious limitation but do not perceive as nullifying the substantive challenge that this new way of doing theology places before both the discipline of theology and the vocation of the theologian.

The focus here will be primarily on the perspectives emerging from Latin America, the home of liberation theology; yet, even within Latin America itself, liberation theology is not monolithic, having emerged from situations as diverse as Chile under the Pinochet regime and Costa Rica with its long tradition of democracy. Liberation theology is ecumenical and diverse in terms of styles and topics. The impact of this movement is reflected in the theological voices emerging from the Caribbean, Africa, Asia, and corners of the first world, voices that take up the liberationist themes but transpose them in their own particular social, cultural, political, and interfaith contexts. The universal implications of liberation theology are evidenced not only in this polyphony of theological voices but also in the sustained critique that has emerged both from within Latin America and elsewhere, including the United States and Europe. This critique includes significant self-criticism by liberation theologians themselves, constructive criticism from a number of other theological perspectives, and criticism by some conservative commentators that tends to caricature liberation theology and define it by its weakness.[2]

Liberation theology has developed through a number of distinct phases since its beginnings in the late 1960s, with each new decade showing developments in its formulation, as well as changes in the political and economic realities of Latin America.[3] This theology must be critiqued in the light of these developments and with an acknowledgment of the intrinsic self-critical dimension within liberation theology itself.[4]

There has been growing systematization of liberation theology, and theologians writing from this perspective have made significant contributions to Christology, ethics, ecclesiology, theological anthropology, epistemology, methodology, and spirituality.[5] This systematization has rendered liberation theology more academically and ecclesiastically respectable, but it could be suggested that liberation theology risks being deradicalized if its roots in historical praxis become more tenuous. The extension of liberation theology into a polyphony of global voices has unveiled both the complexity of poverty and the complexity of oppression, but this extension risks losing liberation theology's radical solidarity with the poor as the concerns of middle class identity politics blunt the sharp socioeconomic analysis that accompanied liberation theology from its beginnings.[6] The Peruvian theologian Gustavo Gutiérrez reminds us that for liberation theology, like any theology, "God and God's love are, ultimately, its only theme."[7]

Liberation theology, as a new way of doing theology, also marks the extension and "correction" of the lineage of Rahner and Metz whose influence many liberation theologians acknowledge.[8] Rahner's positive universalism explored the question of the human person and the challenges of humanism after Kant, and the negative universalism that emanates from Metz's emphasis on the authority of those who suffer is an emphasis that issues from the failure of humanism as exemplified in the Holocaust. Liberation theologians, while recognizing the liberative intentions of the Enlightenment, despite the perceived weakness of the overemphasis on individual liberties, uncover the silent and slow catastrophe that has been another failure of humanism: the structural poverty and injustice that has always constituted the underside of modernity.

Liberation theologians thus echo others who have raised questions about the true beneficiaries of the universalist tradition. Although theologians have long struggled with the implications of the Cartesian *cogito* and Kantian subjectivity, Latin American liberation discourse has shown that the implications of the earlier assertion of the ego, the *ego conquiro* of Cortes and Columbus, were overlooked by modern philosophy and theology.[9] The concern, since Friedrich Schleiermacher (1768–1834), to find a place for theology within the house of modernity resulted in the overlooking of those who had no place and upon whose dislocation and homelessness the very construction of modernity was founded.

Liberation theology thus has its origins in ethical indignation and the demands born of this indignation. It is ethical indignation that prepares in the human person the possibility of recognizing what Metz calls "the authority of those who suffer." Metz asked: "How do we do theology after Auschwitz?" in retroactive indignation at the Holocaust. Liberation theologians ask: "How do we do theology *while Ayacucho lasts?*" in present indignation at human rights violations. Ayacucho, the site of the 1984 massacre of Peruvian peasants by the military, is the example of the persistent violation of human rights that Gutiérrez uses in *On Job: God-Talk and the Suffering of the Innocent*, the key theodical text in liberation theology. Whereas Gutiérrez acknowledges that the Holocaust is "an inescapable challenge to the Christian conscience," the present theological task, he maintains, is to find words to speak about God in the midst of "a cruel present," the immediate experience of human rights violations, torture, and murder.[10] It is outside the scope of this work to discuss the lack of sustained engagement by liberation theologians with the Holocaust, but it could be suggested that the immediacy of the human rights violations, combined with anti-Judaic elements in liberationist Christology, means that they do not necessarily see themselves implicated as *Christian* theologians in the Holocaust, thus undermining Metz's challenge about the interruptive nature of the Auschwitz experience.[11]

Liberation theologians view ethical indignation in the face of the reality of Latin America both as an echo of the indignation of God and as a basic human experience. It is the foundation of empathies and antipathies, a transcendent that marks the new humanism to which *Gaudium et spes* referred, a new humanism "where people are defined before all else by their responsibility to their sisters and brothers and at the court of history."[12]

Vatican II recognized the passion for human dignity, and the protection of that dignity in human rights, as a sign of hope of the times. However, as was noted in chapter 1, *Gaudium et spes* did not have a sufficiently developed theology of the cross and was criticized for intimating that reform and goodwill would bring about justice and peace. This seemingly overconfident humanism is modified by the reading of the oppressive signs of the times offered by liberation theology. Liberation theology also shows that even a confidently realistic humanism moved by ethical indignation is fruitless if it does not find expression in some sort of praxis. We now examine the engagement of liberation theology with the universalist discourse that is human rights.

Liberation Theology and Human Rights

The use of human rights discourse in liberation theology is eclectic, drawing from Catholic, Marxist, and liberal approaches to human rights. The development of the relationship between liberation theology and human rights can be outlined in three phases: initial rejection, gradual development of critique, and theological and practical engagement.[13]

INITIAL REJECTION OF HUMAN RIGHTS DISCOURSE

The first phase of the relationship was marked by a distancing of liberation theology from the language of human rights because of a perceived foundation of human rights discourse on an individualistic liberal anthropology and politics. It was suggested that human rights represented a bourgeois ethic of the self-interested middle classes. Liberation theology focused instead on discussion of a "new humanity" or "new society." In this first phase, there was engagement—both intellectual and practical—with Marxism, and works like José Porfirio Miranda's *Marx and the Bible: A Critique of the Philosophy of Oppression* (Maryknoll, NY: Orbis, 1974) pointed to a desire for Christian-Marxist dialogue in the context of Latin America.

Liberation theologians found that Marxist analysis—influenced not only by Marxist-Leninist socialism, but also by the thought of Antonio Gramsci and the indigenous Marxism of the Peruvian José Carlos Mariátegui—offered an accurate interpretation of the exploitative consequences of capitalism and a social analysis that fired the imagination of those who struggled for social justice. Those theologians who used elements of Marxist analysis did so selectively and, for the most part, engaged these elements, for example, the dialectic between theory and praxis, in a critical manner. The actual influence of Marxism on liberation theology has been exaggerated, overlooking the fact that it was the early "Hegelian Marx" on exploitation and alienation that influenced the economic views of liberation theology rather than the "technicalities of surplus value and industrial progress in *Das Kapital*."[14] It is also clear that the influence of Marxism on liberation theology has diminished over the years.

At a time when socialist movements in other parts of the world had moved beyond the initial Marxist opposition to human rights language, "the spirit of Marx's historicist insight lived on to influence the discussion among Latin American revolutionaries in the early 1970s."[15] A thorough examination of the contentious issue of the Marxist conception of human rights is beyond the scope of this work, but it can be said that although Marx himself was critical of natural rights, the "so called *rights of man*," dismissing them as the "rights of egoistic man" and as the fictions of the bourgeois law that upheld the capitalist economy, he did not so much advocate their abandonment as hold that human rights would be rendered obsolete by the proletarian socialist revolution.[16]

In these early years of liberation theology there was no substantive engagement with human rights discourse. The Sri Lankan theologian Aloysius Pieris juxtaposes the liberationist thesis and the human rights discourse used by the "western church." He says—erroneously—that Gutiérrez makes "absolutely no use of the human rights language . . . and has ignored the whole human rights movement as if to say that it has no relevance in a Third World context."[17] Although there are few references to human rights by Gutiérrez in his seminal work, *A Theology of Liberation*, they are not insignificant.[18] He suggests that peace presupposes the defense of the rights of the poor; that part of knowing and loving God is to be concerned with the establishment of just relationships among persons and with recognizing the rights of the poor; that protest against trampled human rights is an active dimension of hope, an eschatological task; and he challenges our passivity or indifference when the most basic human rights are at risk.[19] Gutiérrez defines the poor as "nonpersons," that is, "those who are not considered to be human beings with full rights, beginning with the right to life and to freedom in various spheres."[20] He clearly links rights with personhood and their violation with dehumanization, and embeds human rights concerns in theological themes in a way that allows for deeper theological engagement with this discourse in later stages of the development of liberation theology. Gutiérrez's concern for human rights is articulated with greater urgency in *The Power of the Poor in History* (London: SCM Press, 1983), when he places emphasis on the rights of the poor.

The suggested juxtaposition between the liberationist thesis and human rights discourse was matched by a perceived juxtaposition between the ethics of liberation theology and Catholic social teaching. Liberation ethics tended to self-identify as an inductive method emerging from praxis and to do so in conscious comparison with the perceived ahistoricity and deductive methodology of Catholic social teaching.

Liberation theology and Catholic social teaching are, in fact, mutually enlightening, with many points of convergence. Catholic social teaching, in general, tends to place greater emphasis on preservation of order and avoidance of conflict than liberation theology does. However, the social teaching of the Church provides legitimacy for a liberationist perspective on the struggle for justice and peace. Hostile critics of liberation theology would substitute Catholic social teaching for all liberationist discourse; thus, it is essential that any discussion of liberation theology both explore the relationship between that theology and the tradition of modern Catholic social teaching, *and* highlight the distinctiveness of the liberationist discourse, especially its critique of universality, its bolder acknowledgment of conflict, and its option for the poor. Such distinctiveness does not, however, suggest that liberation theology can ever replace the Church's social teaching.[21] The initial rejection of human rights discourse by liberation theology is ironic in the light of the comparatively recent endorsement of human rights by the Catholic Church discussed in chapter 1.

GRADUAL DEVELOPMENT OF A CRITIQUE
OF HUMAN RIGHTS DISCOURSE

The critique of human rights by liberation theologians that emerged in the late 1970s focused on unmasking human rights as a new rhetoric of morality that reflected a false universalism of elite first world liberalism. This engaged critique of human rights was also stimulated by ideological suspicion of the use of human rights language in the foreign policy of the United States led by President Carter (1977–81), a suspicion born of a concern with individual freedoms that masked North American complicity in the poverty and oppression of so many.[22] Human rights were seen to uphold a morality that was primarily concerned with political and civil rights enforceable in a judicial context, and as Juan Luis Segundo powerfully articulates, "no court, national or international, will entertain a complaint of hunger."[23] The human rights forum was seen as neither offering the poor a voice nor adequately understanding institutional oppression and violence.

However, although this critique of the rhetoric of rights, particularly as used by the United States, was crucial, it also demonstrated that liberation theologians tended to overlook what was also overlooked in other academic circles, that is, the contribution made by Latin America to human rights discourse. This was accompanied by a focus on the continent primarily as a place in which human rights were violated. However, as noted in chapter 1, Latin America made an important and distinctive contribution both to the United Nations Charter and to the Universal Declaration of Human Rights: the input from the Chapultepec Conference, the proposal to include a bill of rights in the Charter, Latin American delegates' support for the inclusion of a list of duties in the Universal Declaration, and their emphasis on social, economic, and cultural rights.

Historically, although Latin America was influenced by the European Enlightenment and the revolutionary codes of France and North America, these influences were "received and redeployed" in the service of a Latin American perspective on human rights.[24] The tradition of Simon Bolívar, who was a disciple of Rousseau, resulted in the early Latin American nations incorporating individual rights in their constitutions prior to the nations of Europe, and their reception and redeployment of the Rousseauian tradition in particular led to an understanding of the content of rights that was substantively different from the more "libertarian, property based notions" dominant in North America.[25] This distinctively Latin American commitment to human rights is rooted in several historical moments beginning with the sixteenth century advocacy of Bartolomé de las Casas on behalf of the rights of the Indians.[26]

THEOLOGICAL AND PRACTICAL ENGAGEMENT
WITH HUMAN RIGHTS

The political scene in Latin America in the 1970s was marked by the demise of the influence of Marxist groups and increasing repression under "national security" governments, backed by the United States, which initiated neoliberal economic policies implemented through state terror—with a totalitarian view of capitalism, that is, capitalism without the principles of democracy.[27] This doctrine of national security underpinned United States foreign policy from the beginning of the Cold War, and the United States established a number of military academies in the Panama Canal Zone that initiated thousands of Latin American military officers in the ideology and practice of the doctrine of war.[28] The justification for this doctrine of war was the belief that democracy in Latin America was too fragile to win the ideological battle with communism. The ensuing repression was carried out in countries that officially recognized the Universal Declaration of Human Rights.

Although resistance to dictatorships and protection of the victimized were certainly not uniform in the Latin American Church, the praxis of the Church became increasingly involved with the defense of human rights as many Latin American Christians turned to the discourse of rights in an effort to save lives. The Church founded centers and bodies for the protection of human rights, or collaborated with other local and international groups, becoming one of the principal defenders of victims of state terrorism. The multifaceted defense of human rights and resistance to dictatorships by the Church included the use of human rights discourse, the evocative power of symbols and symbolic gestures in liturgy, the legitimization of opposition (thus the "de-legitimizing" of dictatorship), conscientization, acting as a mediator, and creating spaces of protection and participation.[29]

It has been suggested that during this period the process of liberation was reduced to the most urgent task of saving lives, thereby replacing the search for a new humanity with questions of mere survival[30]; however it is not sufficient to suggest that liberationist engagement with human rights discourse was simply the result of the pragmatism of desperation. It also marked a response to challenges from theologians like Jürgen Moltmann to seek the positive in the Western tradition. Thus, liberationist engagement with the discourse of human rights indicates the ongoing development and transformation of liberation theology. However, the biting critique of the supposed universality of human rights and its tendency to become a bourgeois ethic remained as an underlying motif even as liberation theologians engaged positively with human rights. Human rights discourse in liberation theology, during this third phase, became increasingly associated with the preferential option for the poor.

The Preferential Option for the Poor

Liberation theology holds that the interlocutors of traditional academic theology are the bourgeois class and the concerns of this theology are those of the nonbeliever in a secular context. Liberation theology juxtaposes itself with this tradition by positing the poor as its interlocutors and making its concerns those of "nonpersons" in an unjust world. It marks an irruption of the poor into theology. The preferential option for the poor, with its twin of commitment to praxis, is the most important contribution of liberation theology to contemporary theology and ethics. The concept of the preferential option elicits strong responses in terms of both commitment and critique; but it has also been vulnerable to dilution by the absorption of the language of liberation into the mainstream of theology. The preferential option for the poor has been central to the engagement of liberation theology with human rights discourse.

The option for the poor has its roots in the God of the Hebrew scriptures, in Christ's revelation of the Reign of God, and in the radical tradition of the early Church. The modern impetus for the option for the poor can be traced to Pope Leo XIII, who moved the Church in the direction of social and economic rights and brought the sufferings of the poor, especially the exploited industrial workers of the late nineteenth century, into modern Catholic social teaching.[31] The concept of the option for the poor was influenced by the changes in the post–Vatican II Church and the renewed commitment of many people to live and work with the poor. It is not the intention here to suggest that prior to liberation theology Christians were not working with and for the poor, and it is clear that the option is also lived out today by people and communities who would not identify themselves as liberationists. However, the ecclesiological developments after that Council, the commitment to the world born of the spirit of *Gaudium et spes*, and the examination by religious communities of the original charism of their foundation have all led to a gradually more self-conscious and public espousal of the option for the poor. With liberation theology, the explicit dimensions of this scripturally rooted commitment have emerged in new and radical ways.

Liberation theology has a tripartite distinction in its discussion of poverty, a distinction articulated in the "Document on Poverty" adopted by the Latin American Episcopal Conference (CELAM) at Medellín in 1968: (a) the evil of real poverty, caused mainly by injustice; (b) spiritual poverty as openness to the will of God; and (c) solidarity with the poor in imitation of the example of Christ.[32] Despite the efforts of hostile critics to undermine the project of liberation theology, the preferential option for the poor that was endorsed at Medellín was reaffirmed by the CELAM conference at Puebla in 1979, an affirmation that called for a "conversion" to this option and for sustained efforts to comprehend and challenge the mechanisms that generate poverty.[33]

It must be recognized that, as a theological term, the preferential option for the poor is both problematic and challenging; each component—"preferential," "option," and "poor"—is hard to define with precision, comparatively easy to use in theological discourse, but more difficult to structure into praxis. Although the term is vulnerable to reductionistic interpretations, the option for the poor nonetheless is a substantive theological concept, a theocentric and Christological option, which has sound biblical and theological roots. As a "datum of revelation," Schillebeeckx suggests that this option is a matter of Christian orthodoxy, touching as it does all the elements of the Christian credo.[34] Gutiérrez offers a simple insight: "When all is said and done, the option for the poor means an option for the God of the Reign as proclaimed to us by the God of Jesus."[35] The preferential option for the poor has a *telos* that is marked by a vision of human flourishing for all that is offered by the proclaimed Reign of God and is oriented by the deontic implications of that *telos* in the present historical context.

Although liberation theology has sought to maintain a commitment both to the universality of God's love and to God's predilection for the poor, a dual commitment incarnated in the universality of Christ's outreach and his clear self-identification with the least and the vulnerable, it is often viewed as partisan and divisive. However, it has also been suggested that the shift from an emphasis on God's justice to God's gratuitousness as a basis for the option for the poor weakens the option into a simple preference, a priority in the order of charity, and thus no longer a true option rooted in the God of Justice who opts for justice, not preferentially but in a partial and exclusive manner.[36]

When the Hebrew scriptures reflect on the just king, they portray not the regent of impartial judgments but the specific and partial protection he offers to the poor: "that he may defend the oppressed among the people, save the poor and crush the oppressor" (Psalm 72:4).[37] This interpretation of the option for the poor as an "option for justice" is fruitful because it neither contradicts the universality of God's love nor sets that in opposition to God's definitive option for justice. Biblical divine partiality issues from a failure of justice. Ultimately, the notion of a preferential option has its basis in a failure of justice, for most poverty results from a failure of justice.

Who Are the Poor?

A litany of sorrowful identifications points to the complexity of what it means to be poor and oppressed: the poor, the "nonpersons," the socially insignificant, the anonymous, exploited classes, marginalized ethnic groups, and scorned cultures; "history's absent ones";[38] those doubly and triply oppressed by virtue of their race, gender, and class; poor minorities in wealthier nations, the dominated, the despised, the unemployed, and underemployed, migrant workers; "those who have ranged against them all the powers of this world"[39]—those persistently on the brink of poverty, the "new poor" of the middle class, the vulnerable working poor, street children and child laborers; women engaged in prostitution and contemporary slaves, AIDS sufferers without access to medication, and those who are of little or no consequence to the three "publics" of theology—society, the academy, and the church.[40]

However, even with the good intentions of liberation theologians, the multiple expressions of those for whom we are called to opt and with whom we are invited to enter into solidaristic friendship can sound like a generalized proletariat, a homogeneous group of sufferers and victims whose distinct personhood is subsumed for rhetorical purposes, no matter how noble. This overlooking of the complexity of subjectivity was characteristic of Marxist class analysis and the subjectivity of the poor was also overlooked by the Western liberal tradition.

In the first two decades of the movement, liberation theologians too tended to overlook this complexity of the poor, being mainly silent about children and women, about the black and indigenous poor, and about the multidimensional nature of poverty. This silence offers a salutary warning that even a commitment to the underside of history can be blind to other faces and experiences of poverty and oppression, a blindness that has a poignant historical precedent in the initial request by Bartolomé de las Casas that people who were already slaves in Spain would be transported to the Indies because he considered black slaves to be more suited than the Indians to hard physical labor. Although Las Casas completely reversed his position with regard to black slaves when he discovered the reality of the African slave trade and amended his writings to express this reversal and his repentance, his initial stance showed that his view of justice, rights, and flourishing—like all ethical attempts to read and respond to reality—was flawed and provisional.[41]

When the early writings of liberation theologians did mention women, indigenous people, young people, and children, there was little sustained analysis of the differentiation of the experience of poverty or of the resultant lost opportunities and thwarted capacities. The poor have many faces and poverty affects different people differently. We should not attempt to merge all victims of poverty and oppression into a common category; what is common is poverty and oppression, but the expression and experience of these are diverse. The five-hundredth anniversary of the arrival of Columbus was a significant year in terms of the inclusion of the neglected voices of Indians and Afro-Latin Americans in the literature of liberation theology. The year 1992 generated research into the historical memory of Latin America enabling these neglected peoples to explore their memories of suffering and resistance and to claim and articulate their heritage.

Poverty is a complex phenomenon that generates various means of categorization and analysis. The difficulties that theology and philosophy have with the definition of poverty and the place poverty should hold in moral discourse are matched by the disagreement among economists on how best to "measure" poverty.[42] Efforts are made to measure poverty empirically either by income distribution or by composite indices that address the multidimensional nature of poverty. The economist Amartya Sen describes poverty in terms of "capability deprivation," in contrast with seeing poverty merely in terms of lowness of income. A discussion of the breadth and complexity of the capability thesis—as outlined by Sen and developed by Martha Nussbaum—is not possible here, but their understanding of poverty as capability deprivation challenges us to see basic needs not merely as the need for commodities, but to see these commodities as *means* to real ends, inputs for valuable human functionings and capabilities that are needed for human flourishing. Sen's understanding of capability deprivation offers a challenge to theologians concerned about the impact of poverty, not only among the global poor but also on the lives of the poor in richer nations. Although not denying that lack of income is clearly one of the major causes of poverty, he nonetheless suggests that "*relative* deprivation in terms of *incomes* can yield *absolute* deprivation in terms of *capabilities*." To be relatively poor in a rich nation can be an enormous capability handicap, even when one's income might be high in terms of world standards of poverty.[43]

Poverty therefore is the great problem of our world—the poor are the majority of humanity—and although the World Bank poverty line of one dollar per day is open to debate, it nonetheless is a stark reminder to us of the fact that poverty, with all its nuances, complexities, and specificities within different contexts, has a bleak and absolute form.[44] One danger with focusing on the various mutations of poverty is that of making the concept so inclusive and undifferentiated that it renders difficult a critical analysis of the economic dimensions of power. Although there can be an overlapping of categories of oppression and thus a plurality of "options" both theological and praxic, the preferential option for the poor *cannot* exclude the "real poor" and their subjectivity within history.

The condition of poverty can be transitory or persistent; its persistent form, leading to the premature (and thus unjust) death of the poor, constitutes institutionalized violence. Although the argument that poverty causes violence is somewhat simplistic, it must be emphasized that pauperization—the structures, decisions, and actions that generate poverty—is a form of violence that can be perpetrated with the greatest impunity, and that such violence, in certain circumstances, can engender further violence. The impact of urbanization and the poverty in urban slums means that priority must be given to the problems and violence of the city.[45]

However, a concern about poverty is not simply based on self-protection but also on the impoverishment that results for all because of the imposed poverty of so many. Over one billion children suffer the effects of poverty, from the extreme capability deprivation caused by malnutrition, with its ensuing effects on physical and neurological development, to the deprivation caused by lack of education and other opportunities. The consequences of the denial of present quality of life are reflected in diminishment and thwarting of future possibilities, thus denying the human community the gifts of those who never reach their potential.

Poverty, however, is not only about vulnerability and deficiencies. The poor are human beings imbued with the same capacities as other human persons, and more often, witness to a graced resilience that seems almost miraculous to those whose life experience is more privileged than peripheral. Working with street children, one learns that it is often the strong who run away from poverty, abuse, and exploitation. The energy to face adversity with creativity and the capacity to celebrate and to hope in the midst of such adversity are also part of the reality of the poor.

To suggest that it is necessary to take this option seriously is not to objectify the poor but, rather, to acknowledge that poverty and injustice exist and find expression in concrete faces and places and that we can only learn about the underside by taking seriously the perspective of the impoverished and victims of our world. The underside unveils a different reality where decisions about access to education and health, about the price of crops, and the terms of credit are made by someone else. To make theological and pastoral options in response to what is unveiled on this underside is to enter into a relationship that is concerned about resources for the poor, with legitimation of their perspective, and with solidarity in difficulty and danger. It is an option evoked not simply by vulnerability but by a mutual recognition of capacities and desires. Those who work on the underside know that there is reciprocity of enrichment in the meeting point of our mutual existential poverty and wealth.

Liberation theology emphasizes that to opt for the poor is to opt for the Reign of God, for the poor flesh out what that Reign means today and point to the necessity of the intentional, if partial, construction in history of what Jesus told us is very near.

Liberationist perspectives in theology have emerged from those normally absent from history, who have also tended to be the absent and silent ones of theology. The *communidades de base* made a very significant contribution to the emergence of these voices: breaking the silence of the poor in the church, allowing their voices to affect the public of academic theology, sensitizing many who were overlooked in society to their human rights and, through their voices, sensitizing others to the reality of poverty.

However, it must be stressed that liberation theology teaches us that the cry of the poor is not just the representative human voice, not just a cry to God, but also the cry *of* God. God's Revelation is not just *for* the poor and suffering, but *through* the poor and those who suffer. The option for the poor is thus a substantive theological concept; that is, it is scripturally located, developed in the tradition, and systematically conceived in modern theology. It challenges contemporary theology to dislocate itself from its abstract universality and find a *locus theologicus* in the particularity of the reality of our times. To hold this is not to engage in a kind of hagiography of poverty. The poor have no moral superiority. The world of the margins can be a place of great generosity and solidarity, but equally, it is a dangerous place where life is precarious. Oppression and exploitation exist on the underside as much as the underside is constructed by neglect, injustice, and exploitation. This is poignantly exemplified in the violence that street children and child soldiers both endure and perpetuate.

The preferential option for the poor asks theology to identify its *locus theologicus*, and requires ethics to identify from where it is viewing the issues and discerning the appropriate discourse and praxis. It challenges the traditional interpretation of objectivity in the form of invariance with regard to observers and their positions, the idea of a "view from nowhere."[46] Sen, while acknowledging the merits of the classical conception of objectivity, offers a different conception in his position-dependent objectivity, that is, "positional objectivity." "The objectivity of observations must be a position-dependent characteristic: not a 'view from nowhere' but one 'from a delineated somewhere.'"[47] Liberation theology issues a reminder that justice is viewed from somewhere—not from nowhere or everywhere—and that even classic notions of impartiality are always a view from somewhere. Rawls tried to develop a viable Kantian conception of justice removed from its background in transcendental idealism by means of the construction of the "original position," wherein parties are not allowed to know their social position, talents, abilities, and so forth, but deliberate behind a "veil of ignorance."[48] Although limited in perspective, the concept put forth by Rawls does attempt to grant the least advantaged a central, if abstract, place in his conception of justice.

Liberation theology, however, challenges human rights, as a boundary discourse of justice and flourishing, to speak, not "from nowhere," nor from behind an imagined "veil of ignorance," but from the positional objectivity, the delineated somewhere, the revealed knowledge of the reality of the poor and the marginalized. In chapter 1, the issue of the relationship between the particularity of culture and the universal nature of human rights was discussed, suggesting that the formulation and explication of universal human rights is always situated somewhere, that is, a situated universalism. With liberation theology, this universalism of human rights is situated in the specific contexts of poverty.

The Rights of the Poor

The rights of the poor are not another category of rights; they are human rights. The very nature of human rights is that they adhere to people simply by virtue of their being human beings. Liberation theology is built on the conviction that we are called to make a preferential, if not exclusive, option for the poor, introducing a binding partiality in theology and pastoral practice, for the poor are "nonsubjects" of universal human rights. Gutiérrez holds that defending human rights means, above all, defending the rights of the poor, for it is their rights that help us realize what is at stake in the defense of human rights.[49] The poor are the majority of humanity, and liberation theology thus views their lives as the prime analogate of the human race.[50] Taking seriously the rights of the poor necessitates addressing the question of social and economic rights through, at least, the right to subsistence.

A focus on the rights of the poor as the key issue in human rights discourse is not only the preoccupation of liberation theologians. The philosopher Thomas Pogge holds that "the great human rights deficits persisting today are heavily concentrated" among the global poor.[51] Pogge argues that nearly all of the severe poverty in the world today is caused by the conduct of others and that such severe poverty should be considered a human rights violation. The widespread violation of socioeconomic rights also plays a decisive role in explaining "the global deficit in civil and political human rights which demand democracy, due process, and the rule of law: very poor people—often physically and mentally stunted due to malnutrition in infancy, illiterate due to lack of schooling, and much preoccupied with their family's survival—cause little harm or benefit to the politicians or officials who rule them."[52] He conceives human rights narrowly as imposing only negative duties, a stringent negative duty of the global rich not to contribute to the development and implementation of a global economic order that impedes the alleviation of extreme poverty and the fulfillment of basic socioeconomic rights. Pogge believes that relatively small reforms of global institutions—including the World Trade Organization, the International Monetary Fund, and the World Bank—reforms of little consequence for the world's affluent, would suffice to eliminate most of this human rights deficit, whose magnitude makes such reforms our most important moral task."[53]

Henry Shue describes "basic rights" as the "morality of depths," specifying the line beneath which no one is allowed to sink.[54] He is aware that he is outlining the moral minimum, the lower limits on tolerable human conduct, individual and institutional. His three covalent values are freedom, security, and subsistence, that is, sufficient food, clothing, and shelter to enable humans to survive. Shue forcefully contends that taking rights seriously necessitates taking duties seriously. These basic rights must be guaranteed by any society, and such guaranteeing necessitates correlative duties in terms of avoidance of deprivation, protection from deprivation, and aid to the deprived. Shue also argues that we have indirect duties in the form of responsibility for the creation of institutions that will protect these basic rights, a responsibility that indicates a globalization of our moral concerns.

The right to subsistence is always qualified by "at least," not that there is unlimited entitlement to everything that is available (a right to enter more fully into unbridled consumerism) but a qualification that recognizes that subsistence is a minimum that is in need of augmentation toward greater fullness of life and opportunity. These basic rights are human rights, that is, they inhere in a human person by virtue of the person's humanity, nothing else. Because human rights can be appealed to independently of and prior to their acknowledgment by particular states, the acknowledgment of basic rights considerably expands moral communities. The provision of basic rights is a "necessary condition for any model of true economic development based on human dignity."[55] Shue describes these basic rights as a "moral minimum"; when this moral minimum is secured, other rights can be enjoyed, but when this moral minimum is not guaranteed, other rights are rendered fragile.[56]

Liberation theology tends to portray the Western liberal tradition as unconcerned about social and economic rights.[57] It is important to note, however, that subsistence rights only seem new because of the "blind spot" that Western liberalism has had for severe economic need.[58] John Locke, acknowledged as one of the foundational influences on liberal democracy, held that a universal right to subsistence limited the right to accumulate private property and that use and appropriation are sanctioned and limited by the law of nature. In the second treatise of Locke's *Two Treatises of Government* (1689), the right to appropriate whatever one can put to use is matched by a duty to use responsibly. The limit is set by the amount one can use "to any advantage of life before it spoils; so much by his labor he may fix a property in. Whatever is beyond this, is more than his share, and belongs to others."[59] To the limits of use and waste is added the limit of sufficiency: "at least where there is enough and as good left in common for others."[60] This limit of sufficiency is reiterated five times in the *Second Treatise*.[61] Locke's close reading of scripture in the *First Treatise*, although used primarily to refute the patriarchal version of the Divine Right of Kings proposed by Robert Filmer, grounded his defense of the equality of all human beings, and this egalitarian perspective forms the basis of the political theory he developed in the *Second Treatise*.[62]

For Locke, property rights could be overridden in cases of extreme need, thus implying that all human beings have the right at least to subsistence, to the minimum needed for material well being. Individual property rights cannot stand in the way of the right of the desperate to the goods they need to survive. Although Locke would not have envisaged our contemporary discussion of social and economic rights, it could be suggested that his argument could be extended into transnational terms: "If individual property rights should not be allowed to stand in the way of people's survival, why should 'societal' property rights?"[63] It is clear that Locke believed that unlimited accumulation of land and durable capital generates productivity for the benefit of all and that such wealth creation is necessary for all.

In Locke's scheme, the wealth that a man derives from the property created by his labor allows him to acquire the property of others; he may also acquire servants whose labor will create property for him. Thus, Locke's doctrine of the natural right to property, while grounded in natural law and limited by the qualifications of spoilage, use, and sufficiency, could, paradoxically, provide justification for imperial expansion, gross inequality in property ownership, and distortion of the relation between property and labor, thus opening the way for labor exploitation in the market. Nonetheless, Locke's repeated insistence on the right at least to subsistence, and this as a limitation on the rights to the private property of others, cannot be negated.

Thomas Paine, in *The Rights of Man*, advocates support for those in poverty, especially children and "old people past their labour . . . not as a matter of grace and favour, but of right," and this payment would come from surplus taxes.[64] His call for a redistribution of wealth and the establishment of a welfare system in the form of provision for poor families, hardship allowances, donations toward births, marriages, and funerals, and proper funding for education prefigures the modern welfare state. This interconnection of rights and welfare was also found in the thinking of Henri Saint-Simon, Charles Fourier, and Robert Owen. It is also important to note that many traditional societies recognize the right to subsistence, even if this is articulated in language very different from rights discourse.[65]

Liberation theology is, therefore, inaccurate in its portrayal of the liberal tradition as completely unconcerned with social and economic rights. The specific contribution of liberation theology lies in its emphasis on the need for systemic and structural fulfillment of these rights, and its sometimes strident articulation of the rights of the poor also serves as a salutary reminder of the failure of universality and the capacity of democracy to mask enormous social and economic inequity, inequity that can undermine democracy itself. Jon Sobrino stresses the primacy of victims, suggesting that human rights discourse begins with victims and not with abstract human beings. Ignacio Ellacuría, in a rather strident note, posits that human rights are primarily the rights of the oppressed because the "oppressors have no rights insofar as they are oppressors; at most they will have the right to be freed from their oppression."[66] These statements of Sobrino and Ellacuría reflect human rights discourse as it emerges in the actual concrete historical experience of those caught between life and death.

Although we believe that not all social and economic ideals can be formulated as rights, it must be recognized that basic social and economic rights are intrinsic to the boundary discourse of justice and human flourishing.[67] The concept of partiality for the poor, while seemingly paradoxical and problematic within human rights discourse, highlights an already existing implicit prioritization that is often not acknowledged, a prioritization that overlooks basic human rights for the poor. Liberation theology, in positioning the poor as a defining case for human rights, is not holding them up as a freestanding norm, but as a test for the paradox of universality, pointing to the dialectical nature of human rights. Potentially any human person can be such a testing norm, even the least deserving person who has behaved in a despicable way.[68] The affirmation of the rights of the poor, far from eliminating the universality of human rights, actually points toward authentic universality in the form of historical and concrete realization. We now turn to a distinctively theological perspective on human rights found in the work of Jon Sobrino.

A Mysticism of Human Rights

Reference was made in chapter 2 to Jürgen Moltmann's suggestion that the specific task of Christian theology is not the repetition of what other experts have already achieved but that of "grounding fundamental human rights in God's right to—that is, his claim upon—all beings, their human dignity, their fellowship, their rule over the earth, and their future."[69] In liberation theology, the relationship between human rights and the divine is not expressed in terms of the rights of God but in terms of the divine element in the struggle for human rights. Sobrino presents the defense of the rights of the poor and oppressed as a kind of mystagogy into the life of God. His reflections on the

"Mysticism of Human Rights" could be perceived as a crude attempt to justify theological engagement with human rights. His intention, however, is not to engage with the apologetical question of the compatibility of theology with this modern discourse but to show that engagement in the struggle for the rights of the poor and oppressed is a kind of mystagogy.

In Sobrino's work the idea of the radical proximity of Holy Mystery that is no less radically present in suffering (touched on in our reflections on Rahner) finds a tentative articulation. Sobrino draws from what could be described as a low ascending theology of human rights, that is, he does not deduce the importance of the struggle for human rights from a vision of the human person as *Imago Dei* and the ethical imperative born of that vision, but, instead, he begins by engaging with the *reality of human rights violations*, seeing in this reality an initiation into the life of God. The reality of violation is a priori. Those who defend the rights of the poor and oppressed bring the mercy and tenderness of God to bear on situations of suffering and are further initiated into the mystery of God through that experience.

Borrowing from Rudolf Otto's phrase in *The Idea of the Holy* (trans. John W. Harvey [New York: Oxford University Press, 1950]), Sobrino suggests that the *mysterium tremendum et fascinans* is historicized in the experience of those who are poor and oppressed, in the *tremendum* of poverty, oppression and violence, and in the *fascinans* of the hope, joy, and courage that are made manifest in the struggle for a dignified life. "The mysticism of the struggle for human rights depends ultimately on relating them to life, and to the life of the majorities, the crucified peoples."[70] Sobrino offers this position in a paper marking the fiftieth anniversary of the Universal Declaration of Human Rights.

The suffering Christ is not interpreted in terms of the individual victim but in the context of the crucified peoples.[71] The struggle for human rights could also be described as a mystagogy into the life and reality of the human person. It is a mystagogy that humanizes, not just those who have been dehumanized through deprivation or violation, but all who participate in the struggle. We experience an initiation into our humanity in this struggle because the reality of poverty, oppression, victimization, and violence is not simply the result of the contingency and tragedy of life, but they arise from the will of the human person and the personal and structural implications of human selfishness.

Henry Shue described a morality of the depths as reflecting the moral minimum, the lower limits of tolerable human conduct. Liberation theologians offer a reflection on this morality of the depths as a place of encounter with

God. The divine element in the struggle for human rights points to a contrapuntal transcendence, a transcendence beyond and within human history, the radical presence of holy mystery in radical suffering, no place being too hostile for the presence of God.

From Interruptive Realism to the Centrality of La Realidad

The previous chapter explored the "interruption" of theological discourse by stark realism and the way the Holocaust marked an interruption for some into the priorities and concerns of European theology. It was suggested that the idea of "interruptive realism" is not sufficient in itself, for it presupposes theology only as a response to that which interrupts, leading ultimately to a reactive rather than proactive ethic. Liberation theology marks a shift from this interruptive realism to the placing of the reality of violations of the rights of the poor at the center of theological discourse.

However, liberation theology is not only concerned with reality as manifested at the macro level of economics and politics; it is also intricately concerned with the micro reality of daily life and struggle, particularly of the poor and marginalized. Women theologians, in particular, have insisted upon daily life both as a point of departure for theology and as an intrinsic dimension of the struggle for human rights, justice, and peace, thus bridging the public and private in a kind of mundane phenomenology where attention is paid to the quotidian, to the issues of daily struggle that have not been considered—even by liberation theologians—worthy of serious philosophical or theological reflection.[72] As Elsa Tamez reminds us, "the foretastes of utopia are experienced in everyday life, and it is in everyday life that we begin to build this utopia."[73] Normally considered marginal to the historical struggle for justice and social change, women have pointed to the centrality of daily life issues in this struggle. Liberation theology speaks of a "logic of life" wherein the essential criterion of rationality is concrete human life; hunger, poverty, illiteracy, and disease are illogical and irrational.

The Gospels relate the Reign of God to the mundane tasks of feeding, quenching thirst, clothing, welcoming, cleaning, sowing, and reaping. As this evangelical use of the daily points to the Reign of God that is "already but not yet," so too issues of food and clean water, clothes, shoes, and schoolbooks concretize discourse about the inequalities of global capitalism and violations of human rights. Daily life, the heart of the struggle for human rights and justice, is not just a point of departure for theology but intrinsic to its very deliberations and aspirations.[74] These quotidian concerns also point to the search for flourishing beyond the minimum, for a humane life where more than the material can thrive, for beauty as well as justice, marked by a concern for life and its fullness that is normally considered the preserve of eudemonic discussions of a more idealist genre.[75]

This emphasis on *la realidad* reflects both the turn to the subject and the turn to experience in modern philosophy and theology, but liberation theology historicizes and concretizes these "turns" with a very distinct emphasis, eschewing any theological anthropology that situates itself "above" the contingencies and conflicts, hopes and joys of actual human life. Rahner held that every dimension of human life was the realm of encounter with grace, emphasizing the sacramental nature of the ordinary and the daily. Liberation theology is part of this lineage, but it embraces a distinct focus on human life as the realm of encounter not just with grace but also with dis-grace in its myriad and structural forms. It is not the intention here, by highlighting this quotidian realism, to suggest that all theological and philosophical discourse must speak of mundane concerns but to point to the truth that theology cannot be superimposed on reality, cannot place the truths about the mystery of God and the mystery of the human person in an idealist position beyond history.

The Weight of Reality: Ignacio Ellacuría

Ignacio Ellacuría, the martyr philosopher-theologian of the Universidad Centroamericana in San Salvador, offers a helpful methodology of discernment that may move theology from the interruptive realism emerging from Metz's theology to a place where reality, specifically the reality of the poor and vulnerable, is central. A former student of Karl Rahner, he saw his own theology as developing Rahner's theology in the context of Latin America.[76] Ellacuría's abiding theological concern was the historicizing of the notion of salvation, emphasizing that salvation history is salvation in history and that such salvation in history is a sign of the fullness of a salvation that is metahistorical.[77]

Philosophically, the great influence on Ellacuría's work was the philosophy of historical realism of the Spanish philosopher Xavier Zubiri, for whom reality is a primary concept. For Zubiri, "being" must be understood in reference to reality, not vice versa. Zubiri conceived philosophy as a concrete operation carried out from a specific situation.[78] He defines the human person as a "reality animal," in contrast with the Aristotelian definition of the human person as a "rational animal."[79] Ellacuría brought Zubiri's philosophy of historical realism to bear on his work as an academic in El Salvador. Writing on human rights, Ellacuría said that the process of historicization consists, first, in ensuring that what is abstractly affirmed as an "ought to be" is realized in concrete circumstances, and second in the establishment of the "real conditions without which there can be no effective realization of human rights."[80]

Writing a philosophical justification for the method of liberation theology, Ellacuría emphasized that the formal structure of understanding necessitates facing reality, ethically appreciating reality, and responding practically to the demands of that reality. Thus, he offers for consideration a threefold methodological description of our confrontation with and prudential discernment of reality:

> *realizing the weight of reality*, which implies being in the reality of things—and not merely facing the idea of things or being in touch with their meaning—being "real" in the reality of things, which in its active character of being is exactly the opposite of being thing-like and inert, and implies being among them through their material and active mediations; *shouldering the weight of reality*, an expression which points to the fundamentally ethical character of our intelligence, which has not been given to us so that we could evade our real commitments, but rather to take upon ourselves what things really are and what they really demand; *taking charge of the weight of reality*, an expression which points to the practical character of intelligence which only fulfils its function, including its character of knowing reality and understanding its meaning, when it takes as its burden doing something real.[81]

"Realizing the weight of reality" (*el hacerse cargo de la realidad*) means not simply to stand before reality but to situate oneself within it in order to discern a response. It suggests a profound knowledge, a comprehension beyond purely "objective" knowledge, which Ellacuría sees as the formal theological equivalent of reading the signs of the times and interpreting them in the light of the Gospels. This also suggests an expectation of the revelatory character of reality.

"Shouldering the weight of reality" (*el cargar con la realidad*) occurs when we take upon ourselves the actuality of reality and its burdens. Reality places before us a responsibility, which evokes a fundamental option. The responsibility of theology necessitates the choice of the *lugar teológico*, a locus that is not confined to physical spatiality, but never bypasses this question. Ellacuría holds that the primary *lugar teológico* in Latin America is the space marked by the reality of poverty and violations of human rights. His reflections on the historicization of human rights place the struggle for human rights, primarily the rights of the poor, firmly within his abiding theological concern for the historicization of our understanding of salvation.

"Taking charge of the weight of reality" (*el encargarse de la realidad*) occurs when reality is given to human persons as a responsibility, and theologians too must bear its weight.[82] The language of bearing the burden of reality has metaphysical and concrete (physical) historical significance. It suggests a method faithful to a social analysis of reality and reasoned reflection in response. However, it is also a cruciform language—bearing, shouldering, burden, falling under the weight of that burden—that points to the *theologia crucis* that shapes the ethics of liberation theology. This cruciform structure eventually marked Ellacuría's bearing of the burden of the historical reality of El Salvador in the most ultimate way when he was murdered, together with five of his brother Jesuits and two women colleagues, at Universidad Centroamericana on November 16, 1989.[83]

Ellacuría offers a theological method that draws in intelligence, emotion, and volition through a tripartite model of attention to reality, ethical appreciation of that reality, and practical response to the burden of the reality. Holding in tension the dialectic of theory and practice, it also marks a sophistication and internalization of the see-judge-act process.[84] Theology is challenged to be historically conscious and historically responsive through a "fusion of horizons" of academics and the poor, a reciprocal realizing, shouldering, and taking charge of the weight of reality; for only in this reciprocity can the real meaning of justice and human rights, virtue and human flourishing be discerned.[85]

Conclusion

Liberation theology, with its preferential option for the poor and commitment to praxis, challenges human rights discourse to take seriously the "rights of the poor." The concerns of liberation theology are primarily with the implementation of the protections and provisions of human rights and only secondarily with the construction and discussion of foundational theory. However, liberation theology has contributed significantly to the engagement between theology and human rights discourse in the following ways: highlighting the widespread violation of basic socioeconomic rights and the consequent effects on individuals, communities, and society; emphasizing the historicization of ethical theory and human rights; unmasking a false universality in favor of a partiality for the rights of the poor; and the recognition of a mystical dimension to the struggle for human rights based on their relationship to the life of the crucified peoples of Latin America. The affirmation of the rights of the poor—especially social and economic rights—does not negate the universality of human rights, but points toward authentic universality in the form of historical, concrete and evangelical realization. Historicization is thus a principle of verification of human rights.

Although discussion of virtue remains underdeveloped in liberation theology, there is, in fact, an implicit aretaic perspective in the emphasis on humanization through solidaristic praxis and the struggle for human rights. The defense of the rights of the poor and oppressed calls for responsible, courageous, and generous actions with and on behalf of those who suffer. Chapter 3 suggested that Metz's mature theology challenged theologians not just to the practical and the political but to the necessity for the cultivation of a *habitus operativus bonus* of vigilance toward suffering, a prudential sensitivity to the faces of injustice and violations of human dignity, a practical wisdom that includes the capacity to discern the moral significance of concrete situations, and the skill of knowing when to take potentially costly risks for justice or friendship. Ellacuría's threefold method of attention, appreciation, and response to historical reality offers one such way in which this virtue of vigilance toward suffering, prudential sensitivity to injustice, and discernment of risk for solidarity might be cultivated. His passion for reality challenges the theologian to be grounded in reality, to live in expectation of the revelatory character of that reality, to respond to the responsibility evoked by that reality, and to bear the weight of reality in imitation of the one who bore the cross and in solidarity with the crucified peoples of our time—those upon whom reality has placed the heavy burdens of poverty, hunger, and exclusion: "the world tribe of the dispossessed outside the halls of plenty looking in."

This is a hymn
for all recommending
a bootstrap as a way
to rise with effort

on your part
This is a hymn
may it renew
what passes for your heart.

This hymn
is for the must-be-blessed
the victims of the world
who know salt best
the world tribe
of the dispossessed
outside the halls of plenty
looking in
this is a benediction
this is a hymn.[86]

Notes

1. For an overview see Chopp and Regan, "Latin American Liberation Theology," 469–84.
2. For an overview of the early criticisms see Arthur F. McGovern, *Liberation Theology and Its Critics*, 47–61. Michael Novak is representative of criticism that defines liberation theology by its weaknesses. See *Will It Liberate? Questions about Liberation Theology*, 2nd ed. (Lanham, MD: Madison Books, 1991). In *Liberation Theology at the Crossroads*, the political theorist Paul Sigmund offers similar criticisms. One of the most prominent Latin American critics of liberation theology was Cardinal Lopéz Trujillo, past president of CELAM (*Consejo Episcopal Latinoamericano*). See Alfonso Lopéz Trujillo, *De Medellín a Puebla* (Madrid: Biblioteca de Autores Cristianos, 1980). For a twenty-first-century perspective on liberation theology see *Latin American Liberation Theology: The Next Generation*, edited by Ivan Petrella (Maryknoll, NY: Orbis Books, 2005).
3. Catholic and Protestant theologians in Latin America had been meeting in the 1960s to reflect on the relationship between faith and social justice in the light of the social and political situation on the continent. Gustavo Gutiérrez presented a paper to a meeting in Peru in July 1968 titled "Towards a Theology of Liberation." In the same year, Rubem Alves, a Protestant Brazilian theologian studying at Princeton Theological Seminary, submitted his doctoral dissertation, also titled, "Towards a Theology of Liberation." Both men met at a conference in Switzerland the following year and recognized that they shared similar perspectives. Leonardo Boff and Clodovis Boff distinguish four stages in the formulation of

liberation theology: (1) Foundational; (2) Building; (3) Settling-In; and (4) Formalization. See *Introducing Liberation Theology* (London: Burns & Oates, 1987), 66–77. See also David Tombs, "Latin American Liberation Theology Faces the Future," in Stanley E. Porter, Michael A. Hayes, David Tombs, eds., *Faith in the Millennium* (Sheffield: Sheffield Academic Press, 2001), 32–58.

4. In "Founding the Supernatural," chap. 8 in *Theology and Social Theory*, John Milbank offers a critique of liberation theology (and political theology) suggesting that it remains trapped within the terms and unwarranted foundational suppositions of "secular reason." He is also critical of the Rahnerian influence in liberation theology. Milbank bases his assertions on the writings of Gustavo Gutiérrez, Juan Luis Segundo, and Clodovis Boff, whom he considers to be the most important of liberation theologians; however, he makes no reference to developments both within their particular writings and within the broader area of liberation theology.

5. See, for example, *Mysterium Liberationis.* edited by Ellacuría and Sobrino, which aims to offer a fragmentary systematized presentation of the core and nucleus of liberation theology and points to its increased theoretical rigor. This elaboration of the fundamental concepts of liberation theology offers an opening for dialogue between Latin American theologians and with theologians from other parts of the world. However, only two of the essays were authored by women. Liberation theologians who demonstrated openness to new ways of thinking in terms of politics and economics proved to be slower in their willingness to engage with issues of gender and race.

6. Ivan Petrella evaluates liberation theology's responses to the fall of socialism and concludes that it has lost its "distinctive mark," i.e., "relating theological concepts and ideals to institutions in historical projects," in *The Future of Liberation Theology*, 145.

7. "The Task and Content of Liberation Theology," translated by Judith Condor, in Christopher Rowland, ed., *The Cambridge Companion to Liberation Theology* (Cambridge: Cambridge University Press, 1999), 19–38, at 19.

8. Many leading Latin American liberation theologians, including Leonardo Boff, Ignacio Ellacuría, Gustavo Gutiérrez, Juan Luis Segundo, and Jon Sobrino, studied in Europe. They refer to the influence of Metz, Moltmann, and Rahner, whom they both cite and critique.

9. This theme is found in the philosophy of Enrique Dussel. See *The Underside of Modernity: Apel, Ricoeur, Rorty, Taylor, and the Philosophy of Liberation*, Eduardo Mendieta, ed. (Amherst, NY: Humanity Books/Prometheus, 1998).

10. Gustavo Gutiérrez, *On Job: God-Talk and the Suffering of the Innocent*, translated by Matthew J. O'Connell (Maryknoll, NY: Orbis Boooks, 1987), 101–2. The reference to the Holocaust comes only at the very end of the book.

11. John T. Pawlikowski holds that liberation theologians are not free of the shadow of the "deep-seated tradition of anti-Judaic Christology," the *adversus Judaeos* legacy of patristic Christianity. "Christology, Anti-Semitism, and Christian-Jewish

Bonding," in *Reconstructing Christian Theology*, Rebecca S. Chopp and Mark Lewis Taylor, eds. (Minneapolis: Fortress Press, 1994), 245–68, at 249.

12. *Gaudium et spes*, 55. Pedro Casaldáliga and José-Maria Vigil outline the characteristics of political holiness, which include "a passion for reality" and "ethical indignation" in *Political Holiness: A Spirituality of Liberation* (Maryknoll, NY: Orbis, 1994), 17–20, 21–26. The authors conceive ethical indignation as composed of several dynamic components out of which an inescapable demand necessitates a choice.

13. Mark Engler also outlines the response of liberation theologians to human rights initiatives through three distinct stages, describing them in terms of "initial avoidance," "early critique," and "nuanced theological appropriation." See "Towards the 'Rights of the Poor': Human Rights in Liberation Theology," *Journal of Religious Ethics* 28 (Fall 2000): 339–65.

14. Valpy FitzGerald, "The Economics of Liberation Theology," in Rowland, ed., 226–27. However, it must be noted here that the Latin American philosopher Enrique Dussel holds that Marxian theory still provides the best analysis of poverty and calls Latin American philosophy of liberation to a renewed reading of Marx, whose theory, Dussel suggests, can be used in the service of liberation in Latin America and elsewhere. See Dussel, *Towards an Unknown Marx: A Commentary on the "Manuscripts of 1861–63"* (London: Routledge, 2001). Alistair Kee challenges the view that liberation theology is overly dependent on Marx, suggesting that, on the contrary, it is not Marxist enough. For Kee, the crux of the matter is the lack of attention to Marx's criticism of religion, specifically his second ontological critique. *Marx and the Failure of Liberation Theology* (London/ Philadelphia: SCM Press/Trinity Press International, 1990).

15. Engler, "Towards the 'Rights of the Poor,'" 342.

16. Marx's extended discussion of the "rights of man" is in "On the Jewish Question" (1843). See *Karl Marx, Frederick Engels: Collected Works III* (London: Lawrence & Wishart, 1975), 162–64. His treatment of rights emerges from his discussion of the French Revolution, which he saw as a revolution of the bourgeoisie; he held that the doctrine of equal rights was grafted onto a social context of inequality.

17. "Human Rights Language and Liberation Theology" in Marc H. Ellis and Otto Maduro, eds., *Expanding the View: Gustavo Gutiérrez and the Future of Liberation Theology* (Maryknoll, NY: Orbis, 1990), 157–70, at 164.

18. *A Theology of Liberation*, Revised version (London: SCM, 1988). First published in Spanish in 1971.

19. Ibid., 97, 111, 125, 159.

20. Ibid., xxix. Gutiérrez also defines the poor as members of the proletariat who are struggling for the most basic rights (173). With the exception of the reference in the new introduction, all these references to rights are in the 1971 edition.

21. Ricardo Antoncich in *Christians in the Face of Injustice* holds a similar position. He explores hermeneutical criteria for an understanding of the social teaching of the magisterium in the reality of Latin America. Antoncich emphasizes that

although Catholic social teaching and liberation theology have different tasks and employ different, although convergent, approaches, they are vitally related.

22. See Hugo Assmann, ed., *Carter y la Lógica del Imperialism*, 2 vols. (San José, Costa Rica: EDUCA, 1978). However, it should also be noted that within the United States the Carter administration had a distinctive economic rights policy, exemplified in its interpretation of the right to work as a first-generation rather than second-generation right. In *God Bless the Child That's Got Its Own*, 55–101, Darryl M.Trimiew suggests that Carter's economic rights policy acted as a bridge between first- and second-generation accounts of rights.

23. Juan Luis Segundo, *The Liberation of Theology* (Maryknoll, NY: Orbis, 1976), 61.

24. See Carozza, "From Conquest to Constitutions," 281–313.

25. Ibid., 302. Carozza describes this libertarian perspective as "Lockean," but he does not engage directly with Locke's use of the term "property" or consider that Locke's ideas about property were interpreted in the United States by the jurist William Blackstone through the influential American edition of his *Commentaries on the Laws of England*. Blackstone took a less philosophical and more literal approach to property. Mary Ann Glendon in *Rights Talk* critiques the North American version of rights talk, arguing not for an abandonment but a renewal of rights talk. She describes the "near mythic" status of property in the American legal tradition under the influence of Blackstone's reading of Locke.

26. See Bartolomé de las Casas, *A Short Account of the Destruction of the Indies*, edited and translated by Nigel Griffin (London/New York: Penguin Books, 1992). Written in 1542, the first edition was published in 1552.

27. The first "National Security" Coup took place in Brazil in 1964, and this doctrine was dominant by 1973, when the Chilean Coup marked a bitter blow for Christians for Socialism hopeful of a democratic transition to socialism. Not all "national security" governments were military dictatorships, but all national security regimes gave a foundational role to the military. Many of these dictators in the 1980s were disciples of the New Right, and in Chile, under the Pinochet regime, "the lack of democratic constraints facilitated the imposition of painful monetarist economic policies carried out under the guidance of a team of economists from the University of Chicago." See Noreena Hertz, *The Silent Takeover: Global Capitalism and the Death of Democracy* (London: William Heinemann, 2001), 24.

28. Although it was in Central America that the United States had most influence over the military, many of the brutal military officers of Chile, Argentina, Brazil, Uruguay, Bolivia, and Paraguay were schooled in these military academies.

29. See Klaiber, *The Church, Dictatorships, and Democracy in Latin America*, especially "Church, Power, and Popular Legitimacy," 3–19.

30. See Comblin, *Called for Freedom*, 159–62. Comblin continues to be a trenchant critic of human rights, perceiving it as a bourgeois ethic where indignation arises primarily because of the torture of the middle classes, holding that those who

trample the rights of the poor are not in danger of being brought to justice, and suggesting that the human rights of the poor are invoked only if the powerful are willing to defend them. His critique tends to caricature the whole tradition of human rights discourse and shows no appreciation for its complexity and self-critical dimension. However, Comblin challenges both rights discourse and liberation theology to self-examination in the light of the ever-present and changing reality of poverty. I concur with the translator, Phillip Berryman, who, in the foreword, describes the style of Comblin's book as "colloquial to the edge of carelessness"; however, I also agree that the book is significant because it reflects the critique of a theologian who has been consistently faithful to the spirit of Medellín. Elsewhere, Comblin notes that the repression, especially in Brazil, Argentina, Uruguay, Peru, and Colombia, wiped out "the elite of young Catholics," an entire generation of young intellectuals and potential leaders. Under the pretext of eliminating guerrilla movements, young people who were members of, sympathizers, or merely *suspected* of being sympathetic to these movements were tortured or disappeared. This loss to society was keenly felt in the years following the dictatorships. See Comblin's "The Church and Defence of Human Rights" in Dussel, ed., *The Church in Latin America 1492–1992.*

31. For an examination of Catholic social teaching from 1878 to 1992, see Dorr, *Option for the Poor.* Dorr concludes that despite occasional changes of emphasis and one major change of direction—beginning with Pope John XXIII and coming to fruition at Medellín—there is "an organic unity" in the tradition since 1891, an intrinsic dimension of which has been a commitment to the poor (352–79).

32. Second General Conference of Latin American Bishops, *The Church in the Present-Day Transformation of Latin America in the Light of the Council: II Conclusions* (Washington, DC: Secretariat for Latin America, National Conference of Bishops, 3rd ed. 1979), 14.4, 173–74.

33. Third General Conference of Latin American Bishops, *Evangelization at Present and in the Future of Latin America: Conclusions,* Official English Edition (Middlegreen and London: St. Paul's Publications and CIIR, 1980), especially 1134, 1154, 1160. For a discussion of the Puebla conference see Dorr, *Option for the Poor,* 260–66. Dorr maintains that although there was indeed a determined effort by some bishops to "ensure that both the style and outcome of Puebla would be quite different from those of Medellín," some commentators and journalists have exaggerated the tensions behind the scenes prior to Puebla (260).

34. Edward Schillebeeckx, "The Religious and the Human Ecumene," in Ellis and Maduro, eds., *Expanding the View,* 1990, 126–139, at 137.

35. "Option for the Poor," in *Mysterium Liberationis,* 235–50, at 240.

36. Jose Vigil, *The Option for the Poor Is an Option for Justice and Not Preferential,* SEDOS (23 Luglio, 2004): available online at www.sedosmission.org/old/eng/vigil_2.htm [accessed January 5, 2009].

37. *New American Bible* (1990).

38. Gutiérrez, *The Power of the Poor in History,* 186.

39. Sobrino, *The Principle of Mercy*, 5.

40. I am using David Tracy's designation of the three publics to which each theologian is implicitly related. See *The Analogical Imagination: Christian Theology and the Culture of Pluralism* (New York: Crossroad, 1981), 3–28.

41. Las Casas arrived in the "New World" in 1502, a decade after Columbus. In 1516, Las Casas asked for black and white slaves to be sent to maintain the mines. From the early sixteenth century, black slaves were sent to the Indies and then to the Antilles. It was held that these slaves were more suited to hard physical labor than the Indians. It was most likely in Lisbon, around 1547, that Las Casas learned the truth about the brutal reality of the African slave trade. He appended eleven chapters to his *Historia de las Indias* and included a denunciation of African slavery in the same tone and structure as his denunciation of the treatment of the Indians. See Gustavo Gutiérrez, *Las Casas: In Search of the Poor of Jesus Christ* (Maryknoll, NY: Orbis, 1993), 324–30. See also Roger Ruston's *Human Rights and the Image of God* (London: SCM, 2004), a study of the origins of natural rights through the thought of Thomas Aquinas and the work of Francisco de Vitoria and Bartolomé de las Casas in early modern Spain and South America.

42. See "Measuring Income Poverty: Where to Draw the Line?" in United Nations Development Programme, *Human Development Report 2003: Millennium Development Goals: A Compact among Nations to End Poverty* (New York: Oxford University Press, 2003).

43. *Development as Freedom* (Oxford: Oxford University Press, 1999), chapter 4: "Poverty as Capability Deprivation," 87–110, at 89. See also Martha Nussbaum: *Women and Human Development: The Capabilities Approach* (Cambridge: Cambridge University Press, 2000).

44. The World Bank poverty line of about one dollar a day is based on the assumption that "after adjusting for cost of living differences, $1 a day is the average minimum consumption required for subsistence in the developing world. But this approach has been assailed as being conceptually and methodologically inaccurate in capturing minimum subsistence levels across developing countries." Absolute poverty refers to those in a national population living on less than a specific amount of daily income. "Shifting the international poverty line by just a few cents can alter world poverty estimates immensely, 'moving' millions of individuals in or out of poverty." *Human Development Report 2003*, 42.

45. In *Called for Freedom*, José Comblin stresses the need for liberation theology to consider the phenomenon of urbanization, see p. 209.

46. Thomas Nagel, *The View from Nowhere* (Oxford: Clarendon Press, 1986). Examining the validity and limitations of objectivity, Nagel offers both a defense and a critique, for he perceives both as necessary in a climate where objectivity is both underrated and overrated.

47. Amartya Sen, *Rationality and Freedom* (Cambridge, MA/London: Belknap Press, 2002), 463–83, at 464. Sen notes that positional parameters need not be only

locational, but they could include physical positions such as myopia or fluency in a particular language.

48. Rawls, *A Theory of Justice*. Rawls has revised and corrected his account of justice over the years, including a growing acknowledgment that the starting points for the construction of a conception of justice are not pure abstract positions but are socially determinate. He moves toward justice based on the actual ideals of citizenship in liberal democratic societies. However, his earlier work granted the least advantaged a central—if abstract—place. See Rawls, *Justice as Fairness*.

49. See *The Power of the Poor in History*, 87–90, 211–12.

50. Jon Sobrino, *Spirituality of Liberation: Toward Political Holiness* (Maryknoll, NY: Orbis, 1988), 107.

51. "Recognized and Violated by International Law: The Human Rights of the Global Poor," *Leiden Journal of International Law*, 18 (2005): 717–45, at 718.

52. Ibid., 718.

53. Ibid., 745. See also Pogge's *World Poverty and Human Rights*.

54. Shue, *Basic Rights*. see chap. 2, "Correlative Rights," 35–64.

55. Valpy Fitzgerald, in Rowland, ed., *The Cambridge Companion to Liberation Theology*, 221.

56. Shue uses the image of a fabric to describe the intricate weaving of rights of diverse kinds, a rough fabric with threads of different sizes and strengths. "Some of the threads are stronger and more crucial than others—the basic rights—but even the strong threads support each other and are supported by the weaker threads." *Basic Rights*, 156.

57. One example of the dismissal of social and economic rights is a famous piece by Maurice Cranston, "Human Rights, Real and Supposed," in D. D. Raphael, ed., *Political Theory and the Rights of Man* (London: Macmillan, 1967), 43–53. Cranston outlines three evaluative tests on the authenticity of a human right: practicability, universality, and paramount importance. His conclusion is that social and economic rights are rights of the citizen, not of the human person by virtue of their humanity. Shue, however, maintains that Cranston is blind to the "terrible severity of his view's implications." *Basic Rights*, 98–99.

58. Shue, *Basic Rights*, 27.

59. Locke, *Two Treatises of Government*, Second Treatise V: 31.

60. *Second Treatise*, V: 27. There is debate about the practicality of this Lockean "proviso" regarding acquisition of property rights in the state of nature.

61. *Second Treatise*, V: 33–37.

62. For a discussion of the religious foundations of Locke's political thought, particularly his perspectives on human equality, see Waldron, *God, Locke, and Equality*.

63. Peter Jones, *Rights* (Basingstoke: Macmillan, 1994), 169.

64. Paine, "Ways and Means of Improving the Conditions of Europe, Interspersed with Miscellaneous Observations," in *Common Sense and the Rights of Man*, 219–74. Paine also opposed the House of Lords and the established Church.

65. In five years living in the Samoan islands, I never saw anyone begging. The Samoan culture and the *aiga* (extended family) have structures for protection and provision, structures that presume the right to subsistence.

66. Ellacuría, "Human Rights in a Divided Society," 63.

67. Basic economic rights need to be interwoven with other aspects of human rights, e.g., those related to health, education, and employment. However, a commitment to claims regarding economic rights beyond basic economic rights can enmesh a society in an endless chain of "claiming, implementation, and review." See Darryl M. Trimiew, *God Bless the Child That's Got Its Own*, 314.

68. In contradiction to Ellacuría's comments on the oppressors having no rights, it must be stressed that it is oppression that has no rights, but the oppressor remains the subject of basic human rights.

69. Moltmann, *On Human Dignity*, 20.

70. Sobrino, "Human Rights and Oppressed Peoples," 157.

71. The question must be raised as to whether this interpretation—like that of the preferential option for the poor—also runs the risk of abstraction or "massification," thus neglecting the differentiated forms of suffering. This interpretation could potentially overlook the true impact of the damage of deprivation and violence on human persons.

72. In *Sources of the Self: The Making of the Modern Identity* (Cambridge: Cambridge University Press, 1989), the political philosopher Charles Taylor explores the discovery of the significance of ordinary life as one of the facets of modern identity. The subsequent transition from the hierarchy that valued the life of contemplation and political participation moved the world of work and family, i.e., "labour, the making of things needed for life, and our life as sexual beings, including marriage and the family," from the periphery to the center of morality. "Part III: The Affirmation of Ordinary Life," 211–302, at 211. However, Taylor overlooks the underside of modernity and seems unaware that the affirmation of the self in that context was often at the expense of other selves at the periphery of that world, the modernity of slavery, colonialism, and genocide.

73. Rubem Alves and Elsa Tamez, eds., *Against Machismo* (Yorktown Heights, NY: Meyer-Stone Books, 1987), 134.

74. A similar point is made by the political scientist Daniel H. Levine, that even in the midst of poverty and oppression, "a search for meaning and control goes on in the spaces of everyday life." People use all the resources they have, "recombining and reinterpreting ideological and material elements" to make an edge of a difference, no matter how small, to their situation. See *Popular Voices in Latin American Catholicism* (Princeton, NJ: Princeton University Press, 1999), 320.

75. It is clear that aesthetics has not been a central concern of liberation theology. This point is raised by Rubem Alves, who discusses the marginal place of beauty in liberationist theological discussions. In *The Poet, The Warrior, The Prophet: The Edward Cadbury Lectures 1990* (London: SCM Press, 1990), Alves laments the dominance of ethical motifs in theological discourse, noting that the ethical

is not an end but a means to an end. He suggests that the primary purpose of all that we do "from play to politics" is the recovery of the lost garden (131). His reflections are important because it would seem that to be concerned about human rights and justice is to engage primarily with the "ugliness" of life; however, one could also suggest that there is an implicit aesthetic in theological concern with the harshness of reality. It is a pointer to beauty by way of absence. A theological concern with aesthetics can also mark a retreat from reality in its wounded, tawdry, and mundane manifestations. The retrieval of the theological aesthetics of Sor Juana Inés de la Cruz, a seventeenth-century Mexican nun, is an interesting development that has led Hispanic, feminist, and other liberation theologies to reflect on the relationship of aesthetics to the struggle for justice and human rights. See Michelle A. Gonzalez, *Sor Juana: Beauty and Justice in the Americas* (Maryknoll, NY: Orbis, 2003).

76. Ellacuría studied theology in Innsbruck in 1958–62, during the crucial years leading up to Vatican II. On his return to Latin America, Ellacuría described a talk he gave to his fellow Jesuits at the 1969 province retreat as an attempt to apply Rahner's categories to the "mundane reality [of the Third World], and to conceive of it in theological terms." "El Tercer Mundo Como Lugar Optimo de la Vivencia Crístiana de los Ejercícios," quoted in *Love That Produces Hope: The Thought of Ignacio Ellacuría*, Kevin F. Burke and Robert Lassalle-Klein, eds. (Collegeville, MN: Liturgical Press, 2006), xxi.

77. See *Freedom Made Flesh: The Mission of Christ and His Church* (Maryknoll, NY: Orbis, 1976). The last theological essay he completed before his death addressed a historical approach to soteriology: "Utopia y Profetismo," Ignacio Ellacuría and Jon Sobrino, eds., *Mysterium Liberationis: Conceptos Fundamentales de la Teologíca de la Liberación* I (Madrid: Editorial Trotta, 1990), 393–442.

78. See the first book of his mature period, *On Essence* (Washington, DC: The Catholic University of America Press, 1980). The Spanish edition, *Sobre La Esencia*, was published in 1963. His principal systematic work is the three-volume *Sentient Intelligence*, published in the early 1980s. See "Ha desaparecido el último gran matafísico: Xavier Zubiri," *Estudios Centroamericanos* 420 (Octubre 1983): 891–94.

79. This is the translation of *animal de realidades* offered by Kevin F. Burke in his insightful study of Ellacuría's theology, *The Ground beneath the Cross: The Theology of Ignacio Ellacuría* (Washington, DC: Georgetown University Press, 2000). Burke argues that the originality of Ellacuría's work lies in his linking of liberation theology with the philosophy of historical reality.

80. Ellacuría, "Human Rights in a Divided Society," 59.

81. "Hacia Una Fundamentación Filosófica del Método Teológico Latinoamericano," *Estudios Centroamericanos* 322–23 (Agosto/Septiembre, 1975): 409–25, at 419. The translation is mine, and I italicize what Ellacuría has emphasized. Sobrino uses this passage in *Jesus the Liberator* (1993), 34. He translates the three moments as "getting a grip on reality," "taking on the burden of reality," and "taking respon-

sibility for reality." Ellacuría uses a play on words, which can make translation difficult: *cargo* can mean physical load, duty, burden, or accusation.

82. See "Fundamentación Biológica de la Ética," *Estudios Centroamericanos* 368 (1979): 422.

83. Those murdered included Father Segundo Montes, director of UCA's Human Rights Institute.

84. This method of the Young Christian Workers influenced the 1968 Medellín Conference. The conference documents were structured as "Facts/Reflections/Recommendations."

85. The phrase "fusion of horizons" is taken from Hans-Georg Gadamer's *Truth and Method* (New York: Crossroad, 1984). Gadamer proposes an understanding of conversation in which we compare and contrast our various interpretations, thus fostering a common language and a fusion of horizons. This fusion of horizons changes all those involved in the conversation.

86. From "This Is a Hymn" by the Caribbean poet Lorna Goodison, *Heartease* (London/Port of Spain: New Beacon Books, 1988).

Chapter Five

∼

Rights-Holders or Beggars?

RESPONDING TO THE
POSTLIBERAL CRITIQUE

THIS BOOK HAS EXPLORED THE ENGAGEMENT between theology and the discourse of human rights, a dialectical boundary discourse of human flourishing, positioned in ethics as "protective marginality." As a dialectical language, human rights holds in tension the universal and the particular, the individual and the community, the religious and the secular, theory and practice. It draws attention to suffering and sets conditions and guidelines for the exercise of responsibility in response to the awareness of suffering.

Defining and locating human rights discourse as a boundary discourse prevents it from eclipsing other forms of ethical, political, or theological discourse. The argument here has been that human rights can never be the center and goal of ethics but are protective of the *more* of ethics to which we are called, as persons and communities, in a world of globalized moral concerns. Having briefly examined the use of human rights language in both secular and religious public discourse—in the Universal Declaration of Human Rights and in Catholic social teaching—we concluded that, despite significant foundational differences, there is a commonality that is more than pragmatic, and that each can benefit from a reciprocity of critique, particularly in terms of any lessening of what Charles Taylor calls "the impulse of solidarity."[1]

A theological trajectory was then traced from Rahner's concentration on the human, through Metz's political theology and post-Holocaust interruptive realism, to the emphasis on the rights of the poor in liberation theology. It is a complex trajectory that reflects critical, indeed skeptical, engagement with human rights discourse. However there is a clearly identifiable countertrajectory in contemporary theology, one that is marked less by dialectical engagement with secular thought than by dualism, a trajectory whose certainty has a rhetorical appeal in the complicated ethical and theological landscape of our time. It is a theological current in which a number of streams converge in a direction that is not so much post-Kant as post-MacIntyre, a movement identified by Jeffrey Stout as "the new traditionalism."[2]

Within this new traditionalism we can place John Milbank, Stanley Hauerwas, and Daniel M. Bell, aspects of whose theology will be critiqued in this chapter. Notwithstanding John Witte's observation that many "conservative Calvinists and other Protestants" still view human rights discourse "with suspicion, if not derision" because of its association with both Catholic natural law theories and Enlightenment secular individualism, we saw in chapter 2 that theological engagement with this discourse at the start of the twenty-first century is both ecumenical and diverse. Thus, this chapter is not intended to be the critique of a Protestant countertrajectory to the primarily, but not exclusively, Roman Catholic trajectory that was traced from Rahner to liberation theology.[3]

Contemporary philosophical impetus for the new traditionalism comes from the Augustinian Thomism of the Catholic philosopher Alasdair MacIntyre. Although both Hauerwas and Milbank are Protestant theologians, they are ecumenical in their engagement with the Christian tradition, and both have influenced younger Catholic and Protestant theologians including William T. Cavanaugh and Daniel M. Bell.[4] It must be acknowledged that Milbank, Hauerwas, and Bell differ from each other in their perspectives on a number of issues; nonetheless, it is legitimate to identify them as postliberal theologians united in their engagement with an Augustinian view of theological politics and in their opposition to human rights discourse, liberal democracy, and politics as "statecraft."[5] Although the streams in this trajectory are not homogeneous, three common characteristics can be identified: (a) a "disdain" for the secular, including human rights and liberal democracy, (b) a preference for theological politics over political theology, and (c) an impatience with the provisional.

"Disdain" for the Secular: The Refusal of a Rival

The word "disdain" may seem rather strong, but it is evocative of an attitude whereby engagement with the secular, thought to result in "accommodation," is considered a betrayal; indeed, lack of such "accommodation" is considered a measure of authenticity. The disdain is not uniform in all whom we are situating within this current, but it is fair to say that there is a commonality of perspectives wherein such disdain is either explicit or subtly implicit.

The notion of the "secular" can be spoken of in many senses, *saecularis* carrying meanings of worldly or temporal. Primarily understood as a system of thought that denies the spiritual and supernatural, it can be benignly viewed as a neutral influence, which opens a space for religious freedom. Although antitheistic secular humanism is not necessarily antireligious, forms of aggressive secularism deny public space to religion and perceive the secular as the sole voice of rationality. Secular hostility to religion may arise from ecclesiastical dominance or from the betrayal of trust by religious figures or institutions. For many political philosophers, including John Rawls, secularism is seen as a necessary precondition for liberal democracy.[6] Jeffrey Stout views ethical discourse in religiously plural modern democracies as secularized "only in the sense that it does not take for granted a set of agreed-upon assumptions about the nature and existence of God."[7] To advocate engagement with the secular is not to be deluded into believing that such engagement is always welcome.

This section will focus on the work of Anglo-Catholic John Milbank in the movement that describes itself as Radical Orthodoxy. It envisages a richer and more lucid Christianity, rooted in the tradition, as proponents select and interpret that tradition. Radical orthodoxy defines its endeavor—in opposition to the tradition born of Rahner, Metz, and liberation theology—as an attempt to "reclaim the world by situating its concerns and activities within a theological framework."[8] It proclaims a refusal of the secular, the implosion of whose logic is portrayed through the images of theme parks and cyberspace.[9] Positive secular witness, for example, that of *Médecins sans Frontières* or Wangari Maathai and the Green Belt Movement, finds no mention.

Politics is one of the concerns that secularism has claimed, and this movement wishes to resituate politics in relation to Trinity, Christology, Ecclesiology, and the Eucharist; the aim is to move toward a more incarnate, aesthetic, erotic, socialized, even "more Platonic" Christianity.[10] Any attempt to speak of politics apart from a theological framework is to ground it, literally, in nothing. The threads of the Platonic notion of "participation" are woven into a Christian framework offering a vision of participatory reality, the only alternative to which is the unacceptable reservation of a territory independent of God. Participation refuses any reserve of created territory "while allowing finite things their own integrity."[11] Attempted fidelity to the tradition born of Augustine commingles, in radical orthodoxy, with the influence of French poststructuralists, leading to a theological deconstruction of any positive meaning for the secular, coexisting with a placing of ultimate meaning only in the Church and its practice of Eucharist.[12]

Modern attempts to designate a social reality outside of our participation in God's consummating revelation in Christ are seen to rest in primal violence. The secular is a space carved out that is free from divine purpose, and the "will" is at the heart of secular anthropology, grounded as it is in the assumption that to *be* for a human being is to exercise power. John Milbank argues for the conception of social reality governed by the supernatural vocation of fellowship with God. He describes his project in *Theology and Social Theory* as an attempt to critically "radicalize" the work of Alasdair MacIntyre.[13] MacIntyre holds that over a period of four centuries *the acids of individualism* have "eaten into our moral structures, for both good and ill."[14] In chapter 1, we referred to MacIntyre's dismissal of human rights born of his conviction that modern ethical discourse is in ruins and his suggestion that the solution rests in a retrieval of the premodern tradition of the virtues, a tradition displaced by liberal modernity with its emphasis on rights. Belief in rights, for MacIntyre, is akin to believing in witches and unicorns.[15]

We began with Richard Rorty's description of the contemporary moral landscape as inhabited by "Kantians" and "Hegelians."[16] For MacIntyre, this landscape is inhabited by those who speak from within a number of surviving moralities, such as Aristotelianism, primitive Christian, democracy, or socialism, and "those who stand outside all of them," and between all these, no moral conversation is possible.[17] Because of the absence of a shared moral discourse that would facilitate explanation of our reasons for adopting or rejecting moral judgments, MacIntyre holds that our attempts at ethical conversation are reduced to assertion or manipulation, and the only possibility lies in the creation of small communities for virtuous living. The important question of what moral language one speaks echoes throughout the streams in this theological current, as does the formation of communities of virtue as an antidote to an age of moral confusion, fragmentation, and ontological violence.

PATHOS OF MODERN THEOLOGY

For Milbank, the pathos of modern theology in its liberal, liberation, and neoorthodox forms, lies in its humility, which leads it to submit to pagan or heretical traditions. He issues a challenge to theologians of this post-Kantian heritage who hand all exploration of social processes over to the social scientists and reserve for theology only that which secular reason leaves over. Theology is then operative only in what is left over after the anthropological, social, and political have been treated by secular reason. This challenge to theology not to rest content with only left-over space, particularly in public discourse, is one worth our attention. Milbank himself engages with post-Nietzschean social theorists who recognize the intrinsic quality of the mythic-religious dimension of social structures and challenge allegedly secular rationality, a recognition that Milbank says has bypassed theologians who still bow to the autonomy of the "self-torturing circle" of secular reason, a reason that is ultimately based on ontological violence and ethical nihilism.[18]

Milbank's thesis is that theology not only contains social theory, it is social theory; social theory is, in fact, rooted in theology, even if these roots are not acknowledged. He moves, in *Theology and Social Theory*, to a contemporary retrieval of Augustine's *De Civitate Dei*, drawing on its vision of two forms of human association, each of which posits a form of peace: the association of those who live according to the spirit and the community of those who live according to the flesh. Christianity is committed to the ontological priority of nonviolence, harmony, and peace, over those of anarchy, aggression, and war. Yet the oppositional figures in Milbank's narrative tend to be Augustine and Nietzsche, an opposition that contributes to the negative portrayal of power and the conflation of power and violence that seems to underline Milbank's thesis. Positive dimensions of power—the power to enable, empower, retrieve, repair, resist, protest, heal, challenge, envisage alternatives—dimensions of power that are at the heart of movements for human rights, social justice, and peace, are trapped in a Nietzschean hermeneutic.

Milbank narrates four "stories" about the complicity of secular reason with this ontology of violence. He discusses (a) liberalism: the liberalism of Locke, Hume, and Adam Smith; (b) positivism: from Malebranche to Durkheim and from Kant to Weber; (c) dialectics: Hegel and Marx, and the influence of the Hegelian and Marxist traditions on recent Catholic theology; and (d) difference: in postmodern philosophies.[19] For Milbank, these narratives of secular reason cannot, as *mythos*, be refuted, but "only out-narrated" by the Christian story.[20] This chapter is primarily concerned with his critique of the first narrative of liberalism.[21]

LIBERALISM: *DOMINIUM* AND RIGHTS

The invention of the secular was facilitated by the redefinition of Adam's *dominium* (Genesis 1:28) as "power, property, active right, and absolute sovereignty," a collapsing of personhood into a mastery that is uniquely "his own."[22] Liberalism is thus regarded by Milbank as a "Christian heresy."[23] The exaggerated "modern" idea of the human person, who as a rights-bearer can do what she wants with the property that is her own body, is traced to Locke and his treatment of the right to property: "Every man has a property in his own person." Freedom is realized in ownership and self-mastery; thus, human rights are perceived as property rights. The scholastic understanding of *dominium* is reduced to property rights, and individual rights become the starting point for political theory.[24]

Milbank's critique does not consider the matter of Locke's use of the term "property" in three distinct ways: the first refers to possessions or estates; the second, to lives, liberties, and possessions, referred to generally as "property"; the third is property as a synonym for right, meaning "having a right." The function of government is to protect the property of its citizens, and Locke presumably means this to include the broad sense of property and not simply estates, although he does not always make this clear.[25]

However to reduce the Lockean position on property to "self-ownership" is to overlook the fact that Locke also held that all people were the product of God's workmanship and were ultimately God's property.[26] Thus it is a crude summation to say that he simply saw the individual as "absolute Lord of his own Person and Possessions."[27] Self-ownership, in its most extreme form, excludes positive duties of assistance and undermines any concept of responsibility for the well-being of others, leaving the grim specter of a world of negative duties in which my only duty to the other is not to trespass on his property. Despite the fact that Locke understood self-sovereignty as limited by the law of reason, the Lockean individual, the morally sovereign bearer of rights, has been charged with initiating a language of possession or self-sovereignty that is found in the liberal tradition of rights and an objectification of the body that has only contributed to the diminishment of human dignity.

The critique of a reductionistic use of the term *dominium* marks an important caution and corrective, and it raises significant questions about the potential reduction of public interest—via Hobbes and Locke—to the securing of private interests of life, property, and contract. However Milbank never seems cognizant of the reality of dispossession that marks the relationship of many human beings both to the property (home and land) that they tenuously claim or seek to protect and to the question of the disposition of their own bodies: "the world tribe of the dispossessed."[28]

Theologians who engage with human rights discourse are also concerned about the reduction of the body to self-ownership and its subsequent use as a terminus in ethical discussion; nevertheless the "ownership" of one's person is not appropriately treated as a matter of philosophical disdain, especially for the children, women, and men whose bodies are owned in a cycle of abuse and exploitation. Modern *dominium* is a double-edged sword: it has the potential for self-destruction, and it also serves the appeal of the weak and powerless. A legitimate critique of this kind should not be used to render illegitimate the positive and protective functions of human rights.

Milbank's perspective is similar to that of the Italian philosopher Giorgio Agamben, who perceives modern politics as bankrupt. Both have common concerns about the inadequacy of the politics of rights and the dispositions of liberal democracy, and both articulate a desire to replace these through a retrieval of authenticity.[29] Milbank echoes Agamben's warning about the unclear distinction between totalitarianism and liberal democracy, a warning that does not appear unreasonable in the light of derogations from human rights by democracies fighting the "war on terror."[30] The granting of human rights is seen by Milbank—echoing Alain Badiou—as envisaging human persons *primarily* as "passive, if freely wandering animals, who *might* be victimized: the ban actually creates a space for its own violation."[31] However, between a portrait of rights as concerned with reductionistic self-ownership and that of rights as a facilitator of oppression, there is no sustained reflection on the protective dimension of rights or their connection to justice and human flourishing, nor are there any suggestions as to how those who are vulnerable can enjoy the kinds of protections and provisions that the discourse of human rights seeks to uphold.

TELOS

From the perspective of radical orthodoxy, the use of secular reason in the service of a religious vision of justice and peace is thwarted by the very limitations of secular reason. We live in an age of an exhausted and fragmented teleology, and the only way to recover a true sense of an ethical "end" is to revert to traditional Augustinian-Thomist, pre-Enlightenment ethics.[32] The desire and search for the "recovery" of a genuine notion of an ethical *telos* cannot but strike a chord with all who are concerned with the place of ethics in contemporary life, but what is difficult to accept is Milbank's notion that such an end is not possible without reverting to pre-Enlightenment thought. He speaks of a "transvaluation" of teleology in Christian ethics because the Church has far less definite ideas than the *polis* concerning the kind of individuals it desires to produce and the kinds of roles it wishes to foster. Christian universalism, Milbank says, surpasses the liberal teleology of Kant, Hegel, and Marx. It is true that Christian theology, with its focus on the Reign of God, moves in the realm of a *telos* that is ultimately gift, a gift that is already here and still yet to come. However, this gift necessitates concrete, mundane, and quotidian realization, and the bearers of the gift are not limited to those who speak in the Giver's name.

It is also true that a secular eschatology whose credo consists in the belief that human efforts alone can realize a new society is both inadequate and, ultimately, a heavy burden.[33] However, where do we place human hopes and desires for flourishing and well-being—both the desires we have for ourselves and those we have for others? Without equating salvation history with the secular goals of human rights and democracy, it must be acknowledged that the search for a true notion of an "end" surely cannot bypass the creative, provisional, and bruised goals that articulate the protection of the dignity of the human person and the integrity of the world in which we live. Currently, the United Nations is engaged with the effort "to free our fellow men, women and children from the abject poverty and dehumanizing conditions of extreme poverty to which more than a billion of them are currently subjected."[34] By 2015, all member states of the United Nations have pledged to meet the Millennium Development Goals (MDGs) of eradicating extreme poverty and hunger, achieving universal primary education, promoting gender equality, reducing child mortality, improving maternal health, combating disease, ensuring environmental sustainability, and developing a global partnership for development.

The goals are a fragile but nonetheless valuable measure of global solidarity. Again, this is not to suggest an equivalence between these goals and salvation history, nor to reduce salvation history to measurable UN goals, but to ask for a more serious consideration of "secular goals."[35] The MDGs are the end result of national, regional, and international consultations involving millions of people at various levels of society. They articulate a collective commitment to and responsibility for halving poverty by 2015. Achieving the MDGs will advance human rights, which are clearly perceived as carrying counterpart obligations on the part of others; the document speaks of the duty that leaders have to all people, especially the vulnerable and, in particular, children. Yet, the promotion of human rights appears within the "new traditionalism" represented by Milbank as an anti-*telos*.

Jesus forbade the prevention of any driving out of demons in his name by those who are not "one of us": "John said to him, 'Teacher, we saw someone driving out demons in your name, and we tried to prevent him because he does not follow us.' Jesus replied, 'Do not prevent him. There is no one who performs a mighty deed in my name who can at the same time speak ill of me'" (Mark 9:38–39).[36]

The efforts to halve poverty and free people from dehumanizing conditions are not goals articulated "in His name," but the spirit of the response of Jesus is a caution against the "refusal of a rival," against a totalitarian approach that prevents the recognition of goodness in the narratives, words, goals, and praxis of others.

ABSOLUTE CONSENSUS?

Milbank's rejection of the notion of universal reason or law contradicts rather than radicalizes MacIntyre. Milbank holds that all that can be done in response to chaos and conflict is to offer the virtue of nonviolent Christian practice that cannot be grounded in anything external to its own activity.[37] Only the Christian *mythos*—or possibly the Jewish—can save us.[38] He is critical of any ethics that assumes violence and tragedy as part of fundamental reality, but violence and tragedy *are* embodied and embedded as part of reality. The choice is not simply between "pure" ontological peace and Milbank's reading of Niebuhrian realism, or abandonment to secular reason. Does the theologian have to choose between bowing before the autonomy of secular reason and rejecting any validity in secular reason?

The answer is hinted at in the motif of "absolute consensus" that appears in a number of forms in Milbank's work. True society, he contends, implies absolute consensus. Any effort to conceive of justice that is concerned with "less than absolute *social* consensus and harmony"—including the fragile and negotiated consensus of human rights—"is less than justice."[39] The *ecclesia* seeks a more absolute consensus than that demanded by the *polis*, and ethical consensus is to be related to one's role within the Body of Christ.[40] The universality of the Church transcends the universality of the Enlightenment and surpasses the goals of freedom of Kant, Hegel, and Marx. It seeks a work of freedom that is none other than perfect social harmony, "a perfect consensus in which every natural and cultural difference finds its agreed place within the successions of space and time."[41]

Milbank does not outline how this absolute and perfect consensus, this total harmony of natural and cultural difference, is to be achieved. His view does suggest a participation in, rather than an eradication of, difference, but the overall framework of disdain for secular reason and the frequency of language of "overcoming" and "outnarrating" make it difficult to conceive how this absolute consensus can be achieved. The disdain for the secular taints this radical orthodoxy participatory vision of reality, for it is hard to envisage an authentic vision of participation that suppresses the notion of receptivity.[42] The Body of Christ, as true universality, does not negate other authentic forms of universality, yet Milbank's universality presents us with dramatic dualistic choices: paradisal community or hellish society? Leviathan or the Body of Christ?

The Church as a "community of virtue" will train its members teleologically, in contrast with a "community of rights," which Milbank caricatures as founded upon liberal indifference, agnosticism about the common good, and contentment with "mere mutual toleration and noninterference with the liberties of others."[43] Milbank does not consider the communitarian dimension of rights as found in the secular language of the United Nations and in the religious discourse of human rights, nor the *de facto* community of human rights groups characterized by a sense of responsibility and relationality; nor does he trouble to note the significant philosophical thought that has engaged with a positive notion of a "community of rights."[44]

The refusal of leftovers from the table of secular reason can be a challenge to theology to reclaim its place and to question the need for the secular to grant permission for religion to participate in public discussion. The difficulty that emerges is that the mode and kind of reclamation that are envisaged refuse not only the secular in its invidious forms; they refuse the secular in all its forms, including the ethical.[45] Politics and ethics are either grounded in this Christian Platonism or are self-founded and therefore reflective only of a will to power. This disdain for the secular represents a movement from contamination and complicated plurality, a seeking of illusory purity, which does not travel via the "interruptive realism" of Metz's theology or via the more comprehensive engagement with reality that marks liberation theology.

The persistent motif of ontological nihilism, transposed into various keys but nonetheless identifiable in all the streams in this theological current, points to a deeply disturbing and distrustful reading of the world beyond the Church. Distrustfulness of goodness in the form of the other is a pernicious doctrine and reinforces the powers of evil, violence, and oppression. In castigating modernity and its political face of liberal democracy as characterized by the virtual and the pseudo, a negative form of what is immutable and true, radical orthodoxy may end up policing a theology devoid of receptivity and removed from critique.

This book has engaged with the secular not naively or uncritically, not viewing the secular as the benign arbitrator of religious differences, but with a positive and realistic view of the potentiality of the secular. We have seen that to engage with human rights is not simply to "accommodate" political liberalism but to place before ourselves some critical questions of life, death, and flourishing, questions about embodied and embedded damage to individuals and communities. This engagement does not reduce theology to the falsely humble role of *ancilla* to political liberalism; rather, it calls theology to its rightful contribution to public discourse.

The intimate connection between our view of the secular and our operative pneumatology has been alluded to earlier: in relation to the implicit and inductive pneumatology of modern Catholic social teaching, which presumes the working of the Spirit in the hearts of men and women of goodwill and in human efforts to seek peace, human rights, justice, and reconciliation; in Rahner's "anonymous Christianity," which points to the goodness of "others" and the fecundity of God's grace; and, in the recognition of the importance of theological engagement with the reality of loss and damage that takes the forms of human rights violations and the provisional efforts forged from the conscience of humankind to respond to these violations.

The "new traditionalism" serves as an important, indeed, crucial, reminder that we are called to be more fully who we are and to witness to that identity in visible form. It reminds us that our biblical narrative and tradition are rich and resourceful, that we can too easily accommodate ourselves to the point of muting the distinctive theological contribution, that worship is our ultimate vocation, and that all virtue stems from and points to the fullness of persons, humanity, and creation, which worship both celebrates and anticipates. The difficulty lies in the supposition of this "tradition" that there is only one way to "reclaim the world and situate its concerns and activities within a theological framework."[46] What is the "cost" of such a reclaiming of the world in terms of solidaristic conversation and praxis? Ultimately, this current is constituted by a restricted role for the Spirit of God. It undermines God's role in the natural, and therefore questions the engagement of the Church there, of which engagement with human rights is one example.

Can the Spirit—Unrestricted Space—be placed in such a restrictive position?[47] In the Christian scriptures we have two accounts of the coming of the Holy Spirit after the Resurrection: John 20:19–23 and Acts 2:1–41. The first, at the conclusion of John's Gospel, speaks of redemption in embedded damage, a pneumatology born of resurrected woundedness and the Spirit breathed gently in the context of fear and locked doors. The account, in Acts of the Apostles, of the coming of the Spirit on the Feast of Pentecost offers a different narrative of diverse crowds, multilingual comprehension, a drama of fire and tongues. Both accounts speak of peace; neither points to the placing of the Spirit in a restricted position: The Spirit blows where it wills and is outside our control. The Spirit's unrestricted position means that the pain of division and exclusion is more keenly felt.

The gift of discernment enables theology to plot the movement necessary between the pathos of false humility of which modern theology stands accused by Milbank and the apathy of false pride, to which we can also be tempted. There is a time for boldness, and there is a time for respectful listening, for scripture reminds us that our manufactured exclusionary clauses are always open to exposure by surprising pneumatological incisions of witness by the excluded and the "disdained." The revelatory nature of these incisions, the way in which they enlarge our vision of the ethical, makes it difficult to sustain the theological position that the secular human condition is grounded solely in ontological violence and ethical nihilism. The Spirit is never limited to the chosen or the Church; thus, the desire for a located Christendom is forever doomed to be pneumatologically undermined.[48]

A Preference for a Theological Politics over Political Theology

Milbank suggests that what we need is "a new ecclesiology which would also be a post-political theology."[49] Both Milbank and Hauerwas, in different ways, attempt this new ecclesiology, which is simultaneously a postpolitical theology and a challenge to shape a different view of the nature of politics. Although both Milbank and Hauerwas are located within the "new traditionalism," it is important to note that Hauerwas is more theologically driven than most of radical orthodoxy, and he is less concerned with forging a comprehensive political system. His work has been described as "theological politics" as distinct from the European genre of "political theology." This definition of his work, which has been affirmed by Hauerwas himself, is premised on the belief that political theology makes the political struggle for emancipation the horizon in which the Church's theology and practice are interpreted, whereas theological politics makes the Church story the "counter story" that judges and interprets the world's politics.[50]

Hauerwas laments the loss of the political significance of the gospel. The aim of his writings is to challenge Christians to recover the politics of salvation through an emphasis on the significance of the Christian polity as he envisages it. This polity is characterized by separateness and a concern for the development of people of virtue. He aligns himself with political theology in its concern that the meaning and truth of Christian convictions cannot be separated from their political implications. He parts company with political theologians because he sees political theology as associating politics only with social change. For Hauerwas, *the* "political" question is "what kind of community the Church must be to be faithful to the narratives central to Christian convictions?"[51] It is a question that echoes in the work of Bell, Cavanaugh, and other former students of Hauerwas, so it is important to sketch the dimensions of his theological politics. Its traces are definitely evident in the work of Daniel M. Bell, whose perspective on liberation theology and human rights will be addressed later in this chapter.

POLITICS, DEMOCRACY, AND LIBERALISM

Although Hauerwas offers a number of definitions of Church, it is difficult to find an explicit definition of politics in his work. He suggests that he understands politics "in its traditional meaning as the art engaged in to achieve the good society"[52] and says, "genuine politics is about the art of dying."[53] Liberal democracy, built on a denial of death and sacrifice, cannot constitute genuine politics. Political science, the study of the politics of the nation-state, is "politics" only "in the most degraded sense."[54] Politics, for Hauerwas, has abandoned the conversation about the common good in a world where there is no commonality save "the desire to survive."[55] Only "friendship among good people" can help politics to discover true commonality.[56] In stressing that the politics of salvation is the only genuine politics, Hauerwas echoes Augustine's teaching that one cannot have a truthful politics without having as its *telos* the one alone who is worthy of worship.

The democratic society is composed simply of individuals who continu-ally live by bargaining, and the "narrativelessness" of liberal democracy means that it is heavily dependent on war for moral coherence. This is the political system, Hauerwas says, that the Church thinks it must favor because it allows for freedom of religion. He chides theologians who would seek to "rescue the liberal project either in its epistemological or political form."[57] The Church as an international society is placed over the nation-state, reminding us that the latter is not an ontological necessity.

Hauerwas questions the assumption that freedom and equality are the fundamentals of social life, describing them as abstract and inconsistent ideals that lack concrete grounding in the life of Jesus and that find their ultimate justification in violence. He believes that Christian enthusiasm for politi-cal involvement in the secular polity has made us forget the more profound political task of the Church. Christian efforts to promote peace and justice are characterized as social activism that works on the presumption that God is superfluous. Christian political engagement with those of other faiths is seen as ineffective by Hauerwas since there is no common idea of what justice might mean. Thus, Christians are seduced by Kantian, Rawlsian, and other secular conceptions of justice, inevitably leading them to abandon specific Christian convictions.

Hauerwas falls short of equating Gutierrez's "new man" of liberation the-ology with the Kantian "new man," but connects them both by saying that Gutiérrez has unwittingly underwritten "a sense of liberation at odds with the gospel."[58] He also suggests that we engage these secular theories because we desire power more than justice, "power to do good, to be sure, but power just the same."[59] The negative portrayal of power found in Milbank's work finds an echo in Hauerwas, although Hauerwas is responding more to Reinhold Niebuhr than to Nietzsche.[60] Unlike Milbank, Hauerwas does not view liberalism as a heresy, and methodologically his approach to critique is very different from Milbank's "outnarrating."[61] He does suggest that the liberal vision is a secular-ized version of the Christian vision of peace and intimates that liberalism has made a contribution in creating limitations on state power in order to encourage public cooperation for the maintenance of good community.[62]

Hauerwas offers some important critical perspectives on liberalism and its political forms, particularly his critique of the idealized nation state with its quasireligious status; however, these perspectives tend to be given and repeated without development. His view of liberalism and its political forms is matched by an oppositional ecclesiology: whatever liberal democracy denies or distorts, the Church is or potentially should be. The Church is presented as a company of friends, a commonality of memory and narrative, a place of true freedom, with an authentic pluralism born of a genuine tolerance of difference.

THE CHURCH AS *POLIS*

For Hauerwas, the first word Christians have to say about justice is "Church." The Church does not have a social ethic: the Church is a social ethic whose agenda regarding justice and peace should not be set by the world. The Church acts as a social ethic "first by having the patience amid the injustice and violence of this world to care for the widow, the poor, and the orphan. Such care, from the world's perspective, may seem to contribute little to the cause of justice, yet it is our conviction that unless we take time for such care neither we nor the world can know what justice looks like."[63]

Christians should be engaged in politics, but in the politics of the Kingdom that means standing in opposition to all politics based on coercion and falsehood, with the Church as a "contrast model" for all politics that know not God.[64] Hauerwas argues for the primacy of the virtues of patience and hope. Patience is the virtue needed to live "without control" in this violent world as a "peaceable people."[65] Such "living out of control" is simply a reminder that we are an eschatological people and that our promotion of justice in the world does not labor under what Hauerwas would describe as "the illusion of omnipotence," that is, that we do not assume that our job as Christians is to make history come out right. "As Christians, therefore, we seek not so much to be effective as to be faithful."[66] Christians are called to live as resident aliens, as "an adventurous colony in a society of unbelief."[67] It was through martyrdom, Hauerwas says, that the Church triumphed over Rome, but by later taking up Rome's project, Christians attempted to further the Kingdom of God through the power of this world, "an understandable but disastrous strategy that confused the politics of salvation with the idea that in the name of God Christians must rule."[68]

Hauerwas leaves us with a politics that requires friends at common table, with a common story, who participate in a "common adventure."[69] To envisage politics as anything other than this is to stray from his "determinative anti-Constantinian stance."[70] However, many of the struggles for justice, peace, reconciliation, and human rights, for example, the campaign to abolish the death penalty, can lead to enmity with those with whom one shares a common narrative born of baptism and friendship with those with whom table fellowship is not possible.

HUMAN RIGHTS

In his treatment of liberal democracy Hauerwas vacillates between concern that the state does not act in the formation of the good society and concern about the expansion of the state in the name of defense of individual rights.[71] There is no differentiation made between society and state, but Hauerwas speaks of the nation-state as a monolithic whole, paying no attention to the distinction between the various institutions of state and the people who operate them in the service of society. Where, then, would his theological politics place human rights? Hauerwas offers no substantive treatment of human rights, firing mostly passing shots in the midst of his battle against liberalism. One could, perhaps, deduce from his "positive" comments regarding liberalism that Hauerwas might admit to a certain advantage in the notion of rights. However, this deduction would be premature.

In the context of a paper on the question of the use of children in non-therapeutic clinical research, Hauerwas is critical of the use of rights discourse in matters regarding the family and children. Concerned about the placing of the question of this research in the context of the rights of children rather than the duties of parents and the role of their consent, Hauerwas rightly cautious about the reduction of the family to a collection of strangers and the distortion of familial relationships that could result from seeing children as an interest group needing "procedural safeguards in order to be protected from the undue advantage of other interest groups, including their parents."[72]

It is clear that a distorted view of rights as self-ownership can be particularly worrying when it is expressed in a reductive view of the child, the assumption that "the child must own himself."[73] Using the example of a child in an Orthodox Jewish community, Hauerwas contrasts the idea of a child having "rights" with that of the child having "standing" in a particular community. Although Hauerwas would hardly hold, with Richard Rorty, that such a child has no share in human dignity if that community is destroyed, there need not be direct conflict between the "standing" of a child in a family or community and the protective role of human rights.[74] Hauerwas does not adequately explore what protective role rights might need to play in the context of a child in danger, danger that lurks not just in the world of strangers but also in the locations of family and Church. Although in his response to the question of nontherapeutic clinical research on children Hauerwas says that he does not mean "to deny all cogency to rights language" and suggests that the intelligibility of claims to rights is dependent on their correlativity "to specific contexts and institutions" that serve a common good, he does not move from suggestion to elucidation.[75]

Hauerwas's basic position is that liberal societies resort to the language of rights because these societies are only concerned with procedural rules and not with substantive judgments. His basic claims about rights are: (a) rights-based procedural rules abstract individuals from their locations and roles, including their roles within the community called Church; (b) they are embedded in liberal ethics, an ethics based on the autonomous individual and a thin notion of human nature and human flourishing, disengaged from all contingent beliefs and practices; and (c) they are premised on a view of society as a gathering of strangers, devoid of common interests and goals, who only wish to relate to one another in terms of noninterference.

Not only does he associate rights with the worst excesses of liberal political philosophy, Hauerwas also decries human rights as an expression of natural law, an idea he caricatures as a Roman imperial concept developed to serve Christendom. He holds that a natural law position makes violence—in the form of coercion of those who do not agree with us—conceptually intelligible. The natural law, according to Hauerwas, functions too often to sustain Christian (and Western liberal democratic) presuppositions about society. It absolutizes the relative in the name of a universal that makes it more difficult for us to accept the existence of those who do not agree with us, for such differences "in principle should not exist."[76]

Hauerwas suggests that Christians today believe that they must act justly, not out of compassion for the poor but because the poor have rights.[77] Despite his earlier assertion that he did not deny all cogency to rights language, Hauerwas declares that he "does not believe in human rights"[78] as if they were a credo to be affirmed or denied, and he is very critical of Christian ethicists who, as he sees it, distance themselves from theology for the purpose of acting as agents of theoreticians of justice.[79] His theological politics disdains the language of rights and the company of those who engage with this discourse, but he offers no ecclesial substitute for the protections and provisions of human rights, reflection on what might be their role as a boundary discourse in ethics, nor receptivity to their potential contribution to substantive judgments about the common good.

ONLY ONE WAY OF SPEAKING?

Hauerwas offers little that is constructive to a discussion of justice save to say that true justice derives from our receiving what is not due to us. Although correct in his insistence that justice cannot come about through violence, his focus is on the violence that arises when we take up arms, to the neglect of institutional violence in its various forms. Justice remains ultimately the gift of the One who is Just; but the space in which most of the seeking for justice in the sociopolitical sphere occurs is seldom constituted simply by a choice between violence and receptivity to divine gift. It is a space marked by both present urgency *and* eschatological awareness, by consciousness of the fragility of human endeavor *and* confidence in divine fulfillment.

In stating that the Church acts out its social ethics through a caring that may contribute little to the cause of justice, Hauerwas continues what Joan Tronto calls the false dichotomy between care and justice.[80] Care, Tronto reminds us, includes all that we do to "maintain, continue and repair the world."[81] Care serves as "a critical standard" and thus has political implications. Working with those who are poor or marginalized teaches one to view the world through different eyes, allowing one to view anew how the world's social structures and political systems impact the underside of history, how policies and laws touch the lives of the weakest and the most vulnerable.

It is not possible to "care" without also speaking to the many legal, social, and political issues that confront one in the process of caring. A theological awareness of the interrelationship of care and justice, with all the ensuing political implications, does not necessarily consist in a betrayal of the narrative of the Christian community, nor an abandonment of the political significance of the gospel for the politics of power and violence. Such caring for justice requires the virtue of patience; there are, however, different kinds of virtuous patience. The patience of the theologian who struggles with faith seeking understanding in the political context cannot be the same expression of virtuous patience that is required of those who cry out from the depths of war and hunger and oppression.

There is a suggestion in Hauerwas's writings that when theologians engage with policies and strategies for insuring just distribution of resources they lose sight of the role of the Church as a separated community. It is true that policies should not be the prime concern of the theologian, but theological engagement with actual rather than abstract justice means that at times there is no avoiding the questions of policy and strategy. No theologian or Church community engaged in the promotion of justice could deny the importance of avoiding the illusion of omnipotence. If anything, theological involvement at the boundaries of theology and politics heightens one's awareness of contingency and of the fragility of even our best efforts to make a gospel-informed political response to poverty and violence. Thus, the temptation is not to labor under the illusion of omnipotence but to despair at impotence.

There is a consistent and disturbing correlation among power, efficacy, and violence in Hauerwas's work. He contends that as Christians we should seek not so much to be effective as to be faithful. "We need to break the self-deception that justice can only be achieved through a power and violence that seeks to assure its efficacy."[82] Why this dichotomy between efficaciousness and fidelity? Why the supposition that "results" intrinsically compromise Christian justice? The chasm between the *polis* of willful and envious assertion of power on the one hand and the Church as peaceful *alter-polis* on the other seems unbridgeable.

Hauerwas's "Kingdom politics," a politics of understanding rather than one of doing, involves the cultivation of people of virtue and "not simply any virtue, but the virtues necessary for remembering and telling the story of a crucified saviour."[83] We are told by Hauerwas that both oppressed and oppressor must be made aware that the cross determines the meaning of history. "The overriding political task of the Church is to be the community of the cross."[84] But what are the political implications of the cross determining history? How does the cross determine history at a time when many of us, by participation in the global economy, are simultaneously oppressed and oppressive?

However, the Church as the community of the cross cannot mark the outer boundaries of the crucified peoples of our world. The "*ecumene* of suffering humanity" is not just the locus of the Church's witnessing to the truth of Jesus crucified; it is also the locus of revelation of Christ, crucified and risen, whose self-identification with the least in Matthew 25 is disturbingly particular.[85] Of course, if there is an *ecumene* of suffering humanity, is there not also an *ecumene* of the responsive and responsible? The restricted ecclesiology of Hauerwas, like the restricted pneumatology of radical orthodoxy, finds it hard to place this responsive and responsible ethical *ecumene*. A restricted ecclesiology may provide a sanctuary from the world, but not a sanctuary for the world.

The challenge that Hauerwas and the concept of theological politics offer to Christians cannot be denied: the challenge to the Church to *be* a social ethic and a community of nonviolence. However, a theological politics, with its insistence on only one way of speaking, may leave us devoid of language for engagement with the "other" of religious faith or secular conviction. To be left without language at the boundaries of theology and politics in our contemporary world is surely a dangerous thing.

RIGHTS HOLDERS OR BEGGARS?

Hauerwas is critical of what he sees as Christian ethicists distancing themselves from theology for the purpose of acting as agents or theoreticians of justice and charges them with desiring to develop some "third language" for acting and speaking in public. He sees the effort to communicate across the boundaries of difference as a betrayal of what is distinctly Christian.

In the area of ethics, however, it is essential to seek fluency in the many ways human beings articulate concerns about justice and politics in our world. Seeking fluency for the purpose of comprehension and some kind of effective responsive action seems to render theologians guilty, in Hauerwas's eyes, of seeking what could be described as a kind of "ethical Esperanto," wherein God does not matter and natural law or other nontheological sources eliminate an appeal to the Christian narrative. The language of human rights, for example, is not a matter of substituting rights as a moral ideal for fidelity to God; rather, the language of rights often provides an entry into a larger discourse on justice, which, for the theologian, remains rooted in scripture and tradition.

In his response to Jeffrey Stout's *Democracy and Tradition*, a subtle but significant shift is evident in Hauerwas. He specifically mentions that "fresh conversation" is possible between those—like Stout—who support democratic aspirations and those—like Hauerwas himself—who are concerned that the discourse of liberal democracy and human rights excludes, or renders politically irrelevant, strong Christian convictions. Hauerwas acknowledges that Stout takes theology seriously and "his understanding of practical reason, the centrality of the virtues, as well as the democratic tradition not only makes it possible for us to have a conversation, but makes such a conversation imperative."[86]

Milbank completely disdains secular reason, but Hauerwas's disdain coexists with a view of the secular as a gift of humbling that can expose ecclesial pretensions and pride.[87] Hauerwas nuances his critique of liberalism and states that his ire is directed primarily against Christians who have confused Christianity with liberalism.[88] He clarifies that the justice which he considers "a bad idea" includes conceptions of justice that are abstracted "from the practices through which people discover the goods they have in common."[89] Hauerwas also concedes that although Stout's treatment of human rights is "filled with good sense," his underwriting of Annette Baier's linking of human rights discourse with an unwillingness to beg points to the locus of a profound disagreement with Stout and with those who appeal to the notion of human rights.

Baier holds that we are a rights-claiming and rights-recognizing species with a strictly limited willingness both to beg and to give to those who beg. "What we regard as ours by right is what we are unwilling to say thank you for."[90] She also notes that we are traders in rights, relinquishing old rights for new ones and circumscribing some in order to extend others. Baier's exposition of rights is nuanced and critical. She sees them as the tip of an iceberg of morality, supported by a submerged floating mass of cooperatively discharged responsibilities and socially divided labor, for the maintenance of the common goods, such as "civilized speech and civilized ways of settling disputes."[91] Thus, we only have rights as participants in a cooperative practice. In suggesting that "it takes more than rights to settle disputes about rights," Baier ultimately holds a position very similar to our conception of human rights as a dialectical boundary discourse, a protective marginality for human flourishing.

Rights are corrective of the effects of dominance without requiring begging or violence. There should be rights to whatever vital goods people can otherwise only get by violence or begging, that is, food, shelter, and help when we are not yet capable or are incapacitated.[92] Hauerwas, however, reminds Christians that prayer, that which most defines us, renders us "creatures that beg" and therefore can never be content with a politics that assumes "that we are fundamentally not beggars."[93]

The human person begging elicits strong emotions, for there is an almost intuitive protest at this antihuman posture. Often we find ourselves devoid of a hermeneutic to distinguish concocted and improbable stories from genuine tales of desperation: the addict-beggar, the trained child-beggar, the woman who begs with a child at her breast, the placard-bearing disabled beggar, all these manifestations of need or dysfunction in wealthier countries, and the hordes reduced to begging in the poorer cities of our world. It is a despised condition and an addictive one. To return to the touchstone of this book, the children who live and work on the streets: these have to unlearn the art of begging, and the withdrawal can be difficult, for they quickly understand the strange combination of fear and compassion that begging engenders in those who pass by. To advocate an end to the conditions that facilitate begging is not to be concerned with the transformation from beggar to rights holder but with the provision of what is needed so that each human being can be considered a locus of human flourishing. That surely is what Jesus responded to when he heard the insistent cries of Bartimeus whose poverty and blindness left him begging outside Jericho.[94]

Whereas Hauerwas is right to remind us that joyful dependence on God is the proper disposition of the Christian, and that mutual dependence is the hallmark of a Christian community, his presupposition that this renders any politics of human rights incompatible with Christianity could, perhaps, only be held by someone who has never had to stretch out his hand for food, shelter, or safety. "A rights holder is more dignified than a beggar. This is no small consideration."[95]

Impatience with the Provisional

The third characteristic of this postliberal theological current, with its disdain for the secular and preference for a theological politics, is impatience with the provisional, that is, with language and praxis that moves in the realm of the contingencies and provisionality of the historical. Rather than seeing the provisional as the attempt toward concrete, if imperfect, realization of a *telos*, and understanding ethics as a pilgrim practice oriented toward ends, it adopts a reductive view of the provisional, which may lead to a totalizing Christian theological framework.

One example of this impatience with the provisional is Daniel M. Bell's assessment of Latin American liberation theology's vision of Christian resistance to global capitalism. Bell's *Liberation Theology after the End of History* is shaped by study with Stanley Hauerwas and engagement with the radical orthodoxy of John Milbank with his conclusions particularly influenced by the former's theological politics and the near equivalence of power and violence in Milbank.

Bell's basic thesis is that authentic liberation necessitates an understanding of capitalism primarily as a perverted "technology of desire" that reorientates all human goals around "the golden rule of production for the market" that must be replaced by an "ecclesial technology of desire," an alternative political model, characterized by forgiveness, even when this entails the refusal to cease suffering.[96] Although not unsympathetic to liberation theology, Bell critiques its focus on justice and the reduction of justice to "guarantor of rights," a less nuanced reading of liberation theology than was outlined in chapter 4. Indeed, Ivan Petrella suggests that Bell's radical orthodoxy engagement with liberation theology "is merely another example of the cooption previously attempted by the Vatican," a cooption in which the only thing left of liberation theology is its terminology.[97]

Bell is critical of liberation theologians' attention to the state as an agent of transforming "savage capitalism," but he also views their support for civil society as deluded, for it too is an instrument of the regnant capitalist order, forming desire in its own image.[98] Seeming to accept, without challenge, Franz Hinkelammert's bleak analysis of the post-1989 triumph of capitalism and Francis Fukuyama's contentious assessment of the end of history, Bell offers a challenging perspective on the tyranny of capitalism under which we live: "A savage capitalism, repressive states, excluded populations, madness, sacrifice, and the absence of alternatives."[99]

Although Bell's highlighting of "savage capitalism" and "excluded populations" rings true in light of the human suffering that has always persisted on the underside of capitalism and the new suffering caused by the global economic downturn, his reference to the "absence of alternatives" is the most disturbing. Bell states that few liberationists are willing to admit that there are no alternatives.[100] Reminiscent of Milbank's position that all that can be done in response to chaos and conflict is to offer the virtue of nonviolent Christian practice, Bell says that all that can be done is to offer forgiveness.

Part of the impatience with the provisional that is characteristic of this theological current is a tendency to demonize the state or, at the very least, to take demonic examples of state violence and oppression as paradigmatic of the very nature of the nation-state. For Bell, the state is the instrument of this savage capitalism and therefore must be nonviolently abolished. He contends that one should not pursue justice and fight for the rights of the poor and excluded within the citizenship activity of "State" space but, instead, engage in the building of the Church as a "counter-*polis*," an authentic political space. He posits a reductionist reading of both Catholic social teaching and liberation theology as basically theories of rights: "Justice is fundamentally a matter of rendering to each what they are due in accord with their rights."[101] Apart from a few echoes of what could be described as classic antiliberalism, Bell does not offer a substantive treatment of human rights.

For him, liberation theology only attends to doing justice, but more is needed to repair the damage of savage capitalism. Justice as protector of rights is not sufficient for Christian resistance to capitalism, for it is not concerned with the formation of persons in such a way as to redirect their desire. Forming persons to respect rights will not repel capitalism. Liberation theology, he says, has too thin an account of the common good. Justice as the guardian of rights remains problematic because capitalism is quite compatible with such justice, even when it focuses on the rights of the poor.[102] The liberationist conception of justice, according to Bell, forms desire to be acquisitive just as capitalism does, encouraging the poor to be acquisitive, and because there is an emphasis on the distributive dimension, it may actually exacerbate conflict and violence in the name of restoring violated rights. "The liberationists' preference for justice beyond forgiveness only postpones the onset of the terror that plagues justice and ensures that its efforts to resist capitalism fail."[103] Bell fails to comprehend that one of the potential fruits of the preferential option for the poor, for the theologian and those who are not themselves poor, is precisely the reordering of one's desires because of the experience of solidarity with those of the underside of capitalism.

Bell contrasts what he perceives as justice as guarantor of rights with Aquinas's unitive understanding of justice, which he suggests forms desire in such a way that one could forgo what one is due for the sake of the common good. However, it is difficult to envisage a notion of the common good that would require the denial of basic rights. As has been stressed, the denial of what is due, particularly in the case of child poverty, can damage the capacity to forego for the sake of others. Bell suggests that justice can only be redeemed by going beyond itself, or perhaps, biblically prior to itself, that is, to something that is neither the classical conception of *suum cuique* nor assimilable with the modern discourse of rights. Contrary to the liberationist appeal to the resurrection of Christ as a victory of justice, Bell argues that the resurrection is an overcoming that is something other than the terror of justice conceived as *suum cuique*.[104]

Only forgiveness, Bell contends, will transcend this terrorism of justice: "The gift of forgiveness leaves behind the agony of rights and opens a peaceful path of reconciliation by restoring desire in its original mode of donation."[105] Bell suggests that the poor themselves have moved beyond the liberationist view of justice, by offering forgiveness to their oppressors and not demanding what is their due. This is the stance of the crucified people who point to a "justice beyond justice," beyond *suum cuique* and human rights discourse.

Forgiveness is the condition of possibility for this justice "beyond" justice, and forgiveness necessitates setting aside claims to rights and the instruments that are usually invoked in the name of warding off suffering and combating sin. Unjust suffering that is a consequence of sin is "defeated precisely by its being borne."[106] The gift of forgiveness is resistance in the form of the bearing of sin. Bell does suggest that this bearing of sin is not simply the abandonment of the power of justice (nor, for the forgiven oppressor, the renunciation of the power of privilege) but is a bearing of the cross in the hope of bearing suffering away.[107] However, it is difficult to see how suffering can be borne away in such an oppositional positioning of forgiveness and justice.[108]

Milbank posited that there is only one way to respond to oppressors: "to act as if their sin was not there by offering reconciliation."[109] What does the refusal to cease suffering mean to the child who lives on the streets, to parents who cannot feed their families, or to the prisoner of conscience? A less oppositional view is offered by Jon Sobrino who reflects on forgiveness as a paradox of destruction and love: forgiving reality as destroying the sin of poverty and oppression and the personal forgiveness of the sinner.[110] The integration of this tension between love and destruction is a work of love, for the purpose of forgiveness is not to heal guilt but to come into communion.

The poor and the victims of the world can also act as historical mediators of a forgiveness that is acceptance. However, far from advocating an augmentation of suffering, liberation theology understands itself specifically as a praxis of elimination of unjust suffering inflicted by others. "In the presence of such suffering, theology must understand itself as an intellectual exercise whose primary purpose is to eliminate this kind of suffering. Briefly stated, suffering in today's world means primarily the suffering of people who are being crucified, and the purpose of theology is to take this people down from the cross."[111]

Sobrino stresses that to be merciful is to struggle for justice and that mercy is not simply the traditional "works of mercy" but, rather, the basic structure of our response to the victims of the world. It is not simply indignation at injustice or violations of human rights, but to be merciful is to make someone else's pain our own and to allow that pain to move us to respond.[112] He insists that there are not just wounded individuals but also crucified peoples, and mercy means doing everything possible to bring them down from the cross. Bell interprets Sobrino's position as "mercy understood as forgiveness trumps justice."[113] However, Sobrino makes it clear that to respond with mercy is to be passionately concerned with taking the crucified people down from the cross, and this means working for justice, "which is the name love acquires when it comes to entire majorities of people unjustly oppressed."[114]

If injustice is that which damages the human person and human communities, then forgiveness is a constitutive feature of any restorative process. However, Bell, by disregarding both justice as *suum cuique* and the notion of human rights, burdens forgiveness with the repair of all the embedded damage to which we have referred.

As we have seen in the discussion of the ethics of memory in chapter 3, victims of serious human rights violations may not be fully healed simply by the provision of what is lacking or the removal of sources of oppression. Forgiveness, however, does not exclude the need for acknowledging violations and naming injustice, nor does justice exclude forgiveness and reconciliation, which are ultimately gift and not ethical stances that we can mandate or use to outnarrate the provisional.

If some liberation theologians are open to criticism of a collapsed eschatology, then Bell and those working within this radical orthodoxy current run the risk of an overextended ecclesiology that is inevitably insensitive to the pneumatological stirrings for alternatives to the savagery of capitalism evident in all manner of faces and places. Whereas the early Church engaged in a daring use of imperial language to speak of the lordship of Christ, thus challenging the authority of the emperor, and in courageous and imaginative breaking of social boundaries, there does not seem to be any scriptural or patristic justification for envisaging Church as an *alter-polis* in the total way that this current suggests.

Bell's description of our age as devoid of alternatives to savage capitalism—except for the true politic of the ecclesia—is bleakly dualistic. On a practical level, the suggestion that the Works of Mercy, as corporate and communal activities, can somehow constitute an alternative to capitalism fails to address questions of production and distribution. On the level of constructive social and political discourse, the idea that politics parodies the true political space that is the Church, runs the risk of ridiculing concrete, albeit inadequate, efforts on behalf of justice and peace, a ridiculing that could only come from a place of comfort in the academy or the Church. What happens when those with—or those striving to shape—rightly ordered desires abandon the craft of politics?

Statecraft, of course, is limited and flawed. It is clear that many of the conditions essential for human flourishing, conditions such as loving relationships, family stability, and cohesive communities cannot be guaranteed by laws or human rights instruments, but neither can they be guaranteed by ecclesial politics. There is a flourishing beyond human rights and classical *suum cuique*, but this is not possible by passing completely over any notion of justice as rendering each person his or her due. It seems not only intellectually problematic but also politically dangerous to suggest that one does not need to recognize legitimate claims nor acknowledge violations of these claims. Our placing of human rights as a boundary discourse in ethics avoids the reduction of the fuller dimensions of justice to the protection of human rights, yet it reminds us that we cannot bypass these concrete issues of protection and provision in our search for human flourishing.

Conclusion

Like the "new traditionalists" we also know—with Augustine—that our justice is not true justice, our community is not true community, our virtue is not true virtue.[115] However, this does not necessitate a retreat to the fundamentally antipolitical strain of this current: no participation in political processes, no place for alliances or coalitions, rejection of all statecraft and all provisional conceptions of justice, of which human rights is the most despised example. Is everything that is outside perfection "sin"? Eschatology renders all efforts in the pursuit of justice, peace, and reconciliation provisional; but the Word made flesh renders that provisionality crucial.

To accept the provisionality of our positions and responses is also to accept that we now only see in a mirror dimly: our judgments are not final, but nonetheless important; our knowledge, even with the aid of the Holy Spirit, is imperfect. The radical orthodoxy current, with its disdain for the secular, including human rights, its preference for a theological politics, and its impatience with the provisional, marks a quest for perfection that bypasses the messiness of the contingent and the historical. It tempts a placing of theology in the realm of the pure, the permanent, and the certain, a realm that seems more akin to the rigorist elitism of Donatism than to the latitudinal "mixed body" of Augustine's City of God.[116]

As with any other human society, the Church is tinged with sin and contains within itself both the *Civitas Dei* and the *Civitas terrena*, for only at the end of time will the two cities be distinct: "mingled together from the beginning till the end... until they are separated by the final judgment."[117] Augustine thus leaves the relationship between the two cities ambiguous.[118] The depth of this ambiguity is overlooked by the "new traditionalism," which, without denying the sinfulness of the Church, overextends ecclesiology and thereby neutralizes the Augustinian position that the question of the distinction of the cities is ultimately an eschatological one.[119]

These new traditionalists are united in their engagement with an Augustinian view of theological politics; however their disdain for the secular results in a neglect of the ethical possibilities within the overlapping space shared by the "sacred" of the *Civitas Dei* and the "profane" of the *Civitas terrena*. Robert Markus identifies this Augustinian intermediate realm as the "secular," a realm that is not neutral, but "ambivalent": "capable of being linked either with damnation or with salvation, depending on the purpose to which it is harnessed."[120] Where Milbank equates salvation from sin with "liberation from all structures belonging to the *saeculum*," a more positive understanding of the overlapping cities sees that salvation history can be worked out within the overlap.[121]

It is precisely within this overlap of cities that theological engagement with human rights—with its positive discourse and with the reality of violations— takes place. Defenders and violators of human rights inhabit both cities. The justice that is pursued in the overlap by the just pilgrims of both cities may not be *vera iustitia*, but concerns about protection, provision, and governance, concerns even of the State, mark an attempt at justice of a kind. Human rights is a discourse for the provisional time, in the overlapping space of the intermediate realm, an effort "to make it the best city possible" knowing it is not a lasting city.[122] Human rights, in this context, could be interpreted as a boundary discourse of *vera iustitia*.

Notes

1. Taylor, *A Catholic Modernity?* 26. See reference to this in chapter 1. Taylor uses the phrase with specific reference to the impulse of solidarity needed to "transcend the frontier of Christendom itself."

2. Jeffrey Stout, *Democracy and Tradition* (Princeton/Oxford: Princeton University Press, 2004), Chapter 5: "The New Traditionalism," 118–39.

3. Witte, *The Reformation of Rights*, 22.

4. Both of these former students of Hauerwas have contributed to radical orthodoxy publications.

5. Daniel Bell describes the "new traditionalism" as an "emergent tradition" but with the caveat that it "implies no prophecy about the tradition's future status as dominant." "State and Civil Society," in Peter Scott and William Cavanaugh, eds., *The Blackwell Companion to Political Theology* (Oxford: Blackwell, 2004), 423–38, at 437, n. 1.

6. Rawls's views on the relationship between religion and politics are not static. At the end of his late essay, "The Idea of Public Reason Re-Visited," Rawls notes the difference between *A Theory of Justice* (1971) and *Political Liberalism* (1993): "This kind of well-ordered society (of *A Theory of Justice*) contradicts the fact of reasonable pluralism, and hence, *Political Liberalism* regards that society as impossible." He contends that there need be no war between religion and democracy, building on a differentiation between "political liberalism" and "Enlightenment liberalism." In his earlier work, public reason is envisaged as a comprehensive liberal doctrine, whereas his later position presents public reason as "a way of reasoning about political values shared by free and equal citizens that does not trespass on citizens' comprehensive doctrines so long as those doctrines are consistent with" a democratic conception of justice. *The Law of Peoples with "The Idea of Public Reason Revisited*," 131–80, at 179–80. See mention of Rawls's *Theory of Justice*, in chap. 4.

7. Stout, *Democracy and Tradition*, 99.

8. Milbank, Pickstock, and Ward, *Radical Orthodoxy*, 1.

9. Ibid., 1, 3, 14.

10. The other concerns are aesthetics, sex, the body, personhood, visibility, and space. Ibid., 1–3.

11. Ibid., 3.

12. The movement reminds us of the necessity of continually seeking the social and political implications of liturgy as participation in a Divine community, but William Cavanaugh's development of this seems to lead to what I would term a "liturgical supersession of the political." In *Theopolitical Imagination*, Cavanaugh advocates a "Eucharistic Counter-Politics," an anarchic challenging of the false order of the state. He presents the modern state as an alternative soteriology to that of the Church, critiquing the "fable" that liberalism was born of the cruelties of the Wars of Religion in the sixteenth and seventeenth centuries. Without

denying that Christians did kill each other over matters of dogma, Cavanaugh emphasizes that temporal rulers directed these doctrinal conflicts to secular ends. Although this reading of the birth of liberalism offers an important corrective to simplistic comparisons between irenic liberalism and bellicose religion, the conclusions that Cavanaugh draws with regard to the state are disturbing. His politics rests on demonizing the state or at best viewing the function of the state merely as that of preventing individuals from interfering with each other's rights. Cavanaugh also dismisses the distinction between state power and civil society, thus reducing the notion of *res publica*, saying that there is no real free space outside this hegemonic state. He is correct to remind us that the Eucharist generates the Body of Christ, a body that is not reducible to simply another voluntary association of civil society, but his seeming presumption that the Eucharist leads, almost *ex opere operato*, to authentic politics is troubling.

13. Milbank, *Theology and Social Theory*, 5. Milbank is also critical of aspects of MacIntyre's work, in particular his more positive view of the ethics of Ancient Greece.

14. MacIntyre, *A Short History of Ethics*, 266.

15. MacIntyre, *After Virtue*, 67.

16. Richard Rorty, "Postmodernist Bourgeois Liberalism," in *Objectivity, Relativism, and Truth*, 201.

17. MacIntyre, *A Short History of Ethics*, 266, 268. Macintyre's philosophy, in trying to restore virtue to its important position in ethical concern, often results in a dichotomous fracturing of ethical discourse.

18. Milbank, *Theology and Social Theory*, 434.

19. Milbank suggests that American sociology is a form of secular policing whose secret purpose is to ensure that religion remains conceptually at the margins, "both denied influence, and yet acclaimed for its transcendent purity." *Theology and Social Theory*, chap. 5, "Policing the Sublime: A Critique of the Sociology of Religion," 101–43, 109.

20. Milbank contrasts his approach with that of MacIntyre, who "wants to *argue* against this stoic-liberal-nihilist tendency, which is 'secular reason,'" *Theology and Social Theory*, 330.

21. See references to Milbank's critique of Rahner and Metz in chapters 2 and 3.

22. Milbank, *Theology and Social Theory*, 12–15. This redefinition of original *dominium* is accompanied, according to Milbank, by a voluntarist substitution of a theology of participation by a theology of will. On such a redefinition and substitution, modern politics is founded.

23. Ibid., 23, 399.

24. Milbank does not consider that before Locke's engagement with questions of rights, property, and personhood, Francisco de Vitoria, of the sixteenth-century Salamanca School, raised questions about the right to own and the right to rule in the context of Spanish America. Vitoria, in *Relectio de Indis*, asked whether the Amerindians had any true *dominium*, public and private, before the arrival

of the Spaniards. Conscious of the interconnection of freedom, self-mastery, and inherent human right, Vitoria also argued "that all human beings—sinners, infidels, children, even natural slaves as [he] understood the term—could be bearers of rights and did possess certain natural rights." Brian Tierney, *The Idea of Natural Rights*, 256–72, at 271.

25. Locke, *Two Treatises of Government*, Peter Laslett, ed. Hume is critical of Locke's conflation of property itself with the right to property, observing that the relation of the person with the material of his or her labor cannot be the foundation of the right to property. For Hume, property was not a natural right but existed by convention: *A Treatise of Human Nature* (London: Fontana, 1970–72), III. ii 1, 2. Locke held that use and appropriation are sanctioned and limited by the law of nature; the right to appropriate is matched by the duty of responsible use. Limits of use, waste, and sufficiency are part of the Lockean framework, but Rousseau employed a more stringent qualification of property rights, saying that they were always subordinate to the claims of community.

26. "For Men being the Workmanship of the one Omnipotent, and infinitely wise Maker . . . are his Property, whose Workmanship they are, made to last during his, not one another's Pleasure." *Second Treatise*, II: 6.

27. Ibid., IX: 123.

28. From "This is a Hymn" by Lorna Goodison, *Heartease* (London/Port of Spain: New Beacon Books, 1988), quoted at the end of chapter 4.

29. Agamben, *Means without Ends*. Agamben reflects on the corrosion of traditional political juridical categories and the need to "abandon decidedly, without reservation, the fundamental concepts through which we have so far represented the subjects of the political (Man, the Citizen and its rights, but also the sovereign people, the worker, and so forth) and build our political philosophy anew starting from the one and only figure of the refugee." "Refugee" is a "border concept" that radically calls into question the principles of the nation state and the future of the concept "citizen" (16).

30. The decision by the administration of President George W. Bush to engage in coercive interrogation—defined under international law as torture—of prisoners held on suspicion of terrorist activity is outlined in *The Torture Papers*. This collection of "torture memos" and reports written by U.S. government officials details a systematic decision to deconstruct rules and legal constraints against torture, the result of the belief that any means are justified in the fight against terror. The category of "unlawful combatants," applied to those captured in Taliban Afghanistan (designated a "failed state"), deprived them of their rights under the 1949 Third Geneva Convention on the Treatment of Prisoners of War. Decisions regarding the balance of security and freedom are extremely difficult ones, but torture has neither moral justification nor practical usefulness.

31. *Being Reconciled: Ontology and Pardon* (London: Routledge, 2003), 97.

32. "In the true notion of an 'end,' we can recognize that certain actions have a tendency to produce certain results." Milbank, *The Word Made Strange*, 251.

33. Tony Vaux reflects on the inadequacy of secular eschatology, especially the unlimitedness and "superficial optimism" of the concept of humanitarian concern. "The aid worker is condemned to live with dissatisfaction and uneasiness." He also explores the relationship between altruism and power and discusses both the dangers of a strictly human rights approach to aid and the worrying ascendancy of Western governments over aid agencies. *The Selfish Altruist: Relief Work in Famine and War* (London and Sterling, VA: Earthscan Publications Ltd., 2001).

34. United Nations Development Programme, *Human Development Report 2003: Millennium Development Goals: A Compact among Nations to End Human Poverty* (New York: Oxford University Press, 2003). See the UN Millennium Project Report on the implementation of the goals: "Investing in Development: A Practical Plan to Achieve the Millennium Development Goals," issued January 17, 2005, which offers a concrete and utterly affordable plan. This report outlines specific steps toward implementation, acknowledges that there are various human motivations involved in the struggle to end extreme poverty, motivations that include human rights and religious values, but highlights that "all that is needed is action." "The world community has at its disposal the proven technologies, policies, financial resources, and, most importantly, the human courage and compassion to make it happen" (Professor Jeffrey D. Sachs, director of the Millennium Project Report, Preface). Report available online at www.undp.org [accessed November 25, 2008].

35. This is not to deny that certain forms of secular reason are strictly antiteleological, i.e., in the rejection of the notion of a final end or *summum bonum*.

36. *New American Bible* (1990). See also Luke 9:49–50.

37. Milbank, *Theology and Social Theory*, 279.

38. See Milbank, "The End of Dialogue," in *Christian Uniqueness Reconsidered: The Myth of a Pluralistic Theology of Religions*, edited by Gavin D'Costa (Maryknoll, NY: Orbis, 1990), 174–91. Against Raimundo Panikar's desire to fuse neo-Vedantic pluralism with Christian Trinitarianism, Milbank argues, "a postmodern position that respects otherness and locality, and yet at the same time still seeks the goals of justice, peace, and reconciliation, can only, in fact, be a Christian (or possibly a Jewish) position" (176).

39. Milbank, *Theology and Social Theory*, 402.

40. Ibid., 416.

41. Milbank, *Word Made Strange*, 154–55, at 154.

42. Without digressing into the complexity of notions of "participation" and "receptivity," I simply raise the concern that a theology of participation, which emphasizes participation in and through difference, can delineate with such certainty the bounds of truth, goodness, and light, and, in so doing, seem to leave no openness to the possibility of receiving from outside these self-delineated bounds.

43. Milbank, *Word Made Strange*, 154.

44. In *The Community of Rights*, Alan Gewirth challenges the adversarial relation between rights and community, arguing for a community of rights as "a society

whose government actively seeks to fulfill the needs of its members, especially those who are most vulnerable, for the freedom and well-being that are necessary goods of human agency." He holds that when rights are properly understood, they entail a communitarian conception of human relations, "relations of mutual assistance, social solidarity, and important kinds of equality." Gewirth proposes a liberal democratic welfare state, with strong emphasis on the role of government, but also recognizing the importance of civil society independent of the state, both emphasizing the solidaristic characteristics of community as required by the mutuality of rights. *The Community of Rights*, 5, 6, 350, 357.

45. "Christian morality is a thing *so* strange, that it must be declared immoral or amoral according to all other human norms and codes of morality." Milbank contrasts five marks of morality (reaction, sacrifice, complicity with death, scarcity, and generality) with the five notes of the gospel (gift, end of sacrifice, resurrection, plenitude, and confidence). Milbank, *Word Made Strange*, chapter 9, "Can Morality Be Christian?" 219–232, at 219.

46. Milbank, Pickstock, and Ward, *Radical Orthodoxy*, 1.

47. "The wind blows where it wills, and you can hear the sound it makes, but you do not know where it comes from or where it goes; so it is with everyone who is born of the Spirit." John 3:8.

48. Although those promoting radical orthodoxy would deny that they wish to return to the world of Christendom, and Bell and Cavanaugh are very critical of the project of "New Christendom" that is reflected in the work of Jacques Maritain, it is difficult not to see in their own extremely oppositional project of reclamation another search for some sort of located Christendom. Any direct identification of Church and *Polis* risks this.

49. Milbank, *Theology and Social Theory*, 228. Milbank makes this comment as an introduction to his critique of the "Rahnerian version of integralism," that he suggests was pursued by political and liberation theology.

50. Arne Rasmusson offered this definition in *The Church as Polis: From Political Theology to Theological Politics as exemplified by Jürgen Moltmann and Stanley Hauerwas* (Lund: Lund University Press, 1994), 188. Rasmusson sees political theology as a form of mediation between Christianity and modernity, a mediation that necessitates a positive view of the secular. Hauerwas affirms Rasmusson's perspective on his work: see *In Good Company: The Church as Polis* (Notre Dame, IN: University of Notre Dame Press, 1995), 6. A detailed challenge to this articulation of the difference between political theology and theological politics is outside the scope of this work, but it must be stressed that all authentic political theology is concerned with the relationship between Christian faith and the sociopolitical order, with the reading of reality in the light of the Reign of God.

51. Hauerwas, *A Community of Character*, 2.

52. Stanley Hauerwas, *Vision and Virtue: Essays in Christian Ethical Reflection* (Notre Dame, IN: University of Notre Dame Press, 1981), 236.

53. Hauerwas, *After Christendom?* 44.
54. Stanley Hauerwas, *Dispatches from the Front: Theological Engagements with the Secular* (Durham and London: Duke University Press, 1994), 10.
55. Hauerwas, *After Christendom*, 29.
56. Hauerwas, *Dispatches from the Front*, 10.
57. Hauerwas, *After Christendom?* 35.
58. Ibid., 53. Hauerwas suggests that genuine politics is about the art of dying. The extensive martyrology of the Church in Latin America counters the charges of reductionism that both Hauerwas and Milbank level at liberation theology.
59. Ibid., 60.
60. Hauerwas seeks to counter Reinhold Niebuhr's contention that love without power is ineffective, whereas power limits the possibilities of the realization of love.
61. See Stanley Hauerwas, "Creation, Contingency, and Truthful Nonviolence: A Milbankian Reflection," in *Wilderness Wanderings: Probing Twentieth Century Theology and Philosophy* (Boulder, CO/Oxford: Westview, 1997), 188–98. "In my own work I have tried to chip away at liberalism one piece at a time. Milbank, however, may be right that you can only counter a totalizing narrative with another narrative that is equally totalizing, but I fear that in the process the Gospel cannot help but appear as just another 'system' or 'theory'" (190, n. 7). However, it is clear that although Hauerwas resists the temptation to "outnarrate," there is a totalizing trend in his homogeneous use of the terms "Church" and "world." Hauerwas places great emphasis on the call to Christians to "endure," and he suggests that this emphasis marks a most "profound difference" between his work and that of Milbank, saying that the latter "wants to win." *Performing the Faith*, 217.
62. Hauerwas, *Community of Character*, 100ff.
63. Stanley Hauerwas, *The Peaceable Kingdom: A Primer in Christian Ethics* (Notre Dame, IN/London: University of Notre Dame Press, 1983), 99.
64. Hauerwas, *Community of Character*, 84.
65. Hauerwas, *The Peaceable Kingdom*, 103.
66. Ibid., 104.
67. Stanley Hauerwas and William H. Willimon, *Resident Aliens: A Provocative Christian Assessment of Culture and Ministry for People Who Know That Something Is Wrong* (Nashville: Abingdon Press, 1993), 49.
68. Hauerwas, *After Christendom?* 39.
69. Hauerwas, *Community of Character*, 13.
70. Hauerwas, *Dispatches from the Front*, 8.
71. Compare, for example, *Vision and Virtue*, 234, with *After Christendom?* 123–25, and *Resident Aliens*, 33–34.
72. Stanley Hauerwas, "Rights, Duties, and Experimentation," in *Suffering Presence: Theological Reflections on Medicine, the Mentally Handicapped, and the Church* (Notre Dame, IN: University of Notre Dame Press, 1986), 125–41, at 127. This

chapter was a paper prepared for the U.S. National Commission for the Protection of Human Subjects of Biomedical and Behavioral Research.

73. Ibid., 140.

74. "A child found wandering in the woods, the remnant of a slaughtered nation whose temples have been razed and whose books have been burned, has no share in human dignity." Richard Rorty, "Postmodernist Bourgeois Liberalism," in *Objectivity, Relativism, and Truth: Philosophical Papers*, Vol. I (Cambridge: Cambridge University Press, 1991), 201. Hauerwas does not suggest that this "standing" needs to be "conferred," but there is danger that in discarding the language of rights with its reference to "the recognition of inherent dignity" (Universal Declaration of Human Rights: Preamble), dignity becomes something to be conferred by others.

75. Hauerwas, "Rights, Duties, and Experimentation,"130.

76. Hauerwas, *The Peaceable Kingdom*, 51, 61, 63. Hauerwas does not seem to accept that a coherent and distinct ecclesiology can coexist with a natural law ethic.

77. Hauerwas, *After Christendom?* 45.

78. Hauerwas, *Dispatches from the Front*, 6.

79. His particular disdain for theologians who try to find compatibility between Christian belief and a commitment to human rights is exemplified in his comments on the work of Michael Himes and Kenneth Himes in *Fullness of Faith: The Public Significance of Theology*, chap. 3, "The Trinity and Human Rights" (New York/Mahwah, NJ: Paulist Press, 1993), 55–73. Hauerwas comments on the "pathos of such projects as they strive to show that Catholics, too, can be good liberals." *Dispatches from the Front*, 190, n. 7.

80. Joan Tronto, *Moral Boundaries: A Political Argument for an Ethic of Care* (New York/London: Routledge, 1993), 166.

81. Ibid., 145.

82. Hauerwas, *The Peaceable Kingdom*, 104–105.

83. Ibid., 103.

84. Hauerwas, *Resident Aliens*, 43.

85. The phrase "*ecumene* of suffering humanity" is used by Edward Schillebeeckx in *Jesus in our Western Culture: Mysticism, Ethics and Politics* (London: SCM Press Ltd., 1987).

86. Hauerwas, "Postscript: A Response to Jeff Stout's *Democracy and Tradition*," in *Performing the Faith*, 215–41, at 219. See also 215–19. Hauerwas remarks that he and Stout now seem to agree more than disagree.

87. Ibid., 217, n. 4.

88. Ibid., 232.

89. Ibid., 220, 220–32.

90. Annette C. Baier, "Claims, Rights, Responsibilities," in *Moral Prejudices*, 224–46, at 226.

91. Ibid., 241, 246.

92. Ibid., 245. She holds that the language of vital interests is the proper complement, or even successor, to the language of rights.

93. Hauerwas, *Performing the Faith*, 240–41.

94. Mark 10:46–52, *New American Bible* (1990).

95. Trimiew, *God Bless the Child That's Got Its Own*, 24.

96. Bell draws this phrase from John Milbank: "To surpass the tragic, to make the Christian gesture of faith beyond (but not without) renunciation, is not to embark on a premature celebration. On the contrary, it is to 'refuse' to cease to suffer, to become resigned to a loss. Only at the price of an augmentation of suffering does a complete joy and peace begin to shine through." "Enclaves, or Where Is the Church?" in *New Blackfriars* (June 1992): 341–52, 352.

97. Petrella, *The Future of Liberation Theology*, ix. See his discussion of Bell's work on 128–32.

98. Bell, *Liberation Theology after the End of History*, 70–71.

99. Ibid., 12.

100. Ibid., 68.

101. Ibid., 123.

102. Ibid., 126.

103. Ibid., 187.

104. Ibid., 128–30.

105. Ibid., 151.

106. Ibid., 190.

107. Ibid., 190–92.

108. Bell presents forgiveness and justice as diametrically opposed responses to the sin of injustice and poverty. His position is based on a reductionist reading of both concepts. We saw the complex weaving in truth commissions of the threads of truth-telling and justice, anger and lack of remorse, forgiveness and reconciliation. Bell also seems to presuppose that forgiveness is possible only within a Christian or religious framework. In *An Ethic for Enemies: Forgiveness in Politics* (Oxford: Oxford University Press, 1995), Donald W. Shriver describes forgiveness in a political context as a multidimensional human action "that joins moral truth, forbearance, empathy, and a commitment to repair a fractured human relation. Such a combination calls for a collective turning from the past that neither ignores past evil nor excuses it, that neither overlooks justice nor reduces justice to revenge, that insists on the humanity of enemies even in their commission of dehumanizing deeds, and that values the justice that restores political community above the justice that destroys it" (9).

109. Milbank, *Theology and Social Theory*, 411.

110. Sobrino, *Principle of Mercy*, 59–68.

111. Ibid., 29.

112. Ibid., 10.

113. Review of *The Principle of Mercy*, in *Pro Ecclesia* 6 (Winter 1997): 112–14.

114. Sobrino, *Principle of Mercy*, 10.

115. See Milbank, *Theology and Social Theory*, 389.

116. Augustine, *The City of God against the Pagans*, edited and translated by R. W. Dyson. For a discussion of Augustine's controversy with the Donatists regarding the nature of the Church and his relinquishing of the idea of the Church as a spiritual elite in the world, see Robert Markus, *Saeculum*, chap. 5, "*Afer Scribens Afris*: The Church in Augustine and the African Tradition," 105–32.

117. Augustine, *City of God*, XVIII, 54.

118. Eugene TeSelle discusses the lack of clarity in Augustine's distinction between the two cities and the subsequent interpretation of this distinction in the history of the West, outlining three possible interpretations. (a) A dualistic reading that grants the earthly city only provisional significance, and Christians live within it as aliens. TeSelle suggests that this is probably the most authentic reading of Augustine, a reading that is most powerful in contexts where Christians could not imagine being able to change the world around them. (b) The Church, identifying with the city of God, claims for that city an earthly presence, gradually leading to medieval "political Augustinianism" and the views of Wyclif and Hus, who interpreted the earthly presence in a Church that was "not fully identical with the sacramental church." (c) TeSelle, drawing on an interpretation by James Dougherty (*The Fivesquare City: The City in the Religious Imagination*, 1980), contends that it would not be un-Augustinian to envisage that a kind of dual citizenship could be held by Christians, "living in the earthly city with the critical distance of the alien even while trying to make it the best city possible." "The Civic Vision in Augustine's *City of God*," *Thought: A Review of Culture and Idea, Fordham University Quarterly* 62, no. 246 (September 1987): 268–80, at 279.

119. An extension that risks equating the Church with the City of God or, to use a central category of the Christian scriptures, neglecting the difference between the Church and the Reign of God.

120. Robert Markus, "The Sacred and the Secular: From Augustine to Gregory the Great," in *Sacred and Secular: Studies on Augustine and Latin Christianity* (Aldershot: Variorum/Ashgate, 1994), 85.

121. Milbank, *Theology and Social Theory*, 391.

122. Eugene TeSelle, "The Civic Vision in Augustine's *City of God*," 279.

Conclusion

∼

> Contemporary philosophers have been preoccupied with a rather narrow range of issues, which people often refer to today as "morality," in contrast to "ethics." The "moral" concentrates on issues of justice and inter-personal fairness, issues about rights or what is right in our treatment of others, over and against questions of the "good life," of what is a worthwhile way to live, what is fulfilling, valuable to be, and the like.
>
> —Charles Taylor

CHARLES TAYLOR HOLDS THAT THE CONTEMPORARY philosophical preoccupation with issues of rights and justice reflects a narrow concern with "morality" in contrast with broader "ethical" questions about the "good life" and human flourishing.[1] In an argument akin to that of the "new traditionalists," rights are juxtaposed with *eudaimonia* and addressing the latter is proposed as a more worthy pursuit for philosophers and theologians. Two major aims of this book have been to respond to that juxtaposition of rights and flourishing and to challenge the assumption that a concern about human rights is a "preoccupation" with a narrow range of issues. This book has not attempted to construct a theological foundation for human rights nor to present the superiority of theological justifications for human rights over other justifications but, rather, to explore theological engagement with human rights discourse and to show that such engagement should not be characterized as a "narrow preoccupation."

There were a number of reasons—biographical and intellectual—that motivated my tackling the themes addressed in this book. I was brought to reflection on the relationship between rights and *eudaimonia* through the work of my community, the Holy Faith Sisters, with children living and working on the streets of Port of Spain, Trinidad. Engagement in the suffering and the struggle of their lives taught me the importance of maintaining a commitment to human rights *and* a commitment to the exploration of what constitutes human flourishing. These children, one of the most vulnerable human groups, have been the touchstone of my academic research. Many of these are very gifted children who ran away from poverty and abuse; others are visibly marked by the physical and psychological signs of deprivation. But the capabilities of all these children have been, in some way, damaged by poverty and exploitation. When children are denied food, shelter, safety, or education, it is not only a violation of human rights. The far deeper violation is that their capacity to flourish as human beings is impaired. When accompanied by the kinds of exploitation that the most vulnerable children experience, their ability to trust and give of themselves in relationships is profoundly, often irreparably, damaged. The correlation between the denial of basic rights and the flourishing of human persons and communities is not acknowledged by theologians who remain removed from the discourse of human rights.

The response to children in need is not primarily a response to them as "rights-bearers" but comes from the recognition of their inherent human dignity on which those rights are based. From a Christian perspective, it is a response to the disfigurement of *Imago Dei* in the lives of children whose potential is damaged by poverty, exploitation, and violence. The experience of working in Credo Centre, the exposure to the harsh realities of the lives of these children, and the realization of the impact of deprivation and violation on their capacity as human beings to flourish all led me to reflect on the following: the importance of upholding the significance of human rights and of challenging any disdain—political or academic—about their worth; the necessity of articulating a position in which human rights discourse could be located within ethics, a position that takes account of both the strengths and the weaknesses of this discourse while keeping its connection with the teleological dimensions of ethics expressed in terms of *eudaimonia* and *beatitudo*; and the need to ask how theology can engage with this complex and contested discourse.

These biographical and intellectual reasons are located in the larger context of human rights discourse at the beginning of the twenty-first century. Images of handcuffed "unlawful combatants" wearing orange jumpsuits in Guantánamo and humiliated naked prisoners in Abu Ghraib, the visible signs of a more invidious and invisible rehabilitation of torture by the administration of George W. Bush, haunt human rights discourse as examples of derogations from the protective function of rights, derogations built on a shortsighted juxtaposition of liberty and security. These derogations were part of a web of human rights violations that linked perpetrators of terrorist atrocities with illegal belligerent responses to that terror by nation states. Rendition flights drew unsuspecting citizens from other countries into this tangled web of torture as airports, such as Shannon in Ireland, were used to facilitate the exportation of prisoners to secret prisons where torture was practiced on behalf of those whose official commitments to human rights did not permit them to torture. Human rights groups hope that the administration of Barack Obama will usher in "a new era of reformed counterterrorism policies," thus undoing the damage done by the policies of the previous administration.[2]

But human rights discourse is also haunted by the invisible faces of the twenty-five thousand children, men, and women who die each day of hunger and related causes, evidence of the continued derogation from basic social and economic rights.[3] Over the sixty years since the promulgation of the Universal Declaration of Human Rights, there has been considerable formal and theoretical advancement in the area of human rights, but this has not been matched by equal advancement in the conditions in which human beings live. Between the derogations from human rights found in torture and absolute poverty lie a range of violations including discrimination, disappearances, the death penalty, rape as a weapon of war, and the treatment of child soldiers, prisoners of conscience, and refugees. The awful breadth of the violations is evidence that human rights are violated, through omission or commission, by a coalition of national and transnational actors. This coalition of violation needs to be challenged by a similar coalition of responsibility for human rights. As we consider the multiple violations of human rights and the complexity of the damage to human persons and communities resulting from these violations, we posit that it is unacceptable to categorize a concern with these as a preoccupation "with a rather narrow range of issues."

This study of the relationship between theology and human rights began by reflecting on what place human rights discourse should occupy within ethics. It was proposed that human rights be understood as a dialectical boundary discourse of human flourishing, positioned in ethics as "protective marginality." Defining human rights discourse as a dialectical boundary discourse prevents rights discourse from eclipsing other forms of ethical and political discourse, thus challenging the position that rights "trump" all other considerations in ethics.

However, locating human rights discourse to a "marginal" position is not to relegate it to a minor position that is only concerned with minimal protection and provision divorced from consideration of what constitutes the good life and human flourishing. The argument throughout this book has been that rights discourse is also protective of the *more*—virtue, self-transcendence, the good life, personal and communal well-being—to which human beings are called. Human rights discourse emphasizes that *everyone* is included within the potentiality of human flourishing and reminds us that contemporary eudaimonistic reflections cannot bypass the reality of human rights violations in their manifold forms.

The reference to the "dialectical" nature of human rights discourse is not an allusion to the Hegelian understanding of "dialectic" but simply refers to the way human rights discourse holds in tension the universal and the particular, the religious and the secular, the individual and community, theory and practice, emotion and reason, the abstract and the concrete. The dialectical tension between these various elements is necessary in order that human rights not be reduced to the protection of individual rights insofar as those rights do not infringe on the rights of other individuals.

We have attempted to keep this dialectical nature to the fore as we explored theological engagement with human rights. The dialectical relationship between the universality of human rights and the particularity of cultures is tentatively captured in the term "situated universalism." This term does not suggest a contraction of the universalizability of human rights but, rather, an expansion of the capacity of human rights discourse to provide for the conditions in which concrete human beings can flourish in a multiplicity of contexts. It also can facilitate the translation of the principles of human rights into other ethical languages of protection and provision that may, in certain cultures, do more to advance concrete human rights than the sole use of rights discourse.

The brief examination of the use of human rights discourse in the public domain, in the secular foundational documents of the United Nations and in the religious appeal to human rights in Roman Catholic social teaching since Vatican II, showed that, although there are significant foundational differences, there is also significant commonality. Both the difference and the commonality point to the need for a reciprocity of critique between religious and secular use of human rights discourse, a critique that challenges contradictions and any lessening of the "impulse of solidarity."[4]

It is clear that not all ethical and political goals can be formulated in terms of rights nor can rights solve all ethical dilemmas. Human rights can never be the center and goal of ethics, but rights discourse is positioned on the margins of ethics as a discourse of protection of the *more* to which we are called as persons and communities, nationally and internationally.

How then does theology engage with human rights discourse? We have seen that theological engagement with human rights is ecumenical, complex, and diverse. The engagement includes reflection on the connections between the secular language of human rights and biblical perspectives on justice, and Moltmann's position that the specific task of Christian theology is that of grounding fundamental human rights in God's right, that is, God's claim upon all human beings. Theological engagement with human rights discourse emerges from the Latin American experience of poverty and oppression, from postapartheid South Africa in the work of Charles Villa-Vicencio, and from the evangelical theologians in the United States who began engaging with human rights in the context of the War on Terror.

As noted in the introduction, this study has taken a broad understanding of theological engagement with human rights discourse that includes explicit engagement with rights discourse in terms of both foundational questions and historical implementation and implicit engagement in areas of shared concern for both discourses, concerns about the human person and community, about human dignity and freedom, about justice and politics. Some theologians engage explicitly with the discourse of human rights, for example, the work of George Newlands who brings it into dialogue with the claims and dynamics of Christology.[5] Implicit engagement with rights can be identified where theology engages with areas of mutual concern, for example, in Rahner's concentration on human dignity, freedom, and self-transcendence and Metz's response to the unprecedented violations of the Holocaust.

To focus only on the explicit engagement of theology with human rights discourse would limit the possibilities for future theological engagement. The weaving of a more implicit engagement between theology and human rights discourse into a larger picture of that engagement is intended to stretch the moral and theological imagination and to expand that critical engagement beyond the restricted theological constituency that values such engagement.

The ultimate theological justification for engagement with human rights is, of course, the doctrine of *Imago Dei* (Gen. 1:16–17), and the history of theological anthropology has been an attempt to come to terms with the full meaning of this assertion. This study focused first on the theological anthropology of Karl Rahner, suggesting that his concentration on the human makes him an important companion for theological engagement with human rights discourse. Through his reflections on human dignity and freedom, on human goodness that witnesses to the breadth of God and the narrowness of the church and, most importantly, his understanding of the intimate connection between our experience of ourselves and our experience of God, he offers a transcendentalist Thomist version of *Imago*

Dei, which makes an important contribution to understanding the mystery of the human person both in her transcendence and in her historicity. Rahner's theological anthropology needs engagement with the boundary discourse of human rights so that it does not speak too simplistically about the capacity of the human person to live out graced freedom in response to the mystery of God without due regard for the constraints that people experience in living out this freedom or the damage that results from trauma and violation. Despite this, Rahner's reflections on human subjectivity enable us to perceive human rights issues of provision and protection in their radical depth, linking human rights with the ultimate luminosity of the human person.

There is much that theology can learn from understanding human rights as a "realist" discourse in time, located between the memory of suffering and hope for the future. The *Recuperación de la Memoria Historica*, a pastoral theology and human rights project produced by the Human Rights Office of the Catholic Archdiocese of Guatemala, teaches about the impact of human rights violations, not just on individual victims and perpetrators, but also on the fabric of community. This complexity of impact is often overlooked by theologians who disdain engagement with human rights. Theologians can learn much from secular efforts to work toward just memory in postconflict situations, lessons about the relationship between truth and justice and about the capacity of torture to damage both the relationality and the ethical sensitivity of human beings.

Although the theologian Johann Baptist Metz has little explicit theological engagement with the discourse of human rights, his theology has an important implicit engagement with rights through his efforts to forge a political theology in the aftermath of the Second World War. Metz's theological response to the Holocaust is marked by a haunted tardiness as the memory of its victims seep through in his reflections on memory, narrative, and solidarity as essential categories in a postidealist political theology. Auschwitz eventually became an orienting interruption into Metz's theology, an interruptive realism that challenged the more idealist concentration on the human in Rahner's work. With his philosophical companion, Walter Benjamin, Metz offers a critical perspective on the dialectical heritage of the Enlightenment, a perspective that challenges those who would abandon the ideals of universal human rights for political pragmatism or postmodern perspectivalism. The trajectory of Metz's own theology poses a number of challenges for theologians, not least the questions of theological silence in the face of human rights violations and the necessity of developing the virtue of vigilance toward suffering, a virtue that can be developed through constructive engagement with human rights theorists and activists.

Liberation theologians, while pastorally involved with the reality of human rights violations in Latin America, were initially reluctant to engage with the discourse of human rights, a reluctance based on a perception that rights discourse was founded solely on an individualistic liberal anthropology. They gradually began to engage with rights discourse articulating concerns that its focus on civil and political rights, enforceable in a judicial context, overlooked the violations of hunger, poverty, and illiteracy. The Church became increasingly involved in the defense of human rights during periods of repression, and Latin American Christians used the language of human rights to highlight violations in an effort to save lives.

Liberation theology developed a distinctive engagement with rights discourse as human rights became linked with the preferential option for the poor, an option that issued a challenge to theologians to identify their own *locus theologicus*. The liberationist emphasis on the priority of the "rights of the poor" challenges both theologians and human rights scholars to emphasize that most of the extreme poverty in our world is the result of human actions and decisions and should therefore be acknowledged as a violation of human rights. Liberation theology reminds us that human rights discourse begins not with abstract human beings but with concrete and specific victims who are the poor of our world. The specific contribution of liberation theology lies in its emphasis on the need for systemic and structural fulfillment of the rights of the poor, whose rights become the test for the paradox of universality.

The affirmation of the rights of the poor—especially their social and economic rights—does not negate the universality of human rights, but such affirmation points toward authentic universality in the form of historical and concrete realization. A distinctively theological perspective is found in the work of Jon Sobrino, whose reflections on the mysticism of human rights challenge us to understand the struggle for the rights of the poor as a kind of mystagogy into the life of God. The liberationist engagement with human rights presents a challenge to both the data of theology and the theologian, a challenge, expressed in the words of the Ignacio Ellacuría, to bear the burden of the weight of reality.[6]

The theology of the "new traditionalists" in the postliberal radical orthodoxy current shares three common characteristics: (a) a "disdain" for the secular, including human rights and liberal democracy; (b) a preference for theological politics over political theology; and (c) an impatience with the provisional. Although I have challenged the extremity of their critique of human rights discourse, Milbank, Hauerwas, and Bell do offer an important reminder to theologians who engage with issues of rights and justice not to be complacent about that engagement and not to allow theology to be "reserved" only into whatever space secular reason allows it. However the postliberal theological current tends to caricature theologians who engage with rights and social justice. Theologians who engage with human rights, either with the theoretical discourse or with practical advocacy, do so with an awareness that our justice must always be oriented toward true justice, which God alone can bring about. Human rights discourse can thus be understood as a boundary discourse of *vera iustitia*.

George Newlands observes that he is "constantly struck by the disparity between the huge effort put into human rights culture by disciplines other than theology, in comparison with the comparative neglect by theologians."[7] This book attempts to repair some of that neglect, showing theologians that engagement with the discourse of human rights—and the human realities in which that discourse is forged—leads us into areas of crucial concern for both theologians and human rights practitioners. But ultimately it invites us all into solidarity with "the remnant child of a slaughtered nation" and "the world tribe of the dispossessed," the least of the brothers and sisters (Matthew 25:40).[8]

Notes

1. Charles Taylor, Review of Bhikhu Parekh: *Rethinking Multiculturalism: Cultural Diversity and Political Theory* (Basingstoke: Macmillan, 2000), *Times Literary Supplement* (April 20, 2001), 4.
2. See statement by Human Rights Watch, available online at www.hrw.org/en/news/2009/01/19/us-obama-presidency-should-reform-counter-terror-policies [accessed September 30, 2009].
3. "Hunger Stats" from the World Food Programme, available online at www.wfp.org/hunger/stats [accessed April 19, 2009].
4. Charles Taylor, *A Catholic Modernity? Charles Taylor's Marianist Award Lecture*, edited by James L. Heft (New York/Oxford: Oxford University Press, 1999), 26.
5. Newlands, *Christ and Human Rights: The Transformative Engagement*.
6. Ellacuría, "Hacia una fundamentacion del método teológico Latinoamericano," 419.
7. Newlands, *Christ and Human Rights*, 177, n. 5. John Witte Jr. also calls for human rights to have greater prominence "in the theological discourse of modern religions." *The Reformation of Rights*, 339.
8. From "This Is a Hymn" by Lorna Goodison, *Heartease* (London/Port of Spain: New Beacon Books, 1988).

Select Bibliography

∾

Ackerly, Brooke A. *Universal Human Rights in a World of Difference*. Cambridge: Cambridge University Press, 2008.

Adorno, Theodor, and Max Horkheimer. *The Dialectic of Enlightenment*. Translated by John Cumming. London and New York: VERSO (Classics), 1997.

Agamben, Giorgio. *Means without Ends: Notes on Politics*. Translated by Vincenzo Binetti and Cesare Casarino. Minneapolis/London: University of Minnesota Press, 2000.

An-Na'im, Abdullahi A., ed. *Human Rights in Cross-Cultural Perspectives: A Quest for Consensus*. Philadelphia: University of Pennsylvania Press, 1992.

Antoncich, Ricardo. *Christians in the Face of Injustice: A Latin American Reading of Catholic Social Teaching*. Translated by Matthew J. O'Connell. Maryknoll, NY: Orbis Books, 1987.

Archdiocese of Guatemala, Human Rights Office. *Guatemala, Nunca Más: Recovery of Historical Memory Project*. Maryknoll, NY, and London: Orbis Books and Catholic Institute for International Relations, 1999.

Aschheim, Steven E. *Culture and Catastrophe: German and Jewish Confrontations with National Socialism and Other Crises*. London: Macmillan, 1996.

Ashley, James Matthew. *Interruptions: Mysticism, Politics, and Theology in the Work of Johann Baptist Metz*. Notre Dame, IN: University of Notre Dame Press, 1998.

Augustine. *The City of God against the Pagans*. Edited and translated by R. W. Dyson. Cambridge: Cambridge University Press, 2003.

Baier, Annette C. *Moral Prejudices: Essays on Ethics*. Cambridge, MA and London: Harvard University Press, 1994.

Bauman, Zygmunt. *Modernity and the Holocaust*. Cambridge: Polity Press, 1989.

Bell, Daniel A. *East Meets West: Human Rights and Democracy in East Asia*. Princeton, NJ: Princeton University Press, 2000.

Bell, Daniel M. *Liberation Theology after the End of History: The Refusal to Cease Suffering*. London and New York: Routledge, 2001.

Benhabib, Seyla. *Situating the Self: Gender, Community and Postmodernism in Contemporary Feminism*. Oxford: Polity Press, 1992.

Benjamin, Walter. *Illuminations*. Edited and introduced by Hannah Arendt. London: Fontana Press, 1973.

Berlin, Isaiah. *The Proper Study of Mankind: An Anthology of Essays*. Edited by Henry Hardy and Roger Hausheer. London: Chatto & Windus, 1997.

Beste, Jennifer E. *God and the Victim: Traumatic Intrusions on Grace and Freedom*. Oxford and New York: Oxford University Press, 2007.

Burke, Kevin F. *The Ground beneath the Cross: The Theology of Ignacio Ellacuría*. Washington, DC: Georgetown University Press, 2000.

Burleigh, Michael. *Ethics and Extermination: Reflections on Nazi Genocide*. Cambridge: Cambridge University Press, 1997.

Carozza, Paulo G. "From Conquest to Constitutions: Retrieving a Latin American Tradition of the Idea of Human Rights," *Human Rights Quarterly* 25, no. 2 (May 2003): 281–313.

Cavanaugh, William T. *Theopolitical Imagination*. London: T&T Clark, 2002.

Chenu, Marie-Dominique. *La Doctrine Sociale de l'Église Comme Idéologie*. Paris: Les Éditions Du Cerf, 1979.

Chopp, Rebecca S., and Ethna Regan. "Latin American Liberation Theology," in *The Modern Theologians: An Introduction to Christian Theology since 1918*, 3rd ed. Edited by David Ford with Rachel Muers, 469–84. Oxford: Blackwell Publishing, 2005.

Cicero. *De Officiis*. Cambridge: Cambridge University Press, 1991.

Clark, J. C. D. *The Language of Liberty 1660–1832*. Cambridge: Cambridge University Press, 1994.

Comblin, José. *Called for Freedom: The Changing Context of Liberation Theology*. Translated by Phillip Berryman. Maryknoll, NY: Orbis Books, 1998.

Cranston, Maurice. "Pope John XXIII on Peace and the Rights of Man." *The Political Quarterly* 34 (1963): 380–90.

Cronin, Kieran. *Rights and Christian Ethics*. Cambridge: Cambridge University Press, 1992.

Curran, Charles E. "Churches and Human Rights: From Hostility/Reluctance to Acceptability." *Milltown Studies* 42 (1998): 30–58.

Curran, Charles E., and Richard A. McCormick, eds. *John Paul II and Moral Theology* (Readings in Moral Theology, No. 10). New York and Mahwah, NJ: Paulist Press, 1998.

Dietrich, Donald J. *Christian Responses to the Holocaust: Moral and Ethical Issues.* Syracuse, NY: Syracuse University Press, 2003.

Donnelly, Jack. *The Concept of Human Rights.* London and Sydney: Croom Helm, 1985.

———. *International Human Rights.* Boulder, San Francisco, and Oxford: Westview Press, 1993.

———. *Universal Human Rights in Theory and Practice.* Ithaca, NY: Cornell University Press, 1989.

Dorr, Donal. *Option for the Poor: A Hundred Years of Catholic Social Teaching.* Maryknoll, NY: Orbis Books, 2001.

Douglass, R. Bruce, and David Hollenbach. *Catholicism and Liberalism: Contributions to American Public Philosophy.* Cambridge: Cambridge University Press, 1994.

Drinan, Robert F. *The Mobilization of Shame: A Worldview of Human Rights.* New Haven and London: Yale University Press, 2001.

Dunne, Tim, and Nicholas J. Wheeler, eds. *Human Rights in Global Politics.* Cambridge: Cambridge University Press, 1999.

Dussel, Enrique, ed. *The Church in Latin America 1492–1992.* Tunbridge Wells and Maryknoll, NY: Burns & Oates and Orbis Books, 1992.

Dworkin, Ronald. *Taking Rights Seriously.* London: Duckworth, 1978.

Ellacuría, Ignacio. *Freedom Made Flesh: The Mission of Christ and His Church.* Translated by John Drury. Maryknoll, NY: Orbis Books, 1976.

———. "Hacia una fundamentacion del método teológico Latinoamericano," *Estudios centroamericanos.* Agosto/Septiembre 1975, 409–25.

———. "Human Rights in a Divided Society," in *Human Rights in the Americas: The Struggle for Consensus.* Edited by A. Hennelly and J. Langan. Washington, DC: Georgetown University Press, 1982.

Ellacuría, Ignacio, and Jon Sobrino, eds. *Mysterium Liberationis: Fundamental Concepts of Liberation Theology.* Maryknoll, NY: Orbis Books, 1993.

Etzioni, Amitai. *The Spirit of Community: Rights, Responsibilities, and the Communitarian Agenda.* London: Fontana Press, 1995.

Falk, Richard. *Human Rights Horizons: The Pursuit of Justice in a Globalizing World.* London: Routledge, 2000.

Finnis, John. *Natural Law and Natural Rights.* Oxford: Clarendon Press, 1980.

Flannery, Austin, ed. *Vatican II: Constitutions, Decrees, Declarations.* Northport, NY and Dublin, Ireland: Costello Publishing Company and Dominican Publications, 1996.

Gewirth, Alan. *The Community of Rights*. Chicago and London: The University of Chicago Press, 1996.

Ghandi, P. R., ed. *Blackstone's International Human Rights Documents*, 3rd edition. Oxford: Oxford University Press, 2002.

Glendon, Mary Ann. *Rights Talk: The Impoverishment of Political Discourse*. New York: The Free Press, 1991.

———. *A World Made New: Eleanor Roosevelt and the Universal Declaration of Human Rights*. New York: Random House, 2001.

Greenbeerg, Karen J., and Joshua L. Dratel, with an introduction by Anthony Lewis. *The Torture Papers: The Road to Abu Ghraib*. Cambridge: Cambridge University Press, 2005.

Gremillion, Joseph. *The Gospel of Peace and Justice: Catholic Social Teaching since Pope John*. Maryknoll, NY: Orbis Books, 1976.

Griffin, James. *On Human Rights*. Oxford and New York: Oxford University Press, 2008.

Gushee, David P. *The Future of Faith in American Politics: The Public Witness of the Evangelical Centre*. Waco, TX: Baylor University Press, 2008.

Gutiérrez, Gustavo. *A Theology of Liberation: History, Politics, and Salvation*, 15th anniversary edition. Translated by Caridad Inda and John Eagleson. Maryknoll, NY: Orbis Books, 1988.

Hauerwas, Stanley. *After Christendom? How the Church Is to Behave If Freedom, Justice and a Christian Nation Are Bad Ideas*. Nashville, TN: Abingdon Press, 1991.

———. *A Community of Character: Toward a Constructive Christian Social Ethics*. Notre Dame, IN: University of Notre Dame Press, 1981.

———. *Performing the Faith: Bonhoeffer and the Practice of Nonviolence*. Grand Rapids, MI: Brazos Press, 2004.

———. *Suffering Presence: Theological Reflections on Medicine, the Mentally Handicapped, and the Church*. Notre Dame, IN: University of Notre Dame Press, 1986.

Hayes, Michael A., and David Tombs, eds. *Truth and Memory: The Church and Human Rights in El Salvador and Guatemala*. Herefordshire, UK: Gracewing, 2001.

Hayner, Priscilla B. *Unspeakable Truths: Confronting State Terror and Atrocity*. London and New York: Routledge, 2001.

Henkin, Louis. *The Age of Rights*. New York: Columbia University Press, 1990.

Hollenbach, David. *Claims in Conflict: Retrieving and Renewing the Catholic Human Rights Tradition*. New York: Paulist Press, 1979.

———. *The Global Face of Public Faith: Politics, Human Rights, and Christian Ethics*. Washington, DC: Georgetown University Press, 2003.

Holzgrefe, J. L., and Robert O. Keohane, eds. *Humanitarian Intervention: Ethical, Legal, and Political Dilemmas*. Cambridge: Cambridge University Press, 2003.

Ignatieff, Michael. *Human Rights as Politics and Idolatry*. Princeton and Oxford: Princeton University Press, 2001.

Imhof, Paul, and Hubert Biallowons, eds. *Faith in a Wintry Season: Conversations and Interviews with Karl Rahner in the Last Years of His Life*. Translated by Harvey D. Egan. New York: Crossroad Publishing Company, 1990.

Jones, Peter. *Rights*. Basingstoke, UK: Macmillan, 1994.

Kearney, Richard, and Mark Dooley, eds. *Questioning Ethics: Contemporary Debates in Philosophy*. London and New York: Routledge, 1999.

Kerr, Fergus. *Theology after Wittgenstein*, 2nd edition. London: SPCK, 1997.

Kilby, Karen. *Karl Rahner: Theology and Philosophy*. London and New York: Routledge, 2004.

Klaiber, Jeffrey. *The Church, Dictatorships, and Democracy in Latin America*. Maryknoll, NY: Orbis Books, 1998.

Kleinman, Arthur, Veena Das, and Margaret Lock, eds. *Social Suffering*. Berkeley and London: University of California Press, 1997.

Konvitz, Milton R., ed. *Judaism and Human Rights*. London and New Brunswick, NJ: Transaction Publishers and Rutgers University, 2001.

Kritz, Neil J., ed. *Transitional Justice*, Vol. I, *General Considerations*. Washington, DC: U.S. Institute for Peace Press, 1995.

Krog, Antjie. *Country of My Skull*. London: Jonathan Cape, 1998.

Krondorfer, Björn. "Theological Innocence and Family History in the Land of Perpetrators: German Theologians after the Shoah." *Harvard Theological Review* 97, no. 1 (2004): 61–82.

Küng, Hans, and Jürgen Moltmann, eds. *The Ethics of World Religions and Human Rights. Concilium 2*. London and Philadelphia: SCM Press and Trinity Press International, 1990.

Lauren, Paul Gordon. *The Evolution of International Human Rights: Visions Seen*. Philadelphia: University of Pennsylvania Press, 1998.

Lebor, Adam. *"Complicity with Evil": The United Nations in the Age of Modern Genocide*. New Haven and London: Yale University Press, 2006.

Lindholt, Lone. *Questioning the Universality of Human Rights: The African Charter on Human and Peoples' Rights in Botswana, Malawi, and Mozambique.* Aldershot: Ashgate, 1997.

Locke, John. *Two Treatises of Government.* Edited with an introduction and notes by Peter Laslett. Cambridge: Cambridge University Press, 2002.

MacIntyre, Alasdair. *After Virtue: A Study in Moral Theory.* London: Duckworth, 1981.

———. *A Short History of Ethics*, 2nd edition. London: Routledge, 1998.

Mahoney, John. *The Challenge of Human Rights: Origin, Development and Significance.* Malden, MA: Blackwell Publishing, 2007.

Marcel, Gabriel. *The Existential Background of Human Dignity* (The William James Lectures—Harvard, 1961–62). Cambridge, MA: Harvard University Press, 1963.

Margalit, Avishai. *The Ethics of Memory.* Cambridge, MA and London: Harvard University Press, 2002.

Maritain, Jacques. *The Rights of Man and Natural Law.* London: Geoffrey Bles and The Centenary Press, 1944.

Markus, Robert A. *Saeculum: History and Society in the Theology of St. Augustine.* Cambridge: Cambridge University Press, 1970.

Marsh, Charles. *Wayward Christian Soldiers: Freeing the Gospel from Political Captivity.* Oxford: Oxford University Press, 2007.

Marshall, Christopher D. *Crowned with Glory and Honour: Human Rights in the Biblical Tradition.* Telford, PA, and Auckland: Pandora Press, 2001.

Marx, Karl. *Karl Marx, Frederick Engels: Collected Works III.* London: Lawrence & Wishart, 1975.

McGovern, Arthur F. *Liberation Theology and Its Critics: Toward an Assessment.* Maryknoll, NY: Orbis Books, 1990.

Metz, Johann Baptist. "Facing the Jews: Christian Theology after Auschwitz," in *The Holocaust as Interruption*, E. Schüssler Fiorenza and D. Tracy, eds. *Concilium* 5, no. 175 (1984): 26–33.

———. *Faith in History and Society: Toward a Practical Fundamental Theology.* Translated by David Smith. London: Burns & Oates, 1980.

———. *A Passion for God: The Mystical-Political Dimension of Christianity.* Edited and translated by J. Matthew Ashley. New York and Mahwah, NJ: Paulist Press, 1998.

———. "Political Theology," in *Sacramentum Mundi, Vol. V*, Karl Rahner, ed., 34–38. London: Burns & Oates, 1970.

Metz, Johann Baptist, and Jürgen Moltmann. *Faith and the Future: Essays on Theology, Solidarity, and Modernity, Concilium Series.* Translated by Francis Schüssler Fiorenza. Maryknoll, NY: Orbis Books, 1995.

Milbank, John. *Theology and Social Theory: Beyond Secular Reason.* Oxford: Blackwell Publishers, 1993.

———. *The Word Made Strange: Theology, Language, and Culture.* Oxford: Blackwell Publishers, 1997.

Milbank, John, Catherine Pickstock, and Graham Ward. *Radical Orthodoxy: A New Theology.* London and New York: Routledge, 1998.

Minow, Martha. *Between Vengeance and Forgiveness: Facing History after Genocide and Mass Violence.* Boston: Beacon Press, 1998.

Minow, Martha, ed. *Breaking the Cycles of Hatred: Memory, Law, and Repair.* Princeton, NJ: Princeton University Press, 2002.

Moltmann, Jürgen. *On Human Dignity: Political Theology and Ethics.* Translated by M. Douglas Meeks. London: SCM Press Ltd., 1984.

———, ed. *How I Have Changed: Reflections on Thirty Years of Theology.* London: SCM Press, 1997.

Morsink, Johannes. *The Universal Declaration of Human Rights: Origins, Drafting, and Intent.* Philadelphia: University of Pennsylvania Press, 1999.

Mounier, Emmanuel. *Personalism.* Notre Dame, IN, and London: University of Notre Dame Press, 1952.

Murray, John Courtney. "Introduction to the Declaration on Religious Freedom," in *The Documents of Vatican II.* Walter M. Abbott, general editor, 672–74. London: Geoffrey Chapman, 1967.

———. "Things Old and New in *Pacem in Terris*," *America* 108 (April 27, 1963): 612–14.

Newlands, George. *Christ and Human Rights: The Transformative Engagement.* Aldershot: Ashgate, 2006.

Nino, Carlos Santiago. *The Ethics of Human Rights.* Oxford: Clarendon Press, 1991.

Nurser, John S. *For All Peoples and All Nations: The Ecumenical Church and Human Rights.* Washington, DC: Georgetown University Press, 2005.

O'Brien, David J., and Thomas A. Shannon. *Catholic Social Thought: The Documentary Heritage.* Maryknoll, NY: Orbis Books, 1992.

Outka, Gene, and John P. Reeder Jr., eds. *Prospects for a Common Morality.* Princeton, NJ: Princeton University Press, 1993.

Paine, Thomas. *Common Sense and the Rights of Man*. Edited and with a foreword by Tony Benn. London: Phoenix Press, 2000.

Paul, Ellen Frankel, Fred D. Miller, and Jeffrey Paul. *Human Flourishing*. Cambridge: Cambridge University Press, 1999.

Perry, Michael J. *The Idea of Human Rights—Four Inquiries*. New York and Oxford: Oxford University Press, 1998.

Petrella, Ivan. *The Future of Liberation Theology: An Argument and Manifesto*. London: SCM Press, 2006.

Phayer, Michael. *The Catholic Church and the Holocaust, 1930–1965*. Bloomington: Indiana University Press, 2000.

Pogge, Thomas. *World Poverty and Human Rights: Cosmopolitan Responsibilities and Reforms*, 2nd edition. Cambridge: Polity, 2008.

Rahner, Karl. *Foundations of Christian Faith: An Introduction to the Idea of Christianity*. Translated by William V. Dych. New York: Crossroad, 1978/2002.

———. *Hearers of the Word*. Revised by J. B. Metz and translated by Ronald Walls. London and Sydney: Sheed & Ward, 1969.

———. *Spirit in the World*. Translated by William V. Dych. London: Sheed & Ward, 1968.

———. *Theological Investigations*, 23 vols. Various translators. Vols. 1–20, London: Darton, Longman & Todd, 1963–81; vols. 21–23. New York: Crossroad, 1988–92.

Raphael, D. D., ed. *Political Theory and the Rights of Man*. London, Melbourne, and Toronto: Macmillan, 1967.

Rawls, John. *Justice as Fairness: A Restatement*. Edited by Erin Kelly. Cambridge, MA and London: Belknap Press, 2001.

———. *The Law of Peoples: With "The Idea of Public Reason Revisited."* Cambridge, MA and London: Harvard University Press, 1999.

———. *A Theory of Justice*. Cambridge, MA: Harvard University Press, 1971.

Regan, Ethna. "Justice Overshadowed by Charity? *Deus Caritas Est* and the Work of Catholic 'Charitable Organisations,'" in *Who Is My Neighbour? Deus Caritas Est: An Encyclical for Our Times?* Edited by Eoin G. Cassidy, 140–57. Dublin: Veritas, 2009.

Rico, Herminio. *John Paul II and the Legacy of Dignitatis Humanae*. Washington, DC: Georgetown University Press, 2002.

Ricoeur, Paul. "Memory-Forgetfulness-History." ZiF: *Mitteilungen*, Universitat Bielefeld 95, no. 2, (1995): 3–12.

Rorty, Richard. *Objectivity, Relativism, and Truth: Philosophical Papers, Volume I*. Cambridge: Cambridge University Press, 1991.

Rose, Gillian. *Mourning Becomes the Law: Philosophy and Representation*. Cambridge: Cambridge University Press, 1996.

Rosetti, Stephen J. *A Tragic Grace: The Catholic Church and Child Sexual Abuse*. Collegeville, MN: The Liturgical Press, 1996.

Ruston, Roger. *Human Rights and the Image of God*. London: SCM Press, 2004.

Sanchez, José M. *Pius XII and the Holocaust: Understanding the Controversy*. Washington, DC: The Catholic University of America Press, 2002.

Scarry, Elaine. *The Body in Pain: The Making and Unmaking of the World*. New York and Oxford: Oxford University Press, 1985.

Schneewind, J. B. *The Invention of Autonomy: A History of Modern Moral Philosophy*. Cambridge: Cambridge University Press, 1998.

Schuster, Ekkehard, and Reinhold Baschert-Kimmig. *Hope against Hope: Johann Baptist Metz and Elie Wiesel Speak Out on the Holocaust*. Translated by J. Matthew Ashley. New York and Mahwah, NJ: Paulist Press, 1999.

Sen, Amartya. *Development as Freedom*. Oxford: Oxford University Press, 1999.

Shapiro, Ian. *The Evolution of Rights in Liberal Theory*. Cambridge: Cambridge University Press, 1986.

Shue, Henry. *Basic Rights: Subsistence, Affluence, and U.S. Foreign Policy*, 2nd edition. Princeton, NJ: Princeton University Press, 1996.

Shute, Stephen, and Susan Hurley. *On Human Rights: The Oxford Amnesty Lectures, 1993*. New York: Basic Books, 1993.

Sigmund, Paul. *Liberation Theology at the Crossroads: Democracy or Revolution?* Oxford: Oxford University Press, 1990.

Skinner, Quentin. *Liberty before Liberalism*. Cambridge: Cambridge University Press, 1998.

Sobrino, Jon. "Human Rights and Oppressed Peoples: Historical-Theological Reflections," in *Truth and Memory: The Church and Human Rights in El Salvador and Guatemala*. Edited by M. A. Hayes and D. Tombs, 134–58. Herefordshire, UK: Gracewing, 2001.

———. *The Principle of Mercy: Taking the Crucified People from the Cross*. Maryknoll, NY: Orbis Books, 1994.

Steiner, Henry, ed. *Truth Commissions: A Comparative Assessment*. World Peace Federation Reports No. 16, Cambridge, MA, 1997.

Steiner, Henry J., and Philip Alston. *International Human Rights in Context: Law, Politics, Morals*. Oxford: Clarendon Press, 1996.

Stout, Jeffrey. *Democracy and Tradition*. Princeton, NJ, and Oxford: Princeton University Press, 2004.

———. *Ethics after Babel: The Language of Morals and Their Discontents*. Boston: Beacon Press, 1988.

Taylor, Charles. *A Catholic Modernity? Charles Taylor's Marianist Award Lecture*. Edited by James L. Heft. New York and Oxford: Oxford University Press, 1999.

———. *The Ethics of Authenticity*. Cambridge, MA and London: Harvard University Press, 1991.

Tibi, Bassam. *The Challenge of Fundamentalism: Political Islam and the New World Disorder*. Berkeley, Los Angeles, and London: University of California Press, 1998.

Tierney, Brian. *The Idea of Natural Rights: Studies on Natural Rights, Natural Law, and Church Law 1150–1625*. Grand Rapids, MI, and Cambridge: William B. Eerdmans, 2001.

Trimiew, Darryl M. *God Bless the Child That's Got Its Own: The Economic Rights Debate*. Atlanta: Scholars Press, 1997.

United Nations Educational, Scientific and Cultural Organisation (UNESCO), ed. *Human Rights: Comments and Interpretations, A Symposium*, with an Introduction by Jacques Maritain. London and New York: Allan Wingate, 1949.

Villa-Vicencio, Charles. *A Theology of Reconstruction: Nation-Building and Human Rights*. Cambridge: Cambridge University Press, 1992.

Waldron, Jeremy. *God, Locke, and Equality: Christian Foundations in Locke's Political Thought*. Cambridge: Cambridge University Press, 2002.

———. *"Nonsense upon Stilts" Bentham, Burke and Marx on the Rights of Man*. London and New York: Methuen, 1987.

Witte, John Jr. *The Reformation of Rights: Law, Religion, and Human Rights in Early Modern Calvinism*. Cambridge: Cambridge University Press, 2007.

About the Author

~

ETHNA REGAN IS A LECTURER IN THEOLOGY at the Mater Dei Institute of Education, a College of Dublin City University. She studied at the Mater Dei Institute, Fordham University, and holds a PhD from the University of Cambridge. She previously taught at the University of the West Indies in Trinidad and worked with the Credo Foundation for Justice in Port of Spain. She is a Holy Faith Sister, and she also worked for five years in Samoa.

Index

~

A More Secure World: Our Shared Responsibility (United Nations), 23, 44

A Theology of Liberation (Gutiérrez), 147, 168n3

Abu Ghraib, 216

Ackerly, Brooke A., 11

Adorno, Theodor, 17, 116, 122, 139n78

Africa, 18, 43, 101, 144, 154. *See also* South Africa

African Charter on Human and People's Rights, 53n51

After Virtue (MacIntyre), 17–18

Agamben, Giorgio, 184

Aggiornamento, 26

Améry, Jean, 112–13

anamnesis, 120–21, 133

An-Na'im, Abdullahi A., 11

Annan, Kofi, 12, 44

anonymous Christianity, 78–81, 89

apostolate of human rights, 42–43

Aquinas, Thomas, Saint, 68, 71, 74, 106–7, 116, 120, 201

Aristotle, 68

Aristotelian thought, 32, 133, 165

Asad, Talal, 12

Asia, 18, 43, 48n13, 60n147, 144

Augustine of Hippo, Saint 1, 5, 68, 100, 205; *De Civitate Dei*, 1, 5, 182, 205; radical orthodoxy and, 179–80, 182, 185, 190–91, 204–5

Auschwitz, 4, 17, 88, 124, 125–29, 130, 133, 140n96, 145, 220. *See also* Holocaust

autonomy, 12, 64, 86

Badiou, Alain, 184

Baier, Annette, 198

Balkans, postconflict, 105

Balthasar, Hans Urs von, 80–81, 132

Barth, Karl, 70–71, 95n66

beggar versus rights-holder, 198–99

Bell, Daniel M., 5, 179, 190, 222; critique of liberation theology, 199–204

Benedict XVI, Pope, 44–45; address to the UN General Assembly in 2008, 44–45

Benhabib, Seyla, 11

Benjamin, Walter, 116, 118–19, 120, 133, 220

Berlin, Isaiah, 9

Beste, Jennifer, 83–84

Bible, the, 29–30, 64–65; Genesis, 32, 70–71; and human rights, 64; justice, 63, 197; Mark 9:38–39, 186; Mark 10:46–52, 199; Marxism and, 146; Matthew 25:40, 35, 222; Metz on, 120, natural law, 27; Locke on, 159; Psalm 72:4, 152–53; Romans 2:15, 27

Bloch, Ernst, 116

Boff, Clodovis, 168n3, 169n4

Boff, Leonardo, 81, 168n3, 169n8

Bolívar, Simon, 149

Bonhoeffer, Dietrich, 71

Bosnia, 3, 23

boundary discourse, human rights as 13–16, 39, 47, 63, 195, 198, 204–5, 222

Bush, George W., 208n30, 216

Calvinism, contribution to development of human rights, 47n2, 58n119, 179

Canon law, 43; compatibility with UN Convention on the Rights of the Child, 61n154

capability deprivation: poverty as, 154–55

capitalism, 123, 147, 150, 163, 199; "savage capitalism," 200–203

capital punishment, 1, 10, 18. *See also* death penalty

Caribbean, ix, 1, 10, 101, 144

Carter, Jimmy, 149

Cassin, René, 18, 26

Catholic social teaching, 2–3, 16, 23–24, 26, 28, 30, 37, 65, 151, 178, 188, 201, 218; and liberation theology, 148

Cavanaugh, William T., 179, 206n12

CELAM. *See* Conference of Bishops of Latin America.

Centesimus annus (On the Hundredth Anniversary of *Rerum novarum*), 41, 59n130

Chang, Peng–chun, 18, 20

Chapultepec Conference (1945), 51n33, 149

child, rights of, 7, 31, 45–46, 52n45, 61n154, 69–70, 85, 88, 105, 153, 201–2, 215–16; Hauerwas on, 193–95

child sexual abuse: Catholic church and, 3, 45–46; incest, 83–85

children: and war, 105, 109, 217; on the streets, 1, 69–70, 199, 202, 215–16

Chile, 113, 144, 171n27, 171n28

China, 16, 18

Christendom, 24, 46–47, 127, 189, 194

Christian Platonism, 180, 187

Christian-Jewish relations, 125, 133, 145. *See also* Holocaust

Christological humanism, 33, 42. *See also* humanism

Christology: and human rights, 65–66, 219; liberation theology, 144–45; Metz on, 124; Rahner on, 72, 74, 78–81

Cicero, 131

cold war, 28–29

common good, 13, 15, 21, 24, 34, 36, 39–40, 43, 63, 65, 187, 190, 194–95, 201

communitarian, dimension of rights, 2, 20, 187, 209n44

communitarianism, 45, 53n50, 132

Conference of Bishops of Latin America (CELAM), 33, 152, 168n2

Congo, Democratic Republic of, 44

Convention on the Prevention and Punishment of the Crime of Genocide, 23

Costa Rica, 144

Counter–Enlightenment, 9

Cranston, Maurice, 29, 174n57

Credo Centre (Credo Foundation for Justice, Trinidad), ix, 1, 69, 216

Cronin, Kieran, 64

culture, human rights and, 9–12, 19, 110, 157, 218, 222

dangerous memory, 118–22, 133; Auschwitz as, 126; *memoria passionis*, 130

Darfur, Sudan, 23, 44

De Las Casas, Bartolomé, 8, 149, 153–54

De Vitoria, Francisco, 8, 207n24

death penalty, 1, 10, 193, 217. *See also* capital punishment

democracy, 5, 102, 106, 144, 150, 158, 161, 185; Catholic church and, 24–27, 30, 34, 42–43, 60n147; postliberal theological critique of, 68, 179, 181, 184, 186, 188, 190–93, 197, 221

derogations, from human rights, 20, 184, 216–17

Deus Caritas est (God is Love), 45

dialectical discourse, human rights as a 2, 7–47, 161, 178, 198, 217, 218

Dignitatis humanae (Declaration on Religious Freedom), 30, 35–38, 40, 81; John Paul II on, 40–42; methodology of, 36

dignity, human. *See* human dignity

Dominium, 183–84

Donnelly, Jack, 10–11, 69
Dussel, Enrique, 169n9, 170n14
duties, 20, 27
Dworkin, Ronald, 13–14

Eliot, George, 121
Ellacuría, Ignacio, 73, 161, 164–67; on
    historical realism, 165–66; influence
    of Rahner on, 164, 221; theological
    methodology, 165–66
El Salvador, 73, 143, 164–66
Enlightenment, 32, 100–101, 119, 121, 125
eudaimonia, 2, 15, 129, 215–16. *See also*
    human flourishing
evangelical theologians, 66–67, 219
Evangelicals for Human Rights, 66
Evangelium vitae (The Gospel of Life), 41,
    59n43

Faith in History and Society (Metz), 117,
    124
Falk, Richard, 23
fascism, 18, 119
feminist moral philosophy, 11
Finnis, John, 13
forgiveness, 5, 102, 134n7; relationship
    with human rights and justice,
    202–4
Fourier, Charles, 160
France, 16, 24, 149, 180
Frankfurt School, 116, 122
freedom: Catholic social teaching and,
    23–24, 27, 35; Metz on, 117, 127, 130,
    133; postliberal critique, 183, 187,
    191–92; religious freedom, 24, 26,
    40–42, 44; Rahner on, 81–87, 89,
    219–20; Universal Declaration of
    Human Rights on, 19–23
French Revolution, 24; Marx on, 170n16
Fukuyama, Francis, 200

Galtung, Johan, 20
*Gaudium et spes (Pastoral Constitution on
    the Church in the Modern World)*,
    30–35, 146, 151

Genesis, book of, 70–71
genocide, 3, 23, 109, 114, 125, 141n96,
    141n105
Gerardi, Bishop Juan, 107, 114
global ethic and human rights, 65
"Glorious Revolution," 8
God's right, grounding human rights in,
    64, 67–68, 161, 219
Goodison, Lorna, 167–68
Gramsci, Antonio, 147
Great Britain, 16
Gregory XVI, Pope, 24
Guantánamo Bay, 216
Guatemala, 100, 107–14, 220; evangelical
    sects, 110; genocidal policy against
    Mayan Indians, 109; Mayan Indians,
    108–11, 113–14; *Memoria del Silencio*,
    108; Gushee, David P., 66–67
Gutiérrez, Gustavo, 144–45, 152, 169n8,
    191; on human rights, 147–48, 158

Häring, Bernard, 97n84, 132
Hauerwas, Stanley, 5, 15, 68, 179, 189–99,
    222; on Christians as beggars not
    rights-holders, 197–99; on church,
    192–93; on Gutiérrez, 191; on human
    rights, 193–95, 197–99; on justice,
    195–97; on politics, democracy,
    and liberalism, 190–92; theological
    politics, 189–90
Hegel, Georg Wilhelm Friedrich, 127,
    182, 185, 187, 218
"Hegelians," as discussed by Richard
    Rorty, 7, 47, 63, 181
Hehir, Bryan, 24, 61n149
Heidegger, Martin, 72, 76, 88, 116, 123
Herbert, Zbigniew, 114
Hinkelammert, Franz, 200
historical consciousness, approach to
    natural law, 31–32
historical realism, 164–65
Hollenbach, David, 65
Holocaust, 4, 8, 87–88, 100–101, 145,
    163, 219; and foundational UN
    documents, 8, 16–19; and Jewish–

Holocaust (*Cont.*)
  Christian relations, 125, 133, 140n92;
  late theological response, 128–29,
  138n87; liberation theology and, 145,
  163; Metz on, 4, 100, 114–33, 178, 219,
  220; non-Jewish victims, 125–26,
  140n95; as "orienting event," 140n90;
  Pius XII and, 25, 54n69; Rahner on,
  87, 99n101; and theodicy, 87–88, 127;
  as unprecedented, 126–27. *See also*
  Auschwitz
Holy Faith Sisters, 215
Holy Spirit, 30, 35, 38, 78, 188–89, 204
human dignity, 7, 12, 19, 26, 33–36, 42, 70,
  85–87, 89, 104, 146
human flourishing, ix, 1–2, 21, 47, 69–70,
  85, 107, 112, 152, 154, 157, 161, 164,
  166, 185, 188, 194, 199, 204, 215; and
  human rights, 13–16, 178, 184, 198,
  216–18. *See also* eudaimonia
human rights, 1–5, 7–16; Catholic
  Church and, 23–46; civil and
  political, 14, 16, 25, 27, 158, 221;
  communitarian dimensions of, 2,
  20, 187, 209n44; consensus on, 3,
  11, 18, 21, 65, 186; culture and, 9–12,
  19, 110, 157, 218, 222; derogation
  from, 20, 184, 216, 217; a dialectical
  boundary discourse, 13–16, 39, 47,
  63, 195, 198, 204–5, 217–18, 222;
  early modern history of, 8–9,
  47n2, 58n119, 173n41, 207n24; a
  global ethic, 65; Islam and, 11,
  49n14; mysticism of, 161–63; 221; of
  children, 69–70, 105, 192–93, 215–16;
  of the poor, 34, 166–67; postliberal
  critique of, 4–5, 178–205;
  Protestantism and, 24, 29, 46, 64,
  179; secular discourse, 1, 3, 4, 16–23;
  social and economic, 14, 25, 39, 151,
  158–61, 167, 217, 221; subsistence, 14,
  158–60; theological engagement
  with, 64–89; as universal, 8–12, 18,
  26, 33, 46–47, 64–65, 70, 129–30,
  133, 157–59, 185, 218, 220; violations,
  3–4, 10, 12, 14, 19, 22–23, 39, 44–45,
  69–70, 81, 102–14, 125–28, 145, 148,
  158, 162–63, 167, 184, 188, 203, 205
*Human Rights in Cross Cultural
  Perspective: A Quest for Consensus*
  (An-Na'im), 11
Human Rights Office of the Catholic
  Archdiocese of Guatemala, 4, 100,
  107–14
Human Rights Watch, 222n2
humanism, 32–33, 38, 41, 74, 101, 144–46,
  180; christological, 33, 42
Hume, David, 182, 208n25
Humphrey, John, 18
hunger, 14, 104, 149, 163, 167, 185, 196, 217,
  221

Imago Dei, 3, 12, 32, 67, 69–71, 89, 104,
  126, 162, 216, 219
International Covenant on Civil and
  Political Rights, 16, 22
International Covenant on Economic,
  Social and Cultural Rights, 16, 22
International Criminal Court, The
  Hague, 102
international customary law, 21
International Monetary Fund, 158
interruptive realism, 4, 130–31, 163–64,
  178, 187, 220
Ireland, 45, 217
Islam, 11, 49n14. *See also* Muslims on
  human rights

Jesus Christ, 29, 33, 35, 42, 44–45, 65–67,
  78–81, 85, 87, 108, 117–18, 120–23,
  133, 151–52, 156, 162, 181, 186–87, 191,
  196–97, 199, 202–3
Jewish–Christian relations, 125, 133, 145.
  See also Holocaust
John Paul II, Pope: on human dignity, 42;
  on human rights, 38–42; Thomistic
  personalism, 42
John XXIII, Pope, 26–30, 32
Judaism, 119, 120, 124, 145, 193; and
  human rights, 70

justice, 1, 2, 5, 10–11, 15, 20–22, 121, 124, 130, 132, 146–47, 167; Catholic social teaching on, 27–29, 31, 33, 35–38, 63, 65–68, 78; distributive, 14; God's, 152–53; human rights as basis for, 39–40; liberation theology and 157–66; postliberal critique of secular concepts of, 182–204; Rawls on, 11, 157; transitional, 106, 134n7; truth commissions and, 102–7; *vera iustitia*, 204–5; virtue of, 15, 106–7

just memory: culture of 4, 101–2; theology toward, 114–15, 118–25, 129–33; trials and truth commission for, 102–7

Kant, Immanuel, 39, 72, 74, 83, 86, 116–17, 144–45, 182, 185, 187

"Kantians," as discussed by Richard Rorty, 7, 47, 63, 181

Krondorfer, Björn, 128

Lasker–Wallfisch, Anita, 140n96

Latin America, 17, 20, 101, 125, 144, 219; church resistance to dictatorships, 150; Latin American Episcopal Conference (CELAM), 152; "national security" governments, 150; and U.S. foreign policy, 150

Leo XIII, Pope, 24–27, 151

liberal democracy. *See* democracy.

liberalism, 122, 149, 159, 182; Catholic antiliberalism, 24–25; postliberal theological critique of, 183, 188, 191–93, 198, 201; "postmodernist bourgeois," 7

liberation theology, 4, 5, 28, 30, 33, 40, 68, 89, 115, 131, 133, 178, 180, 187, 190, 221; and Catholic social teaching, 148; and *communidades de base*, 156; critique of, 169n6, 199–204 ; and human rights, 146–68; and Marxism, 146–47; on the rights of the poor, 4, 68, 147–48, 157–61; women theologians, 163–64

Locke, John, 8, 14, 159–60, 182–84

Lonergan, Bernard, 31

Maathai, Wangari, 180

MacIntyre, Alasdair, 15, 17–19, 68, 179, 181, 186

Magna Carta, 8

Malik, Charles, 18

Mandlestan, Nadezhda, 104

Marcel, Gabriel, 19

Marcuse, Herbert, 122

Margalit, Avishai, 111

Mariátegui, José Carlos, 147

Maritain, Jacques, 18, 210n48

Markus, Robert, 205

Marx, Karl, 116–17, 123, 182, 185, 187

Marxism and liberation theology, 146–47

Mater et magistra (On Christianity and Social Progress), 28

Mayan Indians, 108–11, 113–14; genocidal policy against, 109

Médecins sans Frontières, 180

Memoria del Silencio, Guatemala, 108

memory, 3, 4, 78, 85, 100, 107–14, 118–23, 154, 192, 202; dangerous, 118–27, 130; destruction of, 120; ethics of, 101–2, 203; Freud on, 101–2; recovery of historical, 4, 107–14, 220; of suffering, 3, 127, 129–30. *See also* just memory

Metz, Johann Baptist, 4, 71, 80, 87, 89, 100, 114–33, 144–45, 167, 178, 180, 187, 219–20; on Auschwitz, 125–33, 140n92, 145; critique of, 118, 141n116, 132–33; and Frankfurt School, 116; "haunted tardiness," 114–15, 124; and the "Hitler Youth Generation," 128–29; influence of Rahner on, 115–16; influence on liberation theology, 144; on Judaism, 119–20, 124; on memory, 118–122, 125, 129–30; on narrative, 122–23, 125; on political theology, 117–18, 127; postidealist theology, 118; on praxis

Metz, Johann Baptist (*Cont.*)
117–18; on solidarity, 123–25; on
theodicy, 127; on the subject, 117–18;
on universalism of human rights,
129–30; and Walter Benjamin, 116,
118–20, 133, 220
Milbank, John, 5, 15, 68, 120–21, 123, 191,
198, 200, 202, 205, 222; on church
186–89; on liberalism and rights,
183–84; on liberation theology,
169n4; on Platonism, 187; on
Rahner, 97n76; on secular ethics,
184–86
Millennium Development Goals,
185–86
Miranda, José Porfirio, 146
Mirari vos, 24
Moltmann, Jürgen, 64, 67–68, 128, 150,
161
Murray, John Courtney, 29, 37
Muslims on human rights, 11

narrative: Metz on 118, 122–23, 133;
Ricoeur on educative function of
101–2, 104; of suffering, 45–46,
104–14
natural law: in *Gaudium et spes*, 31;
Hauerwas on, 94, 197; historical
consciousness, 31–32; and human
rights, 9; John Paul II on, 42, 130;
Locke on, 160; in *Pacem in terries*,
26–27, 29
natural rights, 8, 13, 25, 27–29, 147, 160,
207n24
Nazism, 9, 18, 119, 125
neoliberalism, economic policies, 61n147,
150
Newlands, George, 65, 219, 222
Niebuhr, Reinhold, 29, 41, 186
Nietzsche, Friedrich, 129, 182, 191
nongovernmental organizations (NGOs),
10; influence at 1945 San Francisco
Conference, 16–17
Nuremberg trials, 102
Nussbaum, Martha, 154

O Siadhail, Micheal, 126
Obama, Barack, 90n16, 217
*On Job: God–Talk and the Suffering of the
Innocent* (Gutiérrez), 145
option for the poor. *See* preferential
option for the poor
Origen, 122
Otto, Rudolf, 162
Owen, Robert, 160

Pacem in terris (Peace on Earth), 26–30,
34, 39
Paine, Thomas, 160
Patočka, Jan, 10
personalism, 31–32, 42, 45, 123
philosophical anthropology, 26, 31–32, 70
Pieris, Aloysius, 147
Pius XII, Pope, 24–26; and the Jews, 25,
54n69
Plato, 100, 119, 131
Platonic Christianity, 180
Plotinus, 100
pneumatology, 30, 188–189, 197. *See also*
Holy Spirit
Pogge, Thomas, 4, 158
Polis, 129, 185–86; church as, 192–93, 196,
201, 203
political theology, 4, 5; Metz on, 114–33;
compared with theological politics,
178–79, 189–90, 220, 222
poor, rights of the, 34, 157–61. *See also*
preferential option for the poor
postliberal critique of human rights, 4–5,
178–205
postliberal theology, 2, 4–5, 179, 199,
221–22
postmodernism, 7, 9, 16
poverty, 14, 16, 43, 66, 145, 149, 163, 166–
167, 186, 196, 199, 201–2, 216–17, 219,
221; as capability deprivation 154–55;
complexity of, 144, 153–57; extreme,
158, 173n44, 185, 217, 221; measuring,
154–55; Medellín documents
(CELAM) on, 152; Sen on, 154–55;
Thomas Pogge on, 158

preferential option for the poor, 4, 28, 33, 108, 143, 148, 151–53, 155–58, 166, 201, 221

principle of humanity, 21

protective marginality, ethical position of, 2, 47, 178, 198, 217

Protestantism and human rights, 24, 46, 64, 179

radical orthodoxy, 180, 184–88, 190, 197, 200, 203–4, 221–22

Rahner, Karl, 3, 31, 64, 71–89, 117, 144, 162, 164, 178–80, 188, 219–20; and anonymous Christianity, 78–81, 89; Christology, 78–81; on grace, 81–84, 87, 89; and Heidegger, 72, 76; on human dignity, 85–87, 89; on human experience and the experience of God, 84–85, 89; on human freedom, 81–84, 89; and human rights, 71, 89; on human suffering, 87–89; and Ignatian spirituality, 72; on Imago Dei, 89; influence on feminist theology, 73; influence on Metz, 115–16; and liberation theology, 73; on mystery, 72, 85; and philosophy, 72–73; supernatural existential, 76–78, 89; tendency toward idealism, 3, 80, 131; theological anthropology 71–76, 89; and Thomas Aquinas, 71–72, 74–75, 89

rape as a weapon of war, 105, 109, 217

Rawls, John, 11, 58n116, 157, 180

realism. See historical realism; interruptive realism

Recuperación de la Memoria Historica, 100, 107–14, 220, disappearances, 109, 113; exemplary torture, 110–11; methodology of, 108–9; methodology of horror, 112; perspective on human rights, 112; resistance of women, 113; violence against children, 109–110

Redemptor hominis (Redeemer of Humankind), 39, 42

relativism: cultural, 10–11, 31; ethical, 12; religious, 37, 40

religious freedom, 24, 35–38, 40–42, 44

Rerum novarum (The Condition of Labor), 25, 43, 56n79

responsibility to protect, 23, 44

Ricoeur, Paul, 4, 100–102, 114, 129

Roman Catholic social teaching. See Catholic social teaching

Roncalli, Angelo, 26. See also John XXIII, Pope.

Roosevelt, Eleanor, 55n70

Rorty, Richard, 7, 9, 47, 63, 105, 181, 193–94

Rose, Gillian, 114

Rousseau, Jean–Jacques, 149, 208n25

Rubens, Bernice, 126

Rwandan genocide, 3, 23, 141n105

Ryan, John A., 27

Sacks, Jonathan, 13

Saint–Simon, Henri, 160

Samoa, 1, 175n65

San Francisco Conference (1945), 16–17, 20

Scarry, Elaine, 103–4

Schillebeeckx, Edward, 152, 212n85

Schmitt, Carl, 117

scripture. See Bible

Second Vatican Council. See Vatican Council II

secular, 13, 41, 73, 80; humanism, 41, 180; postliberal "disdain" for, 179–89, 191, 197–98, 204–5; secular-religious allegiances, 1, 3, 20, 35, 43, 46, 108

secular eschatology, 185

secularism, 40–41, 180

Segundo, Juan Luis, 149, 169n4, 169n8

Sen, Amartya, 48n13, 154–55, 157; on positional objectivity, 157

sexual abuse, 83–84, 105–9. See also child sexual abuse

Shannon airport, Ireland: rendition flights, 216–17

Shoah, 115. See also Holocaust

Shue, Henry, 158–59, 162

silence, in the face of injustice, 4, 87, 105, 107–8, 111, 113, 115, 125, 153, 220; and interruptive realism, 130–32

situated universalism, 1, 11, 12, 15, 157, 218

slavery, 66, 70, 101, 120, 153–54

Sobrino, Jon, 161, 169n8; forgiveness and mercy, 202–3 mysticism of human rights, 161–63, 221

social teaching, Catholic. See Catholic social teaching

solidarity, 1, 10, 21, 28, 113, 185, 201, 222; "impulse of solidarity," 47, 178, 218; John Paul II on, 40; liberation theology on, 144, 152, 156, 167; Metz on, 115, 117–19, 121, 123–25, 127, 129, 131, 133, 220

Sollicitudo rei socialis (On Social Concern), 40, 59n127

South Africa, 65, 219; See also Truth and Reconciliation Commission

sovereignty, personal, 183. See also dominium

sovereignty, state, 10, 17, 21, 44, 51n34, 102

Soviet Union, 16, 21, 29

Spes salvi (In hope we were saved), 44

Srebrenica massacre, 3, 23

Stout, Jeffrey, 179–80, 197–98

street children. See children

subsistence, rights to, 14, 158–60

Sudan, Darfur, 23, 44

supernatural existential, 76–79, 81, 88–89, 94n57. See also Rahner, Karl

Tamez, Elsa, 163

Taylor, Charles, 46–47, 124, 178, 215

Telos, 184–86

The Power of the Poor in History (Gutiérrez), 148

theodicy, 87–88, 127

theological anthropology, 31, 35, 70, 219–20; liberation theology on, 144, 164; Metz on, 118; Rahner on, 3, 64, 71–89

Theology and Social Theory (Milbank), 97n76, 169n4, 181–82

Theology of the World (Metz), 117

Third World, 116, 125, 147

Thomism, 3, 32, 42, 63, 71, 107, 115–16, 179, 185, 219; transcendental Thomism, 3, 71, 89, 115–16, 219

Tibi, Bassan, 11

Tierney, Brian, 8

torture, 12, 18, 66–67, 70, 85, 103–4, 110–13, 145, 216–17, 220; therapy after, 113

traditionalism, new traditionalists, 179, 204–5, 215, 221. See also Stout, Jeffrey

transcendence, human capacity for, 34, 37, 71, 74–75, 77–78, 81–82, 87–88, 163, 217, 219–220; and action for human rights, 65; denial of, 46, 87

transitional justice, 106, 134n7

Trinidad and Tobago, 1, 69, 215–16

Tronto, Joan, 195

Truth and Reconciliation Commission, South Africa, 103, 104–5, 107, 135n16, 135n18, 136n34, 137n39

truth commissions, 102–7, 121; Guatemala, 107–14. See also Truth and Reconciliation Commission, South Africa

Tutu, Archbishop Desmond, 107, 134n7

Two Treatises of Government (Locke), 8, 159–60

UNESCO, 22, 26

United Nations: Catholic social teaching and, 26–27, 29, 35–36, 38–39, 44–45; failure to prevent human rights violations, 3, 23; foundational documents, 2, 16–23, 131, 149, 187, 218; Millennium Development Goals, 185–86; peace operations, 22–23; Security Council, 23, 105

United Nations Charter, 16–19, 149

United Nations Commission on Human Rights, 22

United Nations Security Council, 23, 105

United States, 16–17, 23, 29, 66, 144, 149–150, 219; foreign policy, Latin America, 149–50

Universal Declaration of Human Rights, 3, 8, 9, 16–23, 26–27, 38–39, 41, 44, 50n29, 131, 149–50, 162, 178, 217

Universidad Centroamericano, 143; martyrs of the University, 164, 166

U.S. Army School of the Americas, 111

Vatican Council II, 16, 23, 26, 30–38, 41–45, 60n147, 79, 146, 151, 218

Veritatis splendor (The Splendor of Truth), 41

Villa-Vicencio, Charles, 65, 219

Vincent, R. J., 14

virtue, 2, 15, 29, 63, 68, 106, 113, 132, 166, 195–96; liberation theology on, 167;

postliberal theology on, 181–204; of solidarity, 40; of vigilance towards suffering, 4, 132, 167, 220–21

war on terror: derogations from human rights, 184; rendition flights, 216–7; theological response to, 66–67, 219

Western Hemisphere Institute for Security Cooperation. *See* U.S. Army School of the Americas

Wiesel, Elie, 130

Witte, John, 8, 58n119, 179, 222n7

Wojtyla, Karol, 59n144. *See also* John Paul II, Pope

World Bank, 155, 158

World Trade Organization, 158

Zubiri, Xavier, 164–65